National Home
Gardening Club

National Home
Gardening Club

National Home
Gardening Club

National H
Gardening

W9-BMX-324

National Home
Gardening Club

National Home
Gardening Club

National Home
Gardening Club

National Home
Gardening Club

National Home

National Home
Gardening Club

National Home
Gardening Club

National Home
Gardening Club

National Home
Gardening Club

National Home
Gardening Club

National Home
Gardening Club

National Home
Gardening Club

National Home
Gardening Club

National Home
Gardening Club

National Home

National Home
Gardening Club

National Home
Gardening Club

National Home
Gardening Club

National Home
Gardening Club

National Home
Gardening Club

National Home
Gardening Club

National Home
Gardening Club

National Home
Gardening Club

National Home
Gardening Club

National Home

National Home
Gardening Club

National Home
Gardening Club

National Home
Gardening Club

National Home
Gardening Club

National Home
Gardening Club

National Home
Gardening Club

National Home
Gardening Club

National Home
Gardening Club

National Home
Gardening Club

National Home
Gardening Club

National Home
Gardening Club

National Home
Gardening Club

National Home
Gardening Club

National Home
Gardening Club

National Home
Gardening Club

National Home
Gardening Club

National Home
Gardening Club

National Home
Gardening Club

National Home
Gardening Club

National Home
Gardening Club

National Home

National Home

National Home

National Home

National Home

Better Gardens, Less Work

Complete Gardener's Library®

Better Gardens, Less Work

Barbara
Pleasant
National Home
Gardening Club
National Home
Gardening Club
Minnetonka, Minnesota

Better Gardens, Less Work

Printed in 2011.

All rights reserved. No part of this publication may be reproduced, stored in an electronic retrieval system or transmitted in any form or by any means (electronic, mechanical, photocopying, recording or otherwise) without the prior written permission of the copyright owner.

Tom Carpenter
Creative Director

Julie Cisler
Book Design & Production

Michele Stockham
Senior Book Development Coordinator

Gina Germ
Photo Editor

Shari Gross
Production Coordinator

13 14 / 15 14 13 12 11
ISBN 978-1-58159-111-8
© 2001 National Home Gardening Club

National Home Gardening Club
12301 Whitewater Drive
Minnetonka, Minnesota 55343
www.gardeningclub.com

Photo Credits

Joseph DeSciose pp.: cover, 40, 53, 55, 66, 77; **R. Todd Davis pp.:** 1, 6, 10-11, 16-17, 19, 49, 58-59, 66, 71, 73, 94-95, 104, 107, 123, 133, 142, 143; **©Alan and Linda Detrick pp.:** 2-3, 18, 26, 29, 32, 35, 37, 39, 41, 44, 45, 56, 69, 72, 76(2), 88, 102, 103, 109, 110(2), 117, 118(2), 121, 128, 134, 135(2), 141, 144, 156; **Barbara Pleasant pp.:** 7, 13, 19, 22(2), 27, 35, 39, 42, 43, 45, 48, 55(3), 65, 66, 67(2), 68, 73, 75 all, 76(2), 80, 85, 86, 88, 105, 106, 109, 111 both, 113, 115(2), 118, 119(2), 121, 124, 128, 129 all, 131, 137, 138(2), 142, 143, 145, 150, 152, 154, 155, 160; **Saxon Holt pp.:** 12(2), 15(2), 20, 23, 38, 39, 41, 44, 50, 53, 54, 57, 63, 64(2), 68, 71, 72, 86, 89(2), 97 both, 100, 107, 108, 113, 115, 121, 126, 130, 131, 133, 140, 152, 161; **Chuck Crandall and Barbara Crandall pp.:** 12, 18(2), 20, 21, 28(2), 30-31, 33, 35, 36, 37, 38(2), 42(2), 43(2), 46(2), 47(2), 48, 50, 52(2), 55, 56(2), 57, 60(2), 62, 63, 68, 71, 72, 78-79, 84, 85, 88, 89, 90, 93, 98 both, 101, 110, 114, 116, 117, 122(2), 136, 141, 148, 151, 154, 162, 164, 165, 166(2), 167, 168, 169; **Walter Chandoha pp.:** 13, 14, 15, 20, 21(2), 23, 27, 32, 33, 36, 37, 41, 44, 45, 52, 61(2), 63, 74, 80(2), 81, 84, 85(2); **Derek Fell pp.:** 19, 22, 23, 29, 33, 34, 46, 47(2), 49, 51, 53, 54, 62, 65, 70, 80, 83, 87(2), 90, 122, 124, 126, 132 both, 139, 144, 145, 150, 156, 162, 164, 165, 166; **Dency Kane pp.:** 21(2), 24, 28, 33, 40, 49, 51, 55, 61, 63, 64, 69, 73, 77(2), 82, 89, 91 all, 93, 96, 99, 103, 105, 108, 134, 135, 138, 140, 141; **Janet Loughrey pp.:** 34, 74, 92, 96, 112, 114, 116, 117, 120, 126, 134, 144; **NHGC Archive pp.:** 35, 41, 51(3), 55, 60, 61, 65, 67, 84, 120, 137, 146-147, 148, 149 all, 150, 151(3), 153 both, 154, 155(2), 156(2), 157(3), 158 all, 159 all, 160(4), 161(6), 163(3), 164(3), 166, 167, 168; **Bill Johnson pp.:** 41, 48, 77, 92, 101, 112, 123, 128, 166; **Rob Cardillo pp.:** 87(2), 89, 99, 100, 102, 106, 119, 125, 127 both, 130, 131, 136(2), 137, 145; **Amy Sumner p.:** 125.

Illustrators

Eric Bjorlin/Studio Arts pp.: 24 both, 25 all, 45, 81 all, 82 both, 83 all, 151, 153, 155, 157, 162; **NHGC Archive p.:** 51.

CONTENTS

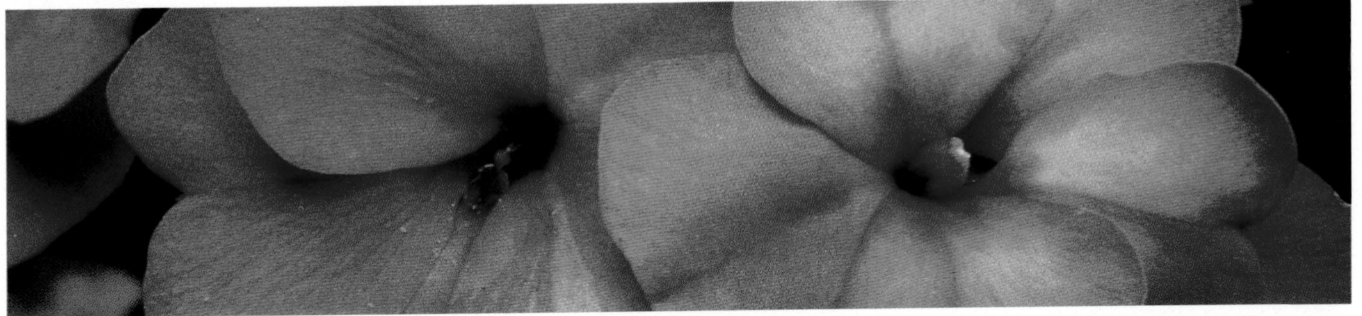

Gardening by Heart

It was a good thing that my parents had so many children, because the home they built to raise us in had a very large yard. Back in the '50s and '60s four children didn't seem like that many, unless you asked my mother, who cooked all the meals and did all the laundry in days when ironing was a mandatory step. So I suppose it only seemed fair that we children should be asked to spend Saturday mornings hand-pulling weeds from our struggling lawn, raking up huge mountains of pine straw and leaves, or fetching tools and gas cans or whatever was needed to help get the job done.

Barbara Pleasant creates better gardens with less work in the yard of her Alabama home, leaving plenty of time to enjoy the results of her efforts. This is the fifth book she has written for the National Home Gardening Club.

With over an acre to keep up, there were many, many jobs clamoring for attention. In summer the mowing never ended, and between Mother's flowers and Dad's vegetables, we quickly learned never to complain that there was nothing to do. Doing so would win us a chore. But because my parents are wise and loving people, the chore would often turn out to be something we didn't really mind doing.

I might be told to deadhead the marigolds and dahlias, an activity that I could be trusted to do correctly. My brothers tended to be given tasks involving mowers, mulch and heavy wheelbarrows, masculine things that built muscles and made loud noises.

Even so, we worked begrudgingly. There never seemed to be a day when all the work was done. But unbeknownst to us at the time, we were all learning important life lessons.

The fact that we all worked, together yet apart, taught us how each of our tasks made the other's accomplishments seem greater. This became a very real if unacknowledged source of family pride. The flower bed I weeded fit with the lawn mowed by my older brother and the walkways cleaned and swept by the younger two. Our yard became a reflection of the fact that we were all parts of a whole.

We also learned to manage our time and to appreciate the satisfaction of a job well done. And, although it has taken many years, all of us also have learned that gardening is most enjoyable when you arrange your life so that you have exactly the right amount of it—not too much and not too little.

We all turned out to be gardeners. Yet we have demanding careers, children, and never enough time to do all that we want to do. So it's not surprising that each of us has discovered different yet related sources of satisfaction. My older brother is a plant explorer at heart, and he seldom gets through a season without becoming impassioned about a new tree, shrub or perennial for his growing collection. My middle brother loves his lawn, and the youngest uses his engineer brain to constantly fine-tune his outdoor spaces to make them more functional. And I'm still in love with flowers, and realize I may never get enough of them.

I tell you this story so you will not be too misled by the title and theme of this book. Yes, it is about making your yard lovelier yet less demanding, but it is also about ways to enjoy a very special part of your life that can build the bonds with your family and your neighborhood, as well as the innate bond that ties you to the natural world. It's about gardening better, perhaps gardening a little smarter, but it's also about weaving your garden into your best possible life. After all, you only get one of those.

Barbara Pleasant

How to Have Better Gardens with Less Work!

Yes, we all love to work outside amongst the glory of our gardens. If we didn't enjoy this labor of love, we wouldn't have become enamored with the wonderful pastime of gardening in the first place.

But these are busy days—time is precious no matter who you are. Your energy has a limit too ... and if your energy isn't limited, daylight surely is! There's nothing wrong with being efficient in gardening—both in the way you plan your landscapes and in the way you maintain them.

That's what *Better Gardens, Less Work* is all about—saving you time, energy and stress. Put all the savings into sitting back a little more to really *enjoy* your gardening creations. You might even find some time to broaden your gardening horizons and start some new gardening ventures.

Nobody ever said you have to be a slave to your garden. A garden is to love and savor. Here's how the pages to come will help you do just that.

Full-Color Photos offer ideas of all kinds, illustrate key concepts, and show you how to save time and effort in the garden.

WATCH OUT Boxes give essential guidelines, warnings and reminders on gardening issues of all kinds. These tips can save you a lot of work and heartache.

Tool Tips tell you about special gardening tools and materials—and how to use them effectively.

26

Better Gardens, Less Work

Design Out Weeds

Shaded areas beneath trees are ideal spots for plants that cover the ground with greenery and choke out weeds in the process. Hostas and pachysandra are perfect plants for the job.

WATCH OUT!

Site Specific Herbicides

Chemicals that kill plants, called herbicides, give some people chills, but you should not be afraid to use herbicides when their use is warranted. Always use good preventive management practices before turning to herbicides for help.

So-called nonselective herbicides will kill any plant they touch, and you will need this much punch to turn dangerous weeds such as poison ivy or stinging nettle into history. Other herbicides do very specific jobs. Crabgrass preventers keep crabgrass (and other seeds) from sprouting. Broadleaf herbicides kill weeds with flat, oval-shaped leaves but do not injure grass when used according to label directions. Grass herbicides, which are sometimes used in wildflower meadows, kill grass rather than broad-leafed flowers.

When using any herbicide, always study the label first. Herbicides are labeled according to which plants they can be used upon safely rather than by which weeds they kill. Very few herbicides are labeled for use on edible plants.

If not for weeds, we would live in a starkly barren world. Equipped to move into any open space, weeds are nature's colonizers of vacant soil, the pioneer plants that begin the process of natural succession in which bare earth is slowly and gradually transformed into a mature ecosystem such as a forest or prairie.

Unfortunately, weeds do not add to the appeal of our yards. Coarse and rangy and downright selfish about space, weeds often outcompete cultivated plants, taking moisture, nutrients and light intended for our peonies and peppers. Anyone who enjoys growing plants quickly comes to resent weeds, which pop up in containers and shrub beds, and are present in amazing numbers in areas that are frequently cultivated, such as vegetable gardens or places planted with annual flowers. Unless you want to spend hours and hours pulling weeds, you will need to use a variety of tricks to prevent the proliferation and spread of weeds.

Natural Edge: Weed Early and Often

Immature weeds have skimpy roots, so they are easy to pull out, especially when the soil is wet. Or simply lop off their heads with a sharp hoe. If you get rid of weeds when they are young, they will never shed seeds in your garden.

How Weeds Work

Weeds bring with them several distinct advantages that make them formidable adversaries. Many species produce hundreds of thousands of seeds, some of which will germinate the following year. Other seeds that manage to get buried in the soil may wait patiently for more than a decade for their place in the sun. In fact, some weed seeds need to be exposed to sunlight to trigger sprouting, which is why newly cultivated soil often gives rise to many more weeds than a nearby spot that has been left untouched for several seasons.

Perennial weeds such as bindweed, greenbrier, Canada thistle and quackgrass spread by seeds and by wandering roots. Pull out or hoe down the main plant, and a few weeks later you can expect a crop of babies to appear a few inches or feet from where the parent weed stood. These new weeds arise from root buds which mobilize and grow even faster when the dominant weed body is removed. Cultivating the soil can make things worse since the root buds often remain viable even when chopped into small 1-inch pieces.

Beating Weeds

What's a weed-weary gardener to do? For starters, design your landscape so that no space is left unoccupied. If some areas refuse to support cultivated plants, either cover them with a hard surface or blanket them with mulch until you think of a more lasting solution. Each time you create a new planting space for any kind of plant, also think of how you will prevent weeds or manage them if they appear.

Designing for Less Work

27

Tool Tip: Landscape Fabrics

Special landscape fabrics, created specifically to prevent weeds, now exist for many different situations. Unlike black plastic, which becomes a barrier to water and soluble plant foods even when perforated, landscape fabrics are porous. Yet their texture is such that they effectively suppress weeds that attempt to grow from beneath them. Although soil and mulch that is spread atop landscape fabrics can support weeds, you will find it easy to pull the weeds from loose organic mulch. Some of the most useful landscape fabrics are circular skirts made to be laid out beneath newly planted trees and shrubs. Installed at planting time, these tree skirts help keep the soil cool and moist while discouraging weeds.

Roll out weed barriers and cover with mulch to prevent weeds from growing.

What to Do with Your Dead Weeds

Even in the best less-work landscapes, weeding days are in order from time to time, during which you may accumulate one or many hefty piles of pulled weeds. What can you do with them? Compost heaps often don't get hot enough to kill weed seeds, though it's perfectly safe to compost weeds pulled when they are young, before they have a chance to develop mature seeds. But with perennial weeds or those holding mature seeds, it may be better to treat the corpses like garbage. Either set them out to be collected as waste, or, if your property is large, find an out-of-the-way place where you can dump them.

Pull weeds and spent plants by hand when the soil is moist. Then set out new plants or cover the soil with mulch.

Natural Edge Boxes present techniques and tips for solving garden challenges in natural and effective ways.

Clear, To-the-Point Text gives strategies, techniques and tips for creating gardening success without working yourself to the bone. This text is friendly to read, and always broken up into logical sections so that you can skim through (if needed) to find the information you need.

Gardening Tips, Techniques, Instructions and Ideas—important ideas that deserve their own special presentation—appear in boxes like this.

50 Less-Work Plants are outlined in detail in Chapter 6. Here's the inside information on selecting, growing and maintaining these great plants that will look wonderful and hang tough in your garden. These are truly all-star plants, in all respects.

A detailed overview explains the specifics of each plant.

Get assistance in choosing a variety that is suitable for you and your growing conditions.

138 Better Gardens, Less Work

SEDUM

Perennial Flower
Sedum species

The flower clusters of 'Autumn Joy' sedum start out pink and gradually age to bronze. Because it blooms late in the season, this is a favorite flower for perennial borders.

The drought tolerance of foolproof sedums will go a long way toward ensuring a successful low-maintenance landscape plan. Persistent and pest free, sedums look good throughout the growing season.

In early spring, fleshy mounds of bright green, blue-green, creamy yellow, or red-tinged foliage emerge. True succulents, sedums' thick, waxy leaves and juicy stems provide unique textural contrast to many other perennials. By midsummer, small, starry flower clusters top those stems in hues of pink, red or white. And when the growing season starts to wane, some sedum flowers even retain their color and form after they have dried.

The variety of sedums is stunning—some can reach 2 feet tall and will hold their own in perennial patches, while others are trailing and look fantastic as groundcovers, growing among rocks or creeping in the crevices of a stone wall.

Choosing Sedums

There are so many sedums to pick from that your main task is to decide where you'd like to have sedums growing, and then select ones that fit the bill and strike your fancy.

Among the sedum hybrids, 'Autumn Joy' is probably the most popular, with 2-foot-tall stems topped with rusty pink flower clusters that persist into fall. 'Ruby Glow' is 1 foot tall with rounded purple-tinged leaves and ruby red flowers. 'Vera Jameson' is similar, but with bronze leaves. The parent species of these cultivars, showy stonecrop (*S. spectabile*), reaches 1 to 2 feet tall with flower heads up to 6 inches across. In perennial catalogs or nurseries, look for rosy-red 'Atropurpureum' or rose-pink 'Brilliant'.

Two-row sedum (*S. spurium*) forms mats of wiry stems about 6 inches tall with rounded leaves; 'Dragon's Blood', 'Red Carpet' and 'Ruby Mantle' all have red-tinged foliage, while 'Tricolor' is variegated pink, white and green. Indestructible *S. acre* grows into a green groundcover topped with yellow flowers in the spring.

Growing Sedums

All sedums are tough, easy-to-grow perennials. They prefer average well-drained soils and full sun. Some of the low-growing types will tolerate partial shade in the North. South of Zone 6, part shade is beneficial for all of the sedums. The taller types may get a bit leggy in shade though, and may need to be pinched back or staked to support the flower heads.

To get more sedums, either dig up and divide established clumps in early spring, or take 1- to 3-inch-long cuttings of the fleshy stems in spring or summer and stick them in a moist (but not too wet) pot of soil until they root. Amazingly fast, cuttings are often nicely rooted within a month.

An eager spreader, S. acre bursts into bloom in late spring, producing numerous flower spikes topped with sunny yellow blossoms.

If you want a spreading sedum for a rock garden or other dry spot, two-row sedums such as 'Red Carpet' are colorful and easy to grow.

Discover the secrets to growing the plant successfully—where to place it, how to care for it … all the insights you need for success.

Full-color photos show you what the plant looks like, and present options and varieties that might suit your needs.

Plant Boxes, such as this one, offer up lists of less-work plants that you can target for your garden and landscape uses. These lists are carefully constructed to offer only the toughest plants that will not only look great, but offer the greatest chance for success.

Time-Saving Tips bring you extra ideas and new gardening strategies for saving time and effort in the garden. It fits our theme: If there's an easier way to do it, and the results are the same, then do it!

54 Better Gardens, Less Work

BETTER GARDENS IN THE SUMMER SUN

Narrow-leaf zinnias are an ideal low-care flower for sun because they resist both drought and disease.

Most of us can't wait for summer to come so that we can feel the warmth of the sun again. But then the days get long and a little too hot, and every minute spent working outside seems to last for an hour. However, with a little planning, you can find yourself enjoying a boisterously beautiful summer garden without spending long steamy hours keeping it up. After all, you probably have plenty of other ways—that don't involve dirt—to enjoy summer!

Because many annual flowers are such strong bloomers, you will definitely want to devote at least a small space to flowers you can pop into the ground as bedding plants, surround them with mulch and then sit back and enjoy. In most climates petunias can be counted upon to bloom continuously all summer, and they come in so many colors that finding ones you like is easy. See pages 66 and 67 for other planting ideas for annuals that come in six-packs, and tips for helping them grow well in your yard.

It's important not to get carried away with a huge flower bed that will undoubtedly need to be weeded, watered, fertilized and groomed often. Using a thick mulch will reduce how much weeding and watering you will need to do, and you may need to fertilize only once if you use an organic or timed-release fertilizer. How much time you spend removing old blossoms or trimming to control leggy growth depends on which flowers you grow. A few, such as melampodium (page 127), portulaca (page 134) and small-flowered zinnias (page 145) need very little attention, and the same is true of the other hot-weather annuals described in the "Summer Replacements" box (next page).

WONDERING WHY?

Bracts vs. Petals

If your flowers seem to fade too fast in the summer sun, switch to species that produce tiny flowers surrounded by bracts rather than petals. True petals, such as those found in roses and peonies, are packed with water. In comparison, the "petals" of gomphrena, strawflowers, sunflower and zinnias are dry and papery, so they are slow to wither in hot sun.

The petals of zinnias and many other sun-tolerant flowers hold only a little moisture. Narrow leaf shape gives plants another edge against heat and drought.

Better Gardens for Special Places 55

SUMMER REPLACEMENTS

The first days of spring are so inspirational that we pack them full of gardening, and fill flower beds with flowers that like cool weather such as pansies, sweet alyssum, snapdragons and other spring bloomers. But then summer comes, and these cool-natured flowers slowly melt away. Here are some prime summer replacements that are widely available at garden centers in late spring, especially in warm climates where they are most needed. When grown in good soil with adequate water and fertilizer, they will bloom through the most torrid of summer heat waves.

Gomphrena – Also called globe amaranth, available in white and many shades of pink.

Gomphrena.

Lantana – A butterfly favorite that bears multicolored clusters of blossoms.

Lantana.

Pentas – In red or pink, this garden newcomer thrives in humid heat.

Pentas.

Purple Heart – With bold purple spiking foliage, this tropical survives winter to Zone 7.

Annual Vinca – Called periwinkle or Madagascar periwinkle, this heat lover hangs tough through torrid summer days.

Purple heart.

Annual vinca.

TIME-SAVING TIP

Drip Irrigation

Water is too precious to waste, and the most efficient way to water is also the healthiest for plants. Drip irrigation, in which water slowly drips into the soil from perforated soaker hoses or from drip irrigation lines equipped with little emitters, supplies moisture to the soil while keeping leaves dry, which helps prevent various leafspots and mildews. Plus, you can turn on a drip hose at night and water your garden without competing with the evaporative power of the sun. Water from a drip line goes exactly where it's needed, unlike a sprinkler that often waters your sidewalk, car or driveway in addition to your garden. But best of all, drip irrigation saves hours and hours of time not spent standing at garden's edge with a hose in your hand.

Drip irrigation lines that include emitters can be arranged so that they drip water right where it's needed, as seen here …

Dress for success when you garden in summer heat. Wear loose-fitting clothing, and don't forget a hat for shade.

Summer Garden Survival Tactics

When summer really gets cooking, you need to take care of yourself before you can take care of your garden. Here are five ways to make summer gardening more enjoyable, and less likely to cause you unnecessary discomfort.

Work Early in the Morning or Late in the Evening

This just makes sense, but it's amazing how many people defy nature by working outside in the heat of the day.

Cover Your Head

A wide-brimmed hat cools your head, and mysteriously discourages gnats and mosquitoes at the same time.

Wear Light Colors

In addition to minimizing solar heating, light colors do not attract bees and other insects. Bright reds, blues and oranges make you a real curiosity to the same critters that visit colorful flowers.

Let Someone Else Mow

It will be worth the cost if you get to spend your time on gardening projects that you truly enjoy.

Sit Back and Smell the Flowers

All work and no play isn't fun. Make time to relax and enjoy the rewards of gardening.

Precise Lists break down the text even further, making this incredible collection of good gardening ideas even more accessible and friendly to use.

Wondering Why Boxes answer gardening questions of all kinds … and provide solutions to the problems at hand.

CHAPTER 1

Six Ways to Work Less

Smart strategies for managing your space, energy and time.

All gardens have as their starting place the dreams and visions we create with our imaginations. Only later do we consider the nuts and bolts of planning and executing landscape projects. And it may be much later that we face the new tasks that we have set before ourselves in terms of maintenance. This book begins with the end in mind, which is to build a landscape that looks good, fulfills your need for enjoyable outdoor spaces and requires minimal time to keep it in top condition.

Such a landscape should be anything but boring. Instead, strive to make your yard a place as enjoyable to be as your favorite room in your house. Chances are this is not a room where you spend all of your time working. Instead, it's probably a room where you do things that make you happy, feel peaceful and relaxed, and don't mind the small amount of energy it takes to keep that room exactly the way you want it.

The best way to begin building satisfaction into your outdoor space is to understand what you do and don't like about it, along with adding important things that may be missing. Review the following six guidelines each time you consider design ideas, plan a project or pursue a new vision that came to you in your sleep. Each strategy is basic to having a better garden with less work.

Hedge pruning can be a source of satisfaction or a headache. Aligning what you like *to do with what you* have *to do makes repetitive tasks like hedge pruning more enjoyable.*

Reduce Repetitive Tasks

What are the things your yard keeps tugging at you to do, over and over again? Most outdoor chores are tolerable the first few times you do them, but then quickly get old. Plus, there is the matter of personal preference, in that you may have some chores that you like (or dislike) more than others. Below is a list of some of the repetitive chores that people complain about most. Review them quickly and try to make a mental guess as to how much time you spend on each of them in a year. Add any repetitive tasks that you find particularly unpleasant.

- Mowing the lawn
- Edging the lawn
- Planting and replanting flowers
- Pruning shrubs or hedges
- Raking leaves
- Gathering up debris from trees
- Managing your vegetable garden
- Sweeping or cleaning entryways
- Weeding beds
- Replenishing mulches
- Watering
- Applying fertilizer
- Applying pesticides

Choose What You Will Do

If you were honest as you contemplated the repetitive tasks list, you probably found yourself smiling as you admitted that you actually like doing some things that other people resent. Go ahead and be pleased if you take pleasure in mowing your grass. Many people do, and for them a landscape with a lush lawn as its centerpiece will be much more rewarding than a no-mow yard furnished with hard surfaces, mulch and groundcovers.

But what if what you really like is edging your lawn? Maybe you only endure mowing so that you can get to that last step. But using an edger or weed trimmer to manicure a clean line between lawn and curb is fun. You may want to redesign your lawn so that it occupies less space but still gives you lots of edges to groom.

Here's another scenario. I have known several people who had trees removed from their yards because the gardeners were so weary of cleaning up after them—something I'd never do, because I always feel happy when I'm in close company with trees. These people were not anti-plant. One couple had a huge vegetable garden and perennial bed, so it wasn't that they didn't like working outdoors. It's just that the fallen leaves and acorns got to them, so they attacked what they considered their biggest maintenance problem at its cause.

Mowing your grass can be one of the pleasures of summer, or you may think of it as pure drudgery. Naturally, small lawns require less time behind a mower than larger ones.

Sculpting topiary requires time and patience, but like other unique types of gardening, it can be a special source of satisfaction.

Sometimes simply reducing, but not eliminating, repetitive tasks turns them into pleasurable activities. I once owned a house with six huge hollies that anchored the foundation beds. At least twice a summer, I would have to prune those prickly monsters, and I hated it. The next house I lived in had only two such hollies, which I could trim in twenty minutes and consider it a job well done. Although I had thought I didn't like hollies, I was mistaken. Having two was fun, but six was four too many.

I also like sweeping, so walkways and patios get a high priority with me. And I always discover a certain feeling of wholeness in weeding small areas, such as a bed of annual flowers. Yet when I see landscapes in which the base of every tree and shrub is carefully mulched, I am tempted to knock on the door and see if the mulcher inside would be interested in a good home-cooked meal in exchange for an hour or two of mulching.

See how many choices you have? The longer you live with your landscape, the more ways you will discover what you can do less of, and what you would be happy doing at least once a week.

Neighborhoods in which one landscape seems to flow into another often showcase plants and design principles worth repeating, with room left over for individual creativity.

Repeat What Works

Most of us live in neighborhoods, and all but a few of us want to do our best to fit in. Your landscape is part of that process too, in that it should blend with its surroundings and reflect your individual tastes and preferences at the same time.

From a less-work point of view, part of blending in might be repeating landscaping ideas you see in nearby yards that seem to work well. Imitation is a form of flattery, so you should not feel embarrassed to copy a shrub grouping, groundcover or flower planting that you have admired at someone else's home. Besides, plants have a way of growing a little differently in variance with the site, so the blue and yellow pansies you plant at the base of your mailbox probably won't look exactly like the same ones down the block that are growing in big concrete planters.

Over time, you will probably make small discoveries within your own yard, such as when you find that a certain daylily likes you as much as you like it. Or, perhaps you will be magically charmed when it comes to growing lilacs. You can be scientific about it and conclude that certain plants are simply good matches to your climate, site and soil, or go with the mystery involved when plants grow well when they should not. Several beloved plants, including roses, clematis and hydrangeas, sometimes show superior growth for no apparent reason, as if the place in which they are grown is a sweet spot intended just for them. If one plant works, why not plant more? Sooner or later, most gardeners do discover that they have green thumbs destined for luck with certain species. Be proud of this and forge ahead.

Also look in commercial landscapes around office buildings, fast food restaurants and gas stations for sure-fire ideas for low-maintenance plantings. Most of these landscapes are designed by professionals and also receive plenty of attention from maintenance companies, yet they tend to be composed of ironclad plants selected for good contrast in color and texture. Two summers ago I saw 'Pink Wave' petunias decking the main streets of Jackson Hole, Wyoming, and Hot Springs, Arkansas. This year I noticed 'Orange Profusion' zinnias outside hamburger restaurants in six states. With an admirable degree of respect, a friend calls these "gas station flowers" since they persist in the polluted asphalt environment of planters stuck between gas pumps. Plants with constitutions this strong should not be ignored in a less-work landscape.

Commercial landscapes are a treasure trove of easy-care landscaping ideas. Here low-care fountain grass and white wax begonias thrive alongside the hot sidewalk of a city street.

Know Your Niches

Your yard is probably made up of several different niches—ecological pockets that vary in terms of light, moisture, wind and possibly even soil. Matching plants to the niches in which they grow best is basic to gardening success, and it's an easy way to align your efforts with the forces of nature.

In North America, the sides of a house that face either south or west normally receive the most intense light, while the east side gets morning light and afternoon shade. Northern exposures are often cool and shaded, and tend to receive the brunt of cold winter winds. Before you launch into a planting project, take the time to study a site and get to know its assets and liabilities.

Drainage is always a paramount matter, because many of the most desirable plants need soil that is sufficiently porous so that water does not stay pooled around roots for extended periods of time. Areas that become receptacles for the rainwater that runs off of your roof may have slow drainage, while high spots drain quickly since water always runs downhill.

To improve drainage, add organic matter to the soil, and dig soil to incorporate air (which makes soil lighter in texture and faster to dry out). Building raised beds improves drainage too, and may be the best way to ensure the success of plantings made where natural drainage is slightly below average.

An important soil characteristic that affects how well plants grow, called pH, has to do with the natural acidity or alkalinity of soil. You can buy inexpensive pH test kits at garden centers and discount stores. If a test indicates that your soil is extreme in either direction, you will want to adjust the pH to bring it closer to neutral. Adding lime raises the pH of acidic soil, and powdered sulfur lowers the pH in soils that are highly alkaline. Still, your soil will nudge itself back into its normal pH range over time, so it's wise to choose plants with their pH preferences in mind. Azaleas, dogwoods, and other plants native to woodland areas usually prefer acidic soil, while many native plants of the interior West are adapted to alkaline conditions.

Also identify areas of your yard that are natural niches for human activity. Places where people like to work or play often become compacted from foot traffic, and it's better to work in harmony with this fact than to try to fight it. Let pathways develop into walkways, and turn sitting areas into patios. Chapters 2 and 3 show dozens of ways to make these changes beautifully, using methods that result in much better gardens with far less work.

In low spots where the soil stays wet much of the time, raised beds improve drainage around plant roots. Result? A garden that grows better.

Tall trees provide filtered shade, creating an ideal spot for low-care pachysandra (an evergreen groundcover), and shade-tolerant shrubs such as viburnum.

Set Nature Free

One of the main ideas to keep in mind when cultivating a low-maintenance landscape is energy—finding ways to balance the energy nature brings to your yard with the energy you want to expend in making it more attractive and functional.

If you live on a windswept slope, it makes sense to accentuate ornamental grasses and sturdy shrubs, which withstand and complement the natural drama of wind. The last thing you would want to do would be to plant lots of upright plants that would constantly need staking or propping up. Similarly, in a woodland setting, nature stands poised to provide cooling shade and natural mulch, a perfect setup for low-light plants that like to have their roots bathed in moisture.

A pergola on pillars enriches the landscape with its elegant architecture and provides a sheltered spot for relaxation amidst plants that thrive in open shade.

At the same time, forge ahead with small things you can do to make your yard more hospitable to both plants and people. Prune low branches from trees to admit more light and fresh air, and keep people from having to duck to avoid obstacles. Plant windbreaks or install a privacy fence to create shelter from persistent wind. Overhead structures such as arbors or pergolas provide welcome respite from the sun in sites that cook a little too much in the summer.

Grow What You Love

Although you may think that the least amount of time you can spend keeping up your yard is what you really want, you may be mistaken. If gardening interests you at all, sooner or later you will find plants or projects you enjoy so much that every moment you spend working with them is pure pleasure. It might be growing a bed of herbs, planting bulbs or perhaps painting your yard with annual flowers. Give in to these sources of enjoyment and take steps to reduce the time you spend doing things that are less gratifying. For example, there is nothing wrong with hiring someone to mow your lawn so that you can have more time to tinker with hostas and ferns in a shade garden!

Gathering baskets of sun-ripened cherry tomatoes or herbs and flowers is so rewarding to many people that they hardly think of the work involved in growing the plants.

We tend to enjoy things that we do well, so it's smart to look for gardening activities that fit your lifestyle. If you tend to have only short spurts of time for playing with plants, container gardening may be your destiny. People who like to set aside widely spaced "dirt days" often enjoy perennials best of all. You will know you are doing something you love when you lose track of time and find yourself smiling. The main thing that makes a good garden better is the joy it brings to the people who create it.

Flower lovers always find happiness among bright blooms. To them, every moment spent weeding, staking and trimming is a real treat.

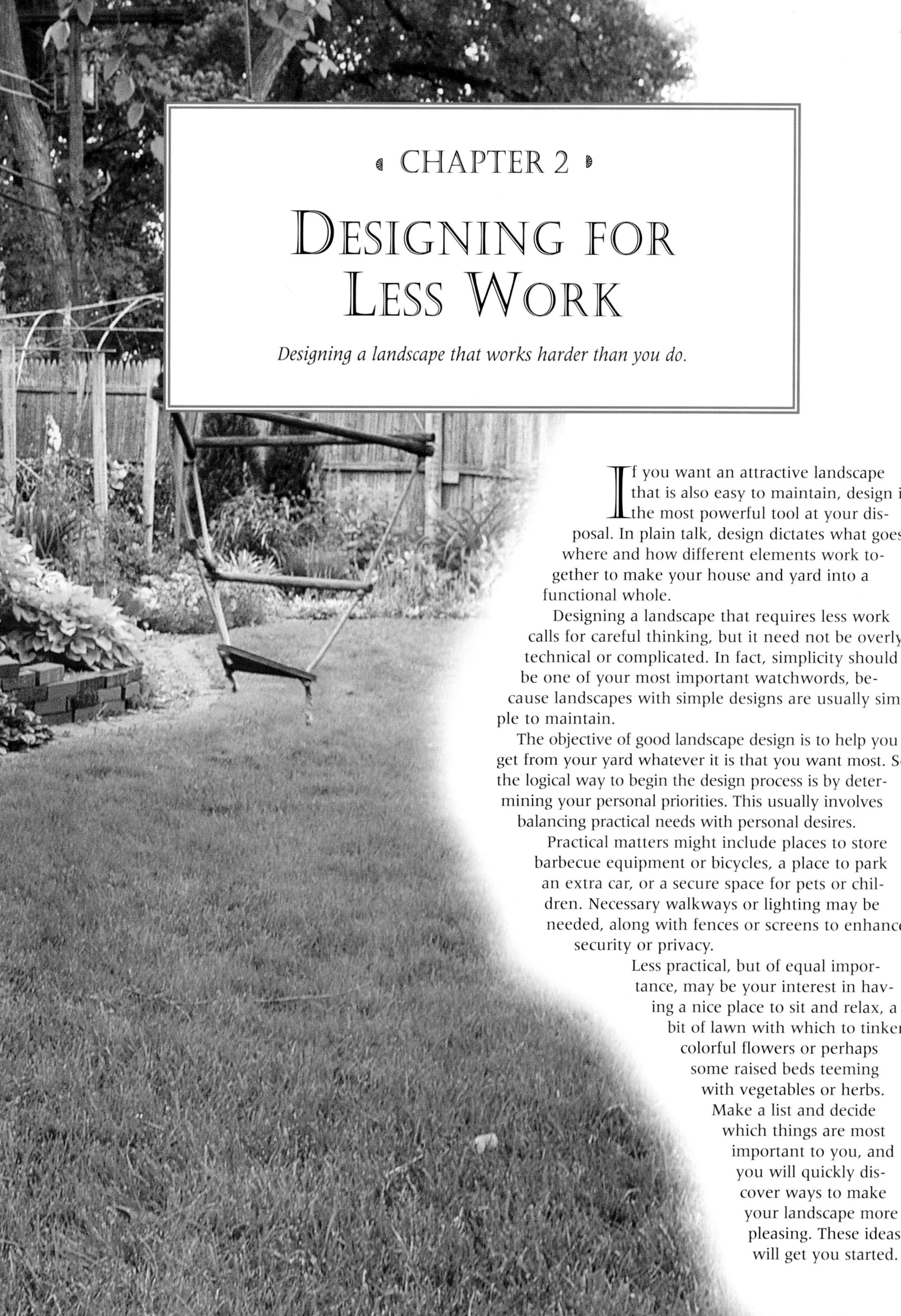

CHAPTER 2

DESIGNING FOR LESS WORK

Designing a landscape that works harder than you do.

If you want an attractive landscape that is also easy to maintain, design is the most powerful tool at your disposal. In plain talk, design dictates what goes where and how different elements work together to make your house and yard into a functional whole.

Designing a landscape that requires less work calls for careful thinking, but it need not be overly technical or complicated. In fact, simplicity should be one of your most important watchwords, because landscapes with simple designs are usually simple to maintain.

The objective of good landscape design is to help you get from your yard whatever it is that you want most. So the logical way to begin the design process is by determining your personal priorities. This usually involves balancing practical needs with personal desires.

Practical matters might include places to store barbecue equipment or bicycles, a place to park an extra car, or a secure space for pets or children. Necessary walkways or lighting may be needed, along with fences or screens to enhance security or privacy.

Less practical, but of equal importance, may be your interest in having a nice place to sit and relax, a bit of lawn with which to tinker, colorful flowers or perhaps some raised beds teeming with vegetables or herbs. Make a list and decide which things are most important to you, and you will quickly discover ways to make your landscape more pleasing. These ideas will get you started.

Limit High-Labor Plants

We are fortunate to live in an age where our choice of plants includes many that are naturally small so that they never need pruning, naturally healthy so that they never get sick, and naturally beautiful because they were bred to bloom like crazy. This is great news if you are installing a new landscape, because you can be assured that the hard work you do digging and preparing planting holes, and the money you pay for state-of-the-art plants, will pay off in less maintenance later on.

But what if you are stuck with a yard stocked with shrubs that seem to need pruning every time it rains, and a yard that takes hours just to mow? Obviously some of those shrubs will need to go, and cutting the lawn back to a more manageable size would definitely be a step in the right direction. Yet older landscapes have assets too. Mature trees are often landscape treasures, and if you wait a season or two you may find many bulbs or dormant perennials lurking in the shadows.

This welcoming entryway has it all—interesting colors and textures, soft framing from trees and large shrubs, and a clear focus toward the front door.

Even well-kept shrubs can become monsters when they grow so large that they block windows. In this landscape, removal of the hollies would be a huge improvement.

The Plants You Keep

To take some of the guesswork out of deciding which plants are worthy of your yard, check out the plants listed in Chapter 6, which begins on page 94. Even older specimens of many of these plants, particularly the trees and shrubs, can give years of satisfaction if you spend a little time weeding, grooming and feeding them. What mature dogwoods and lilacs lack in terms of disease resistance, they more than make up for with their majestic size.

In older landscapes, the most common liability plants are overgrown foundation shrubs that are so huge and unwieldy that they block windows and obstruct walkways. Sometimes they will regain a nice bushy form if you cut them back hard, but you may end up with dead stubs. A better approach is usually to earmark a few keepers that seem in good health and are not placed by doors and windows, then get rid of the others. See the sections on foundation shrubs (pages 44-47) for good ideas on creating foundation beds that need minimal upkeep.

Until they reach mature size, it's easy to underestimate how wide shrubs will grow. Here, mature mugo pines come dangerously close to crowding the entryway.

Headline-Making Plants

Check with your state extension service and at area botanical gardens to learn about plants that perform so well in your area that they have been given awards. Colorado, Texas, and most of the southeastern states sponsor award programs, as do groups such as the Pennsylvania Horticultural Society.

Evaluating Old Trees

Most of us would agree that trees are beautiful, but that opinion may be compromised by the time we spend picking up branches, raking leaves, and washing stains and bird droppings off of our cars. On the positive side, trees provide cooling shade and also give us emotional comfort with their presence and the

Low-maintenance flowering crabapples preside over an informal patio, where they provide color in spring and welcome shade through the summer.

natural drama of seasonal change. Trees also offset air pollution, particularly trees that have dense leaves. Deciding whether to keep a tree or replace it is always a difficult decision, and it's wise to err in favor of the tree unless it is very badly damaged. Even dead trees can be landscape assets because of their form and potential for hosting wildlife—assuming that they are not poised to fall on your house with the next strong gust of wind.

If you decide to sacrifice an old tree, make plans to replace it, perhaps in another part of your yard. When growing a young tree, early pruning and shaping will pay off later by resulting in a stronger, healthier tree. Use pruning shears or a pruning saw to remove branches that cross or take off in awkward directions. Staking, and removing low branches, will help a tree grow straight and tall.

Korean boxwoods pruned into well-defined shapes require close attention, but the payback is an extremely neat, formal effect.

NATURAL EDGE

Naturally Neat Evergreens

It's always a good idea to emphasize evergreens in your landscape because they look attractive year-round and shed very little litter that requires cleanup. Dwarf boxwoods can be left unpruned, and most junipers actually resent pruning. If you live in Zones 7 to 9, consult local nurseries when considering evergreens for your yard, because dozens of beautiful species—including aucuba, camellia and pittosporum—are hardy in these regions but not farther north.

TOOL TIP

Electric Pruning Shears

The easiest way to make peace with hedges or evergreen shrubs that need shaping is to get some electric pruning shears. Lightweight, inexpensive and easy to use, this tool makes quick work of the most intimidating pruning jobs. Catching prunings in a tarp or old blanket spread on the ground under plants saves cleanup time too.

Rechargeable pruning shears make quick work of trimming hedge plants.

WATCH OUT!

Space-Hungry Shrubs

Some plants have no business near walkways or entries because they just can't behave themselves, lurching out or up so that you are constantly running for your pruning shears. Chronic offenders include arborvitae, hollies, privet, rhododendrons and Russian olive. When choosing shrubs for places where humans frequently move about, smaller is always better.

Create Compatible Plantings

Growing summer annuals together in a shared bed makes it simple to keep them weeded, fed and trimmed. Plus, you get to enjoy variations in color and texture.

The main criteria for placing plants together is life cycle. Annual flowers, for example, can be planted together in spring, trimmed, fed and rejuvenated in summer, and pulled out altogether in the fall, so it makes sense to grow them together in an annual bed. Doing so makes growing these flowers more rewarding since you see the results of your efforts so clearly each time you invest some energy in planting or tending your plants.

Any landscape requires some upkeep, and it's always satisfying when you can look back at what you've done in five, fifteen or fifty minutes and see a job that has been completed, with no dangling details. This is the beauty of placing plants together that have common maintenance needs. When those plants also are compatible in terms of their requirements for sun, water and soil type, you can call it a plant guild—a plant association that naturally works well, in which the plants prosper with little help from you.

The same is true with perennials. Much of the work of growing these long-lived flowers comes in the beginning, when you give your back a good workout digging planting holes, amending them with organic matter, and nestling in the best quality plants you can find. After that, upkeep will consist mostly of weeding and renewing mulches, and perhaps providing stakes to keep tall growers upright. If your perennials are located in the same bed, tending to the needs of the group should never take an excessive amount of time.

In a similar way, you can save time mowing if your lawn is in a concentrated space, or at least does not stop and then start again in different parts of your landscape. If you must turn off your mower and wrestle it to a new location to finish the job, or if little strips of grass that poke out here and there are difficult to access, alter the shape of your lawn so that it has a simpler outline with straight or broadly curved edges.

A perennial border requires labor, but placing perennials together in a concentrated space enhances their beauty while easing maintenance chores.

NATURAL EDGE

Gardens of Stone

Not everything in your garden has to be a plant. Large stones are maintenance free, and arrangements of rock can be exquisitely beautiful. Stone is always a strong textural element in a garden, and you can pick up and magnify stones' color with stachys, dusty miller or other plants with gray foliage.

Shallow-rooted dianthus make themselves at home among mosses and sedums.

WATCH OUT!

Taking on Too Much

Besides life cycle, you might want to group plants together for a certain purpose, such as attracting butterflies, creating a strong splash of color or delighting your nose with intoxicating fragrances. Follow your dreams, but keep maintenance at a minimum by limiting the size and number of theme gardens you grow, and don't try to indulge all your gardening fantasies in the same season.

A formal platform lawn is framed with strawberries separated from the turf by a strip of rigid edging. Pots of pink geraniums add height to the composition.

Trees vs. Lawns

Most of us are reluctant to admit that a basic conflict exists between the two types of plants that dominate our yards: trees and lawns. They simply don't go together. Lawngrasses don't like the way trees block light, and trees don't like the way lawns drink up moisture. Pines and other conifers also have an acidifying effect on the soil, which often requires the use of lime to keep the soil pH acceptable to grass. And each time you mow around a tree, there is the risk that you'll slip and smash into the trunk, causing a serious injury to the tree.

Small trees such as crabapples work well as free-standing elements in a lawn, but with larger trees it's wise to give up the fight and transform the area beneath trees into a mulched bed, or perhaps a mass planting of groundcover. This design approach reduces mowing and raking chores; just rake leaves directly into the bed at the tree's base.

Grass is often willing to grow beneath small deciduous trees like this flowering crabapple. Winter sun is abundant beneath its branches, and summer shade is more filtered than dense.

Flowing pachysandra groundcover grows happily in damp shade, protects a tree's trunk from possible mowing injuries, and suppresses weeds.

Go-Anywhere Guilds

These plant combinations always work well together.

- **Dogwood and dwarf azalea** both need moist, acidic soil and enjoy the company of tall shade trees. Plus, they bloom together in the spring.
- **Daffodils and daylilies** are a great duo because emerging daylilies gain size just in time to hide the failing foliage of daffodils.

Long-lived pink azaleas light up spring in a shady landscape.

- **Lavender and roses** are a fine combination for fragrance. Locate them near a wall to help pool their wonderful aromas for your nose.
- **Forsythias and crocus** can turn any space into a spring wonderland. Lavender crocus are especially eye-catching when they bloom at the feet of yellow forsythia.

Purple pansies hold their ground in a bed filled with crocus and pink tulips.

- **Tulips and pansies** can be planted together in the fall in most climates. The tulips will push up between the pansies in the spring, with both flowers blooming in unison.
- **Tomatoes and basil** are a natural partnership for the palate, and they coexist beautifully in a garden too. Both thrive in warm sun.

Make More Hard Surfaces

Spacious and durable, this brick patio requires no maintenance beyond sweeping and occasional cleaning. The water garden makes this a great spot for relaxation.

Sooner or later, the most heavily used areas in your yard will become bare dirt, mud or dusty dog trots. Besides being unattractive, worn-out areas defy good care.

The first fix that most people try—placing steppingstones in the bare places to make them easier to walk upon—often leads to increased maintenance. Weeds and grasses grow up around the steppingstones, requiring the use of a weed trimmer to make them look neat.

The best long-term solution is to install a proper walkway, landing or patio. These are examples of what landscape designers call *hard surfaces,* because they are permanent floors of man-made origin. A number of different materials can be used to create hard surfaces, which vary in their cost and ease of installation. New hard surfaces that occupy only a little space are good projects for do-it-yourselfers, but the installation of a large patio calls for professional help.

As you consider the possibilities described, keep in mind the long-term cost benefits of the project. If you have a small house in a modest neighborhood, it might not be wise to invest your time and money in an expensive patio made of the finest flagstone you can find. In comparison, high-quality hard surfaces that enhance outdoor living in upscale properties are usually a smart investment.

Gravel

Inexpensive and easy to install, a bed of gravel creates a clean walking surface that never needs mowing. Yet because gravel or pebbles move about underfoot, neither provides the most secure walking surface. However, you can have both a clean, less-work outdoor floor as well as solid places to step by combining gravel with steppingstones.

A rough stone walkway set in a bed of pebbles is quick to install, provides secure footing in all types of weather, and enriches the landscape with its texture.

Begin site preparation by getting rid of weeds and grasses manually or with an herbicide. Level the surface, and cover it with a sheet of heavy-weight black plastic with perforations that allow water to percolate through it. Install a frame made of treated wood, treated landscaping timbers, formed concrete edging or some other edging material that will effectively contain a 2-inch-deep layer of gravel. Set steppingstones in place, and fill in around them with gravel.

Maintenance of this type of hard surface is limited to pulling occasional weeds, or zapping them with herbicide. Every year or so, you may need to add additional gravel to make up for settling and loss of material. Depending on the size of the project, you can buy gravel in bags, by the truckload or by the ton.

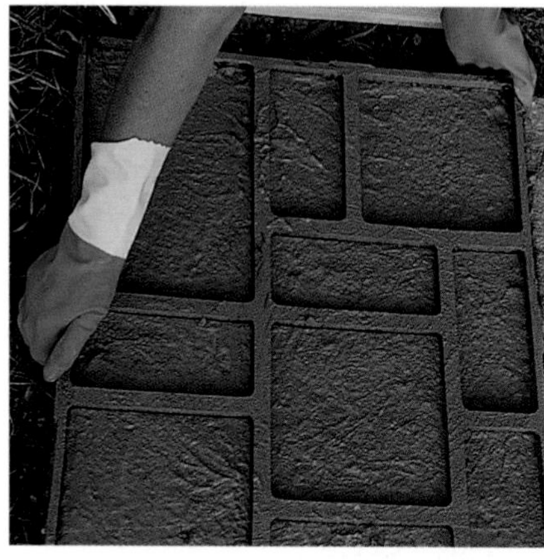

Using plastic molds and inexpensive ready-mixed concrete, it is easy to create a handsome walkway that looks like brick, stone or cobblestone.

Concrete

Permanent and inexpensive, concrete is the most widely used material for walkways and patios. It molds itself to the surface upon which it is poured and becomes harder the longer it cures. For small areas, look into inexpensive plastic molds that you fill with ready-mixed concrete to form natural-

This flagstone patio surrounded by a stone wall warms up quickly on cool days. Flowers in containers add summer color, while evergreen junipers provide winter interest.

looking concrete "bricks" or "cobblestones." Whether molded or poured, the most time-consuming part of installing a concrete walkway or patio is preparing the site and building a frame. You can do this yourself, or have it done by a contractor. Large surfaces more than 100 feet square (10 x 10) are prone to cracking, and should be installed by a professional.

This stone patio works perfectly in combination with the house's stone veneer. The rock garden carries the texture of stone up the hillside.

Brick

Brick pavers are so easy to install, it is no wonder that they are a popular choice for people who want to build a new walkway or patio themselves. Available in a range of colors and textures, there is usually some kind of brick to fill any design need. The installation of a brick walkway is shown in detail on pages 24 and 25. In the interest of reduced maintenance, it is important that the joints between brick pavers be filled with mortar. Otherwise, pavers are prone to pop out of place, and weeds emerging from the joints could become a persistent problem.

Interlocking Pavers

Manufactured from molded concrete, interlocking pavers are more costly than brick pavers, but they also have a more sophisticated appearance. The same site preparation is used to install interlocking pavers as to install brick pavers, but spacing must be much more precise. As each interlocking paver is set in place, it must be firmly tapped so that it locks into adjoining pieces. Because a walkway or patio made from interlocking pavers resembles a symmetrical jigsaw puzzle, some type of permanent frame is needed to support the outside edges. The frame can be made of wood, or you can buy edge pieces that match the pavers.

Flagstone

The natural look of flagstone comes in many colors and textures, which you can preview at the sales lot. Flagstone is sold by the ton, and because the pieces are irregular in size, working with them involves a degree of artistry. You will also need a strong back, because you will be working with pieces of stone 2 inches thick, which can be very heavy. However, because of their weight, flagstones can be set on a thinner bed of crushed stone than is needed for bricks, and a frame is strictly optional. To avoid weed problems, however, it's important to mortar the joints between stones, or to plant them with vigorous crevice plants. Suppliers who sell flagstone can help you calculate how much you will need to buy.

Gentle curves keep this walkway from looking too stiff. The left edge doubles as a mowing strip, eliminating the need for tedious edging.

Build a Brick Walkway

The formal style of this brick walkway gains even more emphasis from symmetrical plantings on both sides. The row of dwarf boxwoods is broken by a planting of culinary herbs.

A brick walkway, landing or patio is a lasting landscape improvement that is also fun to build. Because bricks are not very heavy, you need not be well muscled to handle them. And because the method used here does not require that you mortar each brick into place as you go, you can work at your own speed.

Step 1: Mark the Outline

In most cases, you will be adding onto an existing hard surface, such as a concrete walkway or an asphalt driveway, which will form a fixed edge from which to begin. From there, experiment with laying out the outline of the new hard surface by placing garden hoses or pieces of rope on the ground where the edges will be. Once you are satisfied with your plan, place several cups of all-purpose flour in a plastic bag, snip off one of the corners with scissors, and mark off the edges by laying down a line of flour.

Use a board to level the base layer of crushed stone. Then tamp it well.

Step 2: Prepare the Site

You are now ready to excavate the site to a depth of 4 inches. Use a sharp spade for this task, which involves taking up soil, placing it in a wheelbarrow, and transporting it to a different part of your yard. Avoid cultivating the bottom of the site since you want it to be hard and compacted. Ideally, it should have a very slight slope, or pitch, which you can hardly see but that amounts to about ⅛ inch per foot. This slight pitch is necessary to permit good drainage.

Step 3: Check Width and Fit

Measure as you work to make sure you have the width right, keeping in mind that the excavated area needs to accommodate both the brick pattern and edging material you intend to use. After you have prepared a small area, lay out a "dummy" on the bare ground to make sure the pavers and edging fit according to your plan.

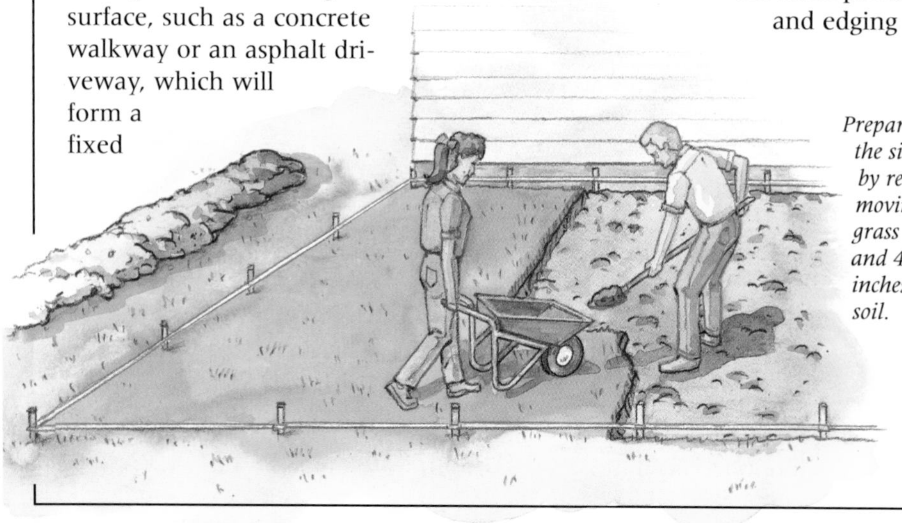

Prepare the site by removing grass and 4 inches of soil.

Step 4: Prepare the Foundation

Fill the excavated site with 2 inches of crushed stone or stone dust, which is sold for this purpose. Level it with a rake, tamp with the back of a shovel to make it smooth, and then use a board pulled over the surface to level it again. As extra insurance against weeds, lay a piece of porous landscaping fabric over the crushed stone, and then install your edging. After the edging is in place, spread a 1-inch layer of clean sand over the landscape fabric.

WATCH OUT!

Minding Your Edges

Because bricks have straight edges, it is easiest to build walkways or patios with straight edges. If your walkway is to include meandering curves, consider making your walkway of free-form flagstones set in a bed of soil topped with a thin base of clean sand. No edging is needed since the weight of flagstone holds it in place with little, if any, natural shifting.

Place each paver, check its position and level, then tap into place.

Step 6: Fill the Joints

In a pail or clean wheelbarrow, mix a half-and-half mixture of clean sand and dry mortar. Carefully sweep this mixture so that the crevices between the bricks are filled. Using a light mist from a garden hose, dampen the surface and allow the water to become absorbed. When the surface has dried completely, repeat the crevice-filling procedure. Allow the walkway or patio to cure for at least two days before walking on it.

After the joints have cured for at least two weeks, enhance the finish of the bricks with a water sealant, which is fast and easy to apply.

When your patio needs cleaning, a stiff scrub brush and water will usually do the job. Or, you can use a high-pressure power washer.

Step 5: Install the Pavers

Lay pavers in the pattern you have chosen, stopping after each paver is placed to tap it tightly into place and to make sure the depth is perfect. Stop after each row and use a level to make sure the surface is not becoming too uneven or wavy. Remember, it should have a very slight slant to one side, and not be absolutely level, for drainage.

Making a Clean Sweep

Clean hard surfaces quickly with a broom, sweeping dust and debris directly into areas that adjoin the hard surface. Mulched beds planted with small shrubs work well for this purpose. Plus, they are ready receptacles for the substantial amounts of rainwater that drain off of hard surfaces.

Paver Patterns

Manufactured especially for hard surfaces, brick pavers resist cracking, though they are thinner than standard building bricks. Most are 4 inches wide and 8 inches long, so you will need about 4½ pavers per square foot. Some patterns require that you score and cut pavers as illustrated below.

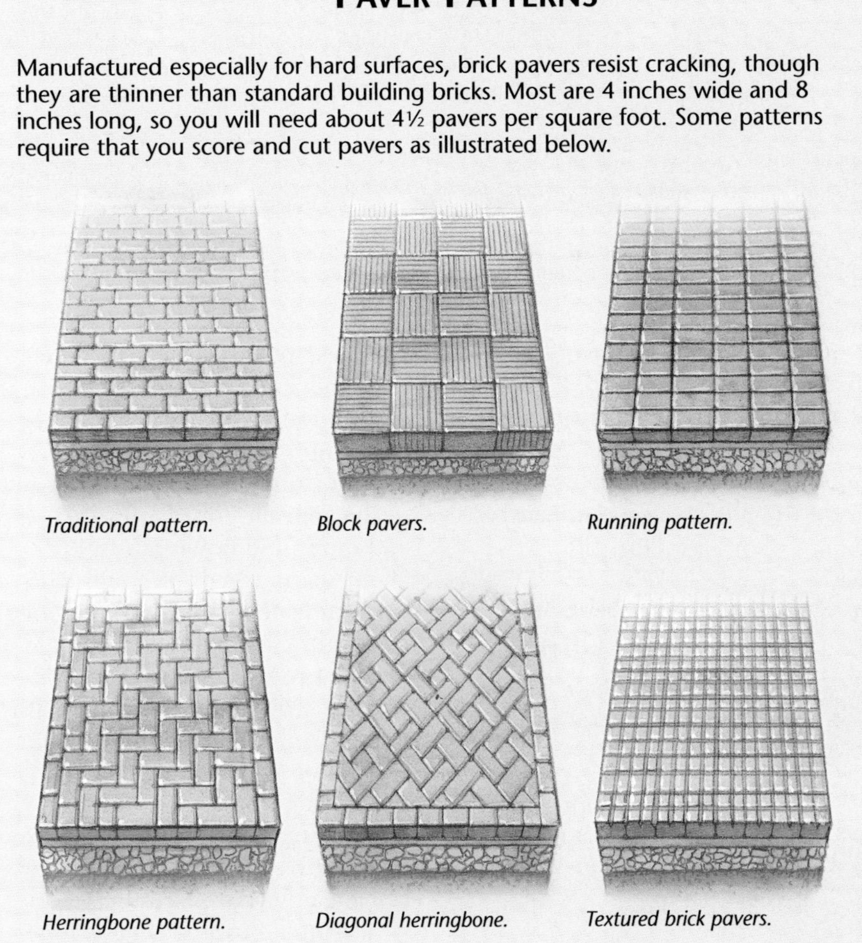

Traditional pattern. *Block pavers.* *Running pattern.*

Herringbone pattern. *Diagonal herringbone.* *Textured brick pavers.*

Design Out Weeds

Shaded areas beneath trees are ideal spots for plants that cover the ground with greenery and choke out weeds in the process. Hostas and pachysandra are perfect plants for the job.

If not for weeds, we would live in a starkly barren world. Equipped to move into any open space, weeds are nature's colonizers of vacant soil, the pioneer plants that begin the process of natural succession in which bare earth is slowly and gradually transformed into a mature ecosystem such as a forest or prairie.

Unfortunately, weeds do not add to the appeal of our yards. Coarse and rangy and downright selfish about space, weeds often outcompete cultivated plants, taking moisture, nutrients and light intended for our peonies and peppers. Anyone who enjoys growing plants quickly comes to resent weeds, which pop up in containers and shrub beds, and are present in amazing numbers in areas that are frequently cultivated, such as vegetable gardens or places planted with annual flowers. Unless you want to spend hours and hours pulling weeds, you will need to use a variety of tricks to prevent the proliferation and spread of weeds.

Weed Early and Often

Immature weeds have skimpy roots, so they are easy to pull out, especially when the soil is wet. Or simply lop off their heads with a sharp hoe. If you get rid of weeds when they are young, they will never shed seeds in your garden.

WATCH OUT!

Site-Specific Herbicides

Chemicals that kill plants, called herbicides, give some people chills, but you should not be afraid to use herbicides when their use is warranted. Always use good preventive management practices before turning to herbicides for help.

So-called nonselective herbicides will kill any plant they touch, and you will need this much punch to turn dangerous weeds such as poison ivy or stinging nettle into history. Other herbicides do very specific jobs. Crabgrass preventers keep crabgrass (and other seeds) from sprouting. Broadleaf herbicides kill weeds with flat, oval-shaped leaves but do not injure grass when used according to label directions. Grass herbicides, which are sometimes used in wildflower meadows, kill grass rather than broad-leafed flowers.

When using any herbicide, always study the label first. Herbicides are labeled according to which plants they can be used upon safely rather than by which weeds they kill. Very few herbicides are labeled for use on edible plants.

How Weeds Work

Weeds bring with them several distinct advantages that make them formidable adversaries. Many species produce hundreds of thousands of seeds, some of which will germinate the following year. Other seeds that manage to get buried in the soil may wait patiently for more than a decade for their place in the sun. In fact, some weed seeds need to be ex-

Tool Tip: Landscape Fabrics

Special landscape fabrics, created specifically to prevent weeds, now exist for many different situations. Unlike black plastic, which becomes a barrier to water and soluble plant foods even when perforated, landscape fabrics are porous. Yet their texture is such that they effectively suppress weeds that attempt to grow from beneath them. Although soil and mulch that is spread atop landscape fabrics can support weeds, you will find it easy to pull the weeds from loose organic mulch. Some of the most useful landscape fabrics are circular skirts made to be laid out beneath newly planted trees and shrubs. Installed at planting time, these tree skirts help keep the soil cool and moist while discouraging weeds.

Roll out weed barriers and cover with mulch to prevent weeds from growing.

posed to sunlight to trigger sprouting, which is why newly cultivated soil often gives rise to many more weeds than a nearby spot that has been left untouched for several seasons.

Perennial weeds such as bindweed, greenbrier, Canada thistle and quackgrass spread by seeds and by wandering roots. Pull out or hoe down the main plant, and a few weeks later you can expect a crop of babies to appear a few inches or feet from where the parent weed stood. These new weeds arise from root buds which mobilize and grow even faster when the dominant weed body is removed. Cultivating the soil can make things worse since the root buds often remain viable even when chopped into small 1-inch pieces.

Beating Weeds

What's a weed-weary gardener to do? For starters, design your landscape so that no space is left unoccupied. If some areas refuse to support cultivated plants, either cover them with a hard surface or blanket them with mulch until you think of a more lasting solution. Each time you create a new planting space for any kind of plant, also think of how you will prevent weeds or manage them if they appear.

What to Do with Your Dead Weeds

Even in the best less-work landscapes, weeding days are in order from time to time, during which you may accumulate one or many hefty piles of pulled weeds. What can you do with them? Compost heaps often don't get hot enough to kill weed seeds, though it's perfectly safe to compost weeds pulled when they are young, before they have a chance to develop mature seeds. But with perennial weeds or those holding mature seeds, it may be better to treat the corpses like garbage. Either set them out to be collected as waste, or, if your property is large, find an out-of-the-way place where you can dump them.

Pull weeds and spent plants by hand when the soil is moist. Then set out new plants or cover the soil with mulch.

Get Real with Your Lawn

This small framed lawn serves as a spacious oasis in the landscape. Because of its modest size and brick frame, it can be mowed and edged in only a few minutes.

We tend to take for granted that most of our yards will be taken up by grass. Yet space filled with scruffy grass is not a lawn, but a burden. A small lawn that is well cared for requires less work and looks much better than a big one that gets grudgingly mowed in summer and neglected the rest of the year.

As you think of practical ways to design or redesign your landscape, you should make a conscious choice to have a lawn of a specific shape and size. In a landscape designed with less work in mind, the lawn should be a working feature that makes everything around it look better. It should be only as big as it needs to be to meet the aesthetic needs of the site and the practical needs of the people who call the place home. This is a very different idea from accepting the grass that came with your yard, seemingly free, but that requires constant summer upkeep and rarely looks its best.

Although there are no hard-and-fast rules on the ideal size and shape of a low-maintenance lawn, simple shapes such as squares, rectangles, circles, ovals or kidneys are common. Indeed, a circular lawn that appears almost like a platform of fine-textured green can be a tremendous problem solver because it unifies everything around it. You can frame a circular lawn with groundcovers, and in doing so drastically reduce mowing time.

Of course, a circle need not be altogether round. If you want your lawn to meet the straight edges of your driveway and the sidewalk, it can always be squared on one side and curved on the other. Also, look for places where grass becomes thin and weak due to shade from trees. You will likely discover a natural outline for a scaled-down lawn.

WATCH OUT!

No Backups

Beware of shapes that require you to stop and back up or change directions with your mower, resulting in missed places. These are trouble spots to solve by reshaping the outline of your lawn. If a lawn must have straight edges, rounding out the corners into broad curves may solve this problem.

NATURAL EDGE

Lawn Alternatives

Chapter 5, which begins on page 78, goes into detail on the nuts and bolts of lawn care and lawn alternatives for climates that are naturally hostile to lawngrasses. If you feel that you're fighting nature by attempting to grow a lawn at all, keep an open mind and look into something a little different such as a casual lawn studded with little bulbs, or an enriched native prairie.

Low-care ornamental grasses and spreading perennials may work better than grass in some climates.

A string trimmer makes quick work of edging chores.

Exploit Important Spaces

A welcoming front yard is a top priority for most of us. Study landscapes in your area to get ideas for making your yard more appealing.

Whether you are designing a new landscape or redesigning an old one, you will accumulate quite a list of projects. Some will excite you from the get-go, and one of the pleasures of living a gardening life is indulging in horticultural projects that stir your passions. At the same time, try to be practical in setting priorities. If you are new to gardening and have plenty of other things to do, like running a family and working a job, you can quickly spread yourself too thin by becoming overly ambitious. Few things are more depressing than a yard full of half-done projects.

Annuals, perennials and bulbs bring color and texture to a spacious patio clearly intended for outdoor living. Brick walls make the space feel more cozy and intimate.

To help you decide which things should come first, read through Chapter 3 (starting on page 30), which addresses landscape concerns associated with the most important parts of your yard—such as entryways and foundation plantings. Taming the maintenance needs of these special places will leave you free to pursue more enjoyable projects such as growing flowers, vegetables or herbs.

Powerful Partnerships

When we embark on a mission to make our yards more beautiful and appealing, yet easier to maintain, we are really trying to form a partnership with the natural world outside our doors. This is an association built upon cooperation among life forms (people and plants) that strives to achieve balance and harmony to the benefit of all. Regardless of your personal views on religion and spirituality, you should know that magical things can happen through this process.

Be prepared to be delighted, and don't expect that all the answers as to how to change or mold your landscape will come to you in one fell swoop. Certainly some challenges will have clear solutions, but others might need to be studied through several seasons before the right idea can germinate and grow.

Meanwhile, keep an open mind and try to appreciate all that unfolds before you. And trust and believe that you were never meant to struggle too hard against nature's energy, but to become a part of it. This is the *real* key to having a better garden with less work.

SECURITY
W
westec

CHAPTER 3

Better Gardens for Special Places

Putting your energy into the spaces that mean the most.

After you have lived in a house for a while, you will probably find yourself naturally attracted to certain parts of your yard. It could be the front entryway, a shady side of a back patio, or perhaps you're so pressed for time that the only part of your landscape you see every day is the walkway that connects the driveway to the door. Then the weekend rolls around and you find yourself faced with upkeep. Where to begin?

Why not start with places that are truly important, either because you actually use them or because they are your property's link with the rest of the world? In this chapter, the timesaving strategies and space-enhancing ideas focus on the most crucial sectors of home landscapes—entryways, traffic corridors, foundation plantings (those shrubs that encircle your house), and areas that are distinctively defined by sun or shade. Concentrating your efforts on these special places ensures that the time you spend working in your yard really counts. As you study your yard's special places, perhaps you will discover something new about yourself and what makes you happy. Is it an alluring entryway that surrounds you with a feeling of welcome? A pretty vine scrambling up a lamppost? A patch of fragrant flowers that greets you when you open your car door?

Discovering new ways to derive pleasure from your yard should always be a goal. It's what makes the work you do more meaningful, and perhaps a little more fun.

A Formal Front Entryway

The front entryway to your home should carry one simple message. It should say welcome, and subtly communicate that your house is a good and comfortable place to be. This message should be clear to you and your family as well as to visitors. Creating such an entryway is easy, because the main thing to keep in mind is simplicity.

A wide landing just outside the front door gives visitors a place to linger, as well as ample space for two people to walk side by side.

Finding Room for Improvement

Begin by studying what you have. Are there obstacles or distractions that can be eliminated or toned down? Is the approach narrow or crowded? Because the purpose of an entryway is to facilitate the movement of people carrying armloads of groceries, meandering and curious guests, or pets on a speed course to their food bowls, an uncomplicated passage is always best.

Come in and out of the entryway several times to get a feel for its assets and drawbacks, and then study it from the curb. Most people with contemporary, colonial or ranch-style houses want their front entryway to look neat and somewhat formal, which makes a good first impression and works well with these architectural styles. You can achieve a formal focus by designing an entryway that has a strong feeling of symmetry. This does not mean that plants on opposite sides of the entryway must match like bookends, but rather that they should be nicely balanced in terms of size and weight. Neatness counts double near the front entry, so a primary goal is to landscape the area so that it looks and feels clean, organized and safe.

You can put these ideas into action—and save many hours spent on maintenance—by following these five guidelines when selecting and placing plants, hard surfaces and accents near your front entryway.

Natural Edge: Dress Your Door

To make a plain front door more noticeable, add a brass kick-plate and matching brass house numbers. Neither are expensive, and you can install them in a matter of minutes.

Urns planted with red geraniums and pink petunias stand as formal sentinels outside the front steps. Lush beds of pachysandra at ground level further the feeling of balance and symmetry.

Give People the Right of Way

An artistic approach is great unless people end up tripping over misplaced objects. If you color your entryway with containers planted with bright flowers, be sure to place them just outside the steps or walkway so people and pets will have more room to move. In the interest of reduced maintenance, consider substituting a flag or banner for hanging baskets, which are chronically thirsty in hot weather.

Portly Pots

TIME-SAVING TIP

You may find that a single large container on one side of the entry is as effective as a matched pair, and one large container requires less watering than two smaller ones. Don't worry if it's too heavy to move. You can refresh the soil in "permanent" containers each time you replant them, and replace all the soil only every three to four years.

A single container planted with bright bloomers such as geranium, heliotrope, browallia and verbena will enhance any entryway with color and texture.

Open It Up

Do not crowd the front entry area. Keep shrubs and tree limbs trimmed back, and replace oversized plants that are constantly pushing their way into walking space. Low-growing, mound-shaped shrubs that need little pruning, such as dwarf boxwoods or barberries, are a logical first choice. Tuck them in with an attractive mulch.

The way these groups of shrubs are repeated several times gives this landscape a strong sense of rhythm that's pleasing to the eye.

Make the Most of Texture Plants

As you choose plants to dress up your entryway, capitalize on differences in leaf texture. Flowers come and go, but foliage texture remains a constant factor, present for months rather than days or weeks. Choose two or three plants with varying texture, such as soft gray stachys, evergreen juniper and bronze-leaved heuchera, and combine them in a simple and logical way. With texture in place, you can add color if you like with a single well-placed container, or clusters of bulbs.

Simplify Plant Groupings

Try to use no more than three different kinds of plants near your entryway, and make one of them an evergreen. Emphasize a single species that's just the right size and texture, such as junipers in the North or dwarf azaleas in the South, neither of which need ongoing pruning. If you hit on a combination of low-care shrubs that works especially well in your climate and soil, feature it by your entryway and repeat it in other parts of your landscape. Besides simplifying maintenance tasks such as pruning and fertilizing, this strategy makes the landscape feel unified and whole.

Upright evergreens help call attention to an entryway year-round. Plenty of variation in texture and form bring grace and charm to a plain house.

Use Concentrated Color

Strategic use of a single accent color can bring an entryway to life and help unify the landscape at the same time. One smart trick is to echo your selected color in two places—one right at the entryway and the second farther away, somewhere along the approach. One maintenance-free trick is to paint your mailbox and front door the same color. Or, use living plants to achieve similar results. For example, pink petunias in a hanging basket or half barrel near the entryway can work as a visual tie-in with a bed of the same flowers closer to the street.

Colorful and compatible, annual flowers such as verbena, marigolds, zinnias and petunias can be used to create bright puddles of color near doors and other high-visibility spots.

Enhance a Front Porch

There's no question that this porch belongs to a gardener. When it blooms in spring, a clematis vine will make any modest home the star of the neighborhood.

Keep It Light

Because porches already block natural light that comes into your house, it's important to stick with light colors, which reflect more light, when painting and furnishing a front porch. White, pale yellow, light gray and other near-neutral colors usually work best.

A front porch is much more than a place to stand while you open your front door. It doubles as an outdoor foyer year-round, and in nice weather it's an extra room with a view. This special type of entryway deserves careful attention since it has so much to offer. And, as with low-maintenance strategies in other parts of your yard, enhancing your porch without adding to your chore list calls for a simple approach.

Begin by considering your porch as a room. What is the condition of the floor, the walls, the ceiling? Clean what needs cleaning, paint what needs painting, and assess special needs for ventilation or screening from sun, wind or neighbors. A small ceiling fan adds ambience while moving stuffy air, and you can use vines or other types of screens to extend walls seasonally or year-round.

You will also need comfortable seating, or perhaps an old-fashioned porch swing. Whatever furniture you choose, be sure to keep as much open space as possible so that you never have to squeeze or bend to get around objects. Fabrics used for chair cushions present a great opportunity for bringing color to your porch, which can be played out further with your choice of plants.

Prime Porch Plantings

Three categories of easy-care plants can help your porch feel like a garden—vines, anchor plants for the entry to the porch, and a few low-care "porch plants" to grow in containers.

Lightweight Vines

If your porch is surrounded by a wood railing, you have a ready-made trellis for vines that will soften the appearance of the porch, make it look more cozy and provide seasonal color and fragrance as well. Clematis (page 105) is ideal for this job. It never becomes so rank that it contributes to rotting wood, it adapts beautifully to places where its roots are shaded, and its stems stretch into the sun. Some honeysuckles (page 117) make good porch vines too, particularly everblooming honeysuckle (*Lonicera heckrottii*). Look at your neighbors' porches to get ideas for other perennial vines that grow well in your area.

Is your porch a hot spot? That's good in winter, but in summer you'll want to cool it down with a bamboo shade screen or a simple string trellis covered with vigorous annual vines. Starting with a packet of seed and a bed or a roomy planting box, any of these plants are sure to please: morning glory, scarlet runner bean, black-eyed-Susan vine or even tiny gourds.

Clematis, larkspur and a climbing 'Blaze' rose give this entryway garden plenty of vertical interest that works well with the house's rustic look.

Foxgloves have a strong upright posture, so they are often used near porches or entryways. These grow in the happy company of iris and later-blooming lilies and coreopsis.

Shade-tolerant coleus bring welcome color to porches and patios. Regular pinching helps the plants to grow bushy and full.

Light and Upright Anchors

Most porches have at least a few steps leading up to them, and it's customary to frame the steps with plants. In keeping with the upward theme, this is a fine place to use vertical plants such as foxglove or cleome (page 106), or perhaps dwarf columnar junipers (page 122).

If lighting at the base of the steps is weak, you can get help from light-colored flowers or plants with gray or variegated leaves. Variegated hostas (page 118) are always a good bet in partial shade, or you can lighten up the look of dark evergreen foundation shrubs by giving them companion plants with gray foliage such as annual dusty miller (page 111) or perennial stachys (page 141). Do at least attempt to fine-tune entry lighting to eliminate spooky pockets of darkness, paying close attention to steps or other changes in elevation.

The felted gray leaves of stachys glow in the moonlight, and their downy texture is wonderful to touch.

Porch Plants for Low Light

If you grow indoor houseplants, you will surely want to move some of them outdoors where they can enjoy summer on the porch. A few weeks basking in warm fresh air is like a tonic to many tropical houseplants such as philodendrons, jades and cacti. But weeping figs and African violets may resent the move, preferring to stay in the cool indoors.

Fortunately there are several easily grown plants that are ideal for providing summer color on shady porches. Coleus, an annual sold as a spring bedding plant, features colorful leaves in a rainbow of colors and patterns. Most impatiens (page 120) have green leaves, but the color range is so extensive that you can easily find the perfect one for any porch.

Light pastel pinks and lavenders are great in deep shade, or you can coordinate reds or hot pinks with colors in your chair cushions. In late spring, check nurseries for potted caladiums—tropical corms that produce big, heart-shaped leaves in white, red, pink and green. Caladiums can make any porch feel like a tropical hideaway.

All three of these plants need constant moisture, and you will save much time spent watering if you plant them in plastic pots. Plastic pots retain moisture better than terra-cotta, and are widely available in natural-looking colors.

Cool-looking caladiums run on warmth, but they are easily grown from corms and require little direct light in order to thrive.

An Inviting Front Walkway

An attractive walkway makes people want to use it. The gentle curves in this unmortared brick walk make it impossible to resist.

If you think there is nothing you can do to induce yourself and your friends to use your front door instead of more utilitarian side or garage doors, think again. Sometimes changing traffic patterns is a simple matter of improving connections. Or perhaps you need to change your landscape to make sure people get the message of which door they are supposed to use. Either way, the goal is to make your primary walkway more inviting, safe and enjoyable to use. Of course, it needs to be so carefree that it is almost self-maintaining.

When houses are built, the builder usually installs a concrete walkway to the front door, which typically connects to the street. But unless the street is the customary parking area, your front door still needs to be connected to where cars are most often parked. You can link the parking area to the approach to your front door by adding an additional concrete walkway, installing a pathway paved with steppingstones, or creating any other type of well-defined walkway. (See page 38 for tips on working with steppingstones.) Sometimes a change of texture, using a material other than or in addition to concrete, gives the walkway an air of cozy mystery that makes it even more enjoyable to use.

Think Wide

Perhaps you are fortunate in having a walkway that originates in the right place and leads where it needs to go, but seldom gets used anyway. It's a big project, but you will be amazed at how much better your entryway looks and works if the walkway is at least 48 inches wide. Most concrete walkways are much narrower than this, but you can widen them with rectangular concrete steppingstones laid edge to edge, mortared flagstone, or a frame of brick or interlocking pavers. And if more of your yard is hard surfaces, the less grass there is to mow, so widening your walkway will save time on mowing chores. See pages 22-25 for information on expanding hard surfaces in your landscape.

Even if you decide you haven't the time or money to widen your walkway, you can make it look wider using special design strategies. Especially if one side of your front walkway is flanked with foundation shrubs, consider letting the other side simply flow into lawn instead of defining the edge with flowers. A swath of lawn that adjoins one side of the walkway makes the walkway feel wider and the yard seem more spacious. However, it's important that the lawn join the walkway at the same level, so that you don't feel like you're in imminent danger of falling over the edge. Plus, you'll mow faster, with less follow-up edging work, if the grass is flush with the walkway.

Easy Plants for Edging a Walkway

Begonias	Pachysandra
Dwarf boxwood	Pansy
Dusty miller	Dwarf petunia
Dwarf hosta	Portulaca
Liriope	Dwarf zinnia

Other options: Petite annuals including lobelia, sweet alyssum and phlox in cool climates, or dwarf marigold, impatiens or ageratum where summers are warm. Avoid vining plants, which need frequent trimming back, or any plant that grows more than 12 to 14 inches tall.

Variegated liriope, with creamy stripes in its leaves, is a naturally neat edging plant that helps light up walkways.

A clipped edging of dwarf boxwood separates a bed of 'Misty Lilac Wave' petunias from a brick walkway.

Well-Dressed Edges

If the main problem with your main walkway is boredom, jazz it up with color. Create planting beds down one or both sides of the walkway by digging the soil deeply, mixing in a 2-inch-deep layer of compost, humus or other organic matter, and filling it with plants that will enrich the site with color and texture.

Choose plants that are right for the job. Since this is such a high-visibility area, you will want plants that are naturally neat and uniform. The smallest of dwarf boxwoods are useful for year-round interest, but in areas where they are not hardy, or if you simply don't like them, there is a large selection of dwarf bedding plants and well-behaved groundcovers to fill this niche. The box on page 36 names ten excellent edging plants, or you can go low, low maintenance and use a band of pebbles or decorative stones.

Edgings Undercover

Need to do a little string trimmer work close to your edging, or do you have to move in close with an herbicide? Protect your plants from possible injury by covering them with upside-down plastic nursery liners or small pails. Lightweight and stackable, these are great for emergency frost protection too.

Dainty blue forget-me-nots and other woodland plants line a walkway paved with shredded bark. The bark mulch extends into the planting bed.

Use Rhythm and Repetition

You can arrange edging plants to create surprising special effects. A long run of a single plant in one color makes the walkway seem longer, while a repeating pattern with uniform texture (such as two white begonias, one pink one, over and over) has a pull-along effect. The more complex the edging, the more likely people are to slow down to take it in. Still, to simplify upkeep, it's always best to use only one or two different plants, and to stick with those with strong talents as edgings. The plants on page 36 stay small, need little maintenance and keep their good looks for a long time.

A repeating pattern of petunias and dwarf snapdragons keeps a long, straight walkway interesting, and pulls you forward like magic.

Informal Passageways

Large steppingstones made of mortared brick set in the ground nearly flush with adjacent grass provide firm footing and can be mowed over with ease.

Take a careful look at the back and side of your house, and you will quickly see where natural traffic patterns have developed—places where people and pets walk over and over again, wearing away grass to bare, compacted ground.

You can easily enhance these informal passageways to make them look and work better, or you can create new pathways to connect different parts of your landscape. The emphasis here should be less on how things look and more on practical factors such as keeping your shoes clean when you want to walk around your house in wet weather. And of course, any changes you make should reduce, rather than increase, a need for ongoing maintenance or upkeep.

The simplest and least expensive fix is to buy some concrete steppingstones and place them on the ground. However, if the site is a sunny one, it won't take long for weeds to find the new protected places around the edges of the steppingstones. So you will do better to excavate the soil sufficiently to install the steppingstones ½ inch above ground level; this way you can mow right over them. Alternatively, surround them with a bed of pebbles or mulch.

Which approach you use hinges on whether the site is level or sloped, as well as how much sun it receives.

Custom-made steppingstones set in a bed of river gravel transform each step down this pathway into a sentimental journey.

Loose mulches in sun are easy targets for weeds, which must either be removed by hand or controlled with herbicides. Even if you lay down a plastic or fabric weed barrier beneath a mulch of pebbles or bark, weeds are likely to move in if there is sufficient sun to power their growth. Loose mulches also don't work well on slopes since they are easily carried downhill by heavy rain.

Yet steppingstones that are set firmly into the ground always stay put, especially large ones. Although they are heavier to handle, steppingstones at least 18 inches across are more stable once set in place, and they are easier to walk on as well. Because setting steppingstones in the ground is hard work, make sure you space them properly. Normal adult strides call for steppingstones to measure 24 inches between centers. Children willingly make a game of hopping and skipping from one steppingstone to the next.

This stone walkway's width varies with the importance of the corridor. Notice how the narrow secondary path forks off through beds of hardy geranium.

A gravel path winds through a perennial garden, toward a small water feature. More small surprises such as specimen stones or statuary await around every corner.

WATCH OUT!

Slip and Slide

Laying a sheet of black plastic beneath a loose mulch will retard weed growth, but it also tends to get slippery when wet. To reduce this risk, use perforated plastic or punch drainage holes in it to keep water from puddling between the plastic and the mulch. Or use more porous landscaping fabrics sold for this purpose.

Loose Materials for Mulched Pathways

Any material you might use to mulch a flower bed also can be used to mulch a pathway. But loose materials are easily tracked into the house, so avoid using them to pave pathways close to doors. It's a different story for pathways that wind through a woodland garden, or for important yet seldom-used pathways through narrow sideyards. In shady spots like these, loose mulches are inexpensive and easy to maintain. They also make good temporary pathways, which you might replace with lower-maintenance hard surfaces when your budget allows.

To install a new mulched pathway, clear away weeds and grasses with a spade or herbicide, install a plastic edging (which is pounded into the ground) to keep the material in place, and fill with your material of choice. Once a year you will probably need to refresh the surface by adding new material.

Following are some of the materials you should consider for mulched pathways.

Pine needles may be free for the raking, or you can buy them in bales. Their rich red-brown color gives a lush look to shady pathways. Pine needles also are long-wearing, and they tend to knit themselves together and stay put on gentle slopes.

Pebbles or river stones are inexpensive when purchased by the truckload, and they bring an attractive texture to the garden. But they are uncomfortable to walk on with bare feet, and somewhat unstable too. Pathways that will be used by elderly people, or that will frequently bear the weight of heavy wheelbarrows, benefit from the added stability of flat steppingstones added to a loose pebble mulch.

Wood chips are free when you can get them from tree-trimming crews, though more attractive versions are sold at garden centers. Expect wood chips to gradually weather to gray over time.

Bark nuggets are widely available in bags or in bulk, and vary in the size of the nuggets. Very large nuggets are suitable only for level sites since they so easily float away. Smaller nuggets have a more comfortable feel underfoot too.

A soft bed of pine needles flanked with hardy ferns give this lovely pathway the feeling of a woodland glade.

NATURAL EDGE

Woodland Wonders

Part of the fun of having a well-defined woodland path is flanking it with low-care plants that thrive in partial shade. Some excellent choices include azaleas (page 96), dogwoods (page 110), ferns (page 113), heuchera (page 116), hostas (page 118), impatiens (page 120), ivy (page 121), pachysandra (page 128), plumbago (page 133) and pulmonaria (page 135).

This woodland garden pathway is little more than an opening in the plants, paved with the same mulch used in the garden.

Well-Dressed Verticals: Mailboxes and Lampposts

In daylight a lamppost clothed with a vine such as this honeysuckle brings its elegant presence to the landscape. By night the foliage appears even more dramatic.

Gravity keeps people well anchored toward the ground, and we naturally keep our eyes focused low so we can see where we are going. Indeed, most of your efforts to develop your home landscape will take place at levels only a few inches to a few feet high. A break from this low horizontal plane is always a welcome diversion, so features with vertical lines have both practical and aesthetic benefits in the landscape.

You can add vertical features for their looks alone, such as an arbor clothed with fragrant climbing roses, but in doing so you are signing up for ongoing upkeep. Instead, capitalize on vertical structures that already exist, such as a streetside mailbox or a lamppost near your entry. Most yards have one or the other.

Any vertical structure naturally draws the eye upward and beyond, so the first step is to consider what kind of new views you can create by dressing your mailbox or lamppost with attractive plants. If the view beyond the mailbox is desirable, such as the entrance to your house, then a vine or other plant that grows upward is in order. However, if the backdrop is less attractive (for example, your neighbor's utility area) you can concentrate on dressing the ground with a skirt of flowers and painting the mailbox or lamppost dark green so that it will fade into the landscape.

The most carefree way to cover the ground around a mailbox or lamppost is to plant a groundcover such as liriope (page 124), ivy (page 121), pachysandra (page 128) or vinca (page 144). A flowing bed of healthy groundcover plants eliminates awkward mowing and weed-trimming around the base, and always looks neat and well groomed.

You will probably need to invest some time and energy in the site if you expect groundcovers—or any other plants for that matter—to grow well. Follow the standard procedure for establishing any new planting bed, which involves digging the soil at least 12 inches deep, working in a 2- to 4-inch-deep layer of organic matter (such as compost or humus), and finally adding a standard application of an organic or timed-release fertilizer, applied according to the rate given on the package. Now you are ready to plug in groundcover plants, perhaps flowers if you want more color, or a vine if you want to draw attention to your vertical feature.

Natural Edge

Reseeding Flowers

If you want flowers around your mailbox but don't want to have to plant and water them, there are three drought-tolerant annuals that often reseed so heavily that you'll never have to replant again—melampodium (page 127), portulaca (page 134) and special varieties of zinnia (page 145). Because the seedlings will not appear until the weather is warm in early summer, you can underplant the bed with daffodils and other spring-flowering bulbs. The bulb foliage will fade just as the volunteer flowers appear on the scene.

Snuggled up against a painted chainlink fence, a mailbox gets a lift from hand-painted folk art and a halo of Japanese honeysuckle.

It's always delightful to encounter the unexpected form of a blooming pillar, especially when it's as charming as this combination of clematis, geranium and birdhouse art.

Plants for Pillars

The best vines for small vertical structures such as mailboxes or lampposts are restrained in size and vigor. Two excellent choices include clematis (page 105) and honeysuckle (page 117), both of which produce beautiful flowers and attractive foliage, and need only minor pruning and yearly feeding. Either of these vines will gladly scramble up a pole if given a little help. Clematis clings to support with curling leaf stems, while honeysuckle gently twines. To help these vines run up a vertical post, you will need to provide guide wires attached to the post and the ground. How you attach wires to the post will depend on its material, but you can easily anchor the ends in the soil with metal tent stakes.

If you want to try an annual vine before committing to a perennial, or if you want the long bloom time that you get with annuals, here are three easy annual vines that can be grown from seed planted in warm spring soil:

Scarlet Runner Bean

Scarlet runners look like pole-type snap beans, and they are. However, the orange-red flowers are numerous and showy, and are usually produced nonstop for six weeks or more. The little beans are edible, and picking them off as soon as they form pushes the plants to produce more flowers.

The pocketbook blossoms of scarlet runner bean keep this sprightly twining vine in full color all summer. A few varieties even bloom white or pink.

Thunbergia

Commonly called black-eyed-Susan vine, this vigorous annual produces a lush cover of foliage punctuated with numerous orange, yellow or white flowers. Volunteer seedlings often appear year after year, so you can count on thunbergia to replant itself.

Thunbergias are usually orange or white, but some varieties include purple in their color range. Blooms close at night and open by day.

Sweet Pea

If you live in a climate where summer nights stay cool, you can easily grow fragrant, old-fashioned sweet peas. Sweet peas thrive in cool weather and stop flowering when temperatures rise. They make fine cut flowers too.

Lacy and refined, sweet peas quickly win the hearts of gardeners. You may need to try old-fashioned varieties such as 'Old Spice' to experience the best fragrance.

TIME-SAVING TIP

Backyard Mailbox

To save lots of trips to your utility room, station an old mailbox at the edge of your flower or vegetable garden and use it as a handy storage compartment for gloves, hand tools or half-empty packets of seeds. It also can double as a support for low-maintenance vines, so it will look as good as it works.

You don't have to worry about a utility mailbox filling up with bills. Instead, use it to store small tools, plant markers and a dry pair of gloves.

Enhance Your Driveway Entrance

Broader is better when it comes to driveways, especially if you need to turn your car around in an enclosed space. This driveway is almost like a stable yard for cars.

WATCH OUT!

Messy Trees

It's nice to be able to park your car in cooling shade on hot days, but not if the shade tree weeps sap, drops fruit or nuts, or otherwise leaves your car a mess. If one of these trees presides over your driveway, you may want to change where cars are parked. Eliminating trees—even messy ones—should always be a last resort.

Hickory
Mulberry
Pecan
Pine
Walnut

The first contact you or anyone else has with your home and landscape is your driveway. We come and go in our cars, a fact that has important implications for a major portion of our yards.

We all want to make the most of first impressions, so it's important that the driveway entrance be easy to see. If the edges give way to a ditch, curb or other structure that might cause problems for first encounters, mark the trouble spot with reflectors. Home supply stores sell many decorative types in addition to traditional safety reflectors, which work well at night but are often hard to see in daylight. Another safety precaution that works in any light is to paint guidelines on the edges of the driveway in a high-contrast color—white on dark asphalt, or dark green on light-colored concrete. Bands of light or dark-colored gravel laid down along the driveway's edge can serve the same purpose, and provide a safety shoulder for tires that miss their mark.

It is not a good idea to define the entrance to your driveway with walls or pillars made of stone or brick, because sooner or later a visitor or delivery truck will damage

A small reflector installed at the end your driveway makes dark edges easy to see at night, and also serves as a marker for which driveway is yours.

Hear Them Coming

If you are installing a new driveway or making repairs to an old one due to unexpected damage or utility work, consider incorporating a band of brick or other textured surface so that a distinctive sound is heard when cars run over it. In addition to enhanced security, this little texture trick can unify your landscape if you use brick or stone that is present in other parts of your yard.

Ribbons of brick make an attractive pattern in a concrete driveway, and cars driving over any textured surface make a distinctive sound that's easy to hear.

TIME-SAVING TIP

Drip Buckets

Whenever you plant shrubs or trees some distance from your house, such as at the end of your driveway, it can be a challenge to get water to them their first year, when even the most drought-tolerant species benefit from regular water. Rather than dragging hoses long distances, use milk jugs or other plastic containers with small holes punched in them to slowly drip water to the root zones of the plants. Make the holes about an inch above the bottoms so that the containers will retain enough water to keep them from blowing about on windy days.

A newly planted azalea won't go thirsty when water is slowly dripped to its root zone from a drip bucket. The cypress mulch helps retain soil moisture.

them. Instead, you might define and beautify the entrance with evergreen shrubs spaced several feet outside your driveway turn-in. Or, if you want more color, use large containers planted with flowers for the same purpose.

Because these containers will be so highly visible, you may want to change the flowers frequently to make sure something is always in bloom. For example, you might fill them with pansies in early spring, petunias in the summer and chrysanthemums in fall. Just be sure to place the containers where they will not obstruct the driveway or your view of street traffic. Set the containers on a bed of mulch to avoid tedious mowing or weed-trimming around them. Choose a mulch material that flatters the containers and works well with other textures in your yard.

Once you or your visitors have made it into your driveway, it is crucial that there be adequate space to get in and out of cars. Lining the edges of the driveway with tall plants or bushy shrubs is usually a mistake, because these plants enclose the space and make it more difficult to use. Unless your driveway is very broad, allow plenty of open space along its edges so that there is adequate room for opening car doors. People should be able to walk around an open car door without having to dodge bushes or step into flowers. If the driveway is hopelessly narrow, let it flow into lawn, or expand the hard surface so that it seems wider. See pages 22 to 25 for ideas on adding onto an existing concrete surface to make it work better and require less maintenance.

If your driveway is enclosed by walls, keep it clear of other obstructions so you will still have ample room to get in and out of your car.

Drought-Tolerant Accent Plants

A pair of low, mound-forming shrubs that do not block views of oncoming traffic provides an easy way to mark the entrance to your driveway. However, because these shrubs may be quite distant from your house, choose drought-tolerant species that rarely need watering. Good choices include dwarf boxwood (page 101), bluebeard or caryopteris (page 102), cotoneaster (page 107) or juniper (page 122).

Drifts of creeping groundcover plants are ideal for flanking your driveway entrance too. For this job, consider English ivy (page 121), liriope (page 124), pachysandra (page 128), creeping juniper (page 122) or vinca minor (page 144).

Low groundcovers such as English ivy never impair your view of oncoming traffic, and make a narrow driveway seem more spacious.

The Basics of Foundation Plantings

A low stone wall helps tame a moderate slope while framing the view of the house. Conical plants emphasize this house's architectural style.

Even if you garden hardly at all, chances are excellent that you will find yourself charged with the care of shrubs or flowers planted around your house by previous residents. Commonly called foundation plantings, the purpose of these plants is to hide unattractive parts of your house's foundation from view while anchoring the house to the site.

Whether you are choosing a foundation planting scheme for a new house or are renovating an old one that requires too much work, use the design strategies described here to guide your thinking toward a landscape plan that works beautifully and requires little maintenance.

Simplicity

How much of your house's foundation do you really need to hide from view? There is no rule that says every square inch of your house's foundation must be covered by bushes. Mask only what you have to, thus reducing the time you'll need to spend caring for plants. If the foundation is not unattractive yet tends to pick up mud stains after heavy rains, dwarf shrubs tucked in with a roll-out fabric or plastic mulch topped with bark nuggets should do the trick. Plus, there is always the option of creating a high-quality planting bed for pretty perennials or bulbs by building a low retaining wall several feet outside the part of your foundation that is most unsightly and filling it with topsoil to form a lovely raised bed.

Keep foundation shrubs low, so that they do not block windows or the view of your house from the street. Vary plant forms to help keep foundation plantings interesting.

Style

Let the style of your foundation plantings echo the style of your house. Because it naturally seems to grow out of the earth, a Southwestern stucco house needs very little anchoring. However, a Midwestern ranch house with two feet of concrete block basement showing obviously needs more help. If your house looks formal, the landscape should repeat that style. Similarly, cozy cottage-style homes look best when the foundation plantings set a warm, intimate mood.

Southwestern-style stucco needs little help from foundation shrubs, so the garden can flow naturally away from the house and courtyard walls.

Natural Edge

Round Out Corners

Because the walls of your house form straight lines and angles, it's tempting to outline foundation beds that way too. But rounding out the edges, especially at corners, makes for much easier mowing. To further reduce time spent manicuring edges, keep the curves as broad as possible, and edge them with plants, mulch or a brick mowing strip.

Set Your Shrubs Free

Have you let certain shrubs make you a slave to your pruning shears? Try letting yews, boxwoods or other fine-textured shrubs grow out more between prunings. You may be surprised at how nice they look when they are not tightly trimmed into strict forms.

Every plant near your house need not conform to a tight shape. Letting plants follow their natural form also means less pruning.

Scale

The plants you choose for your foundation plantings should be the right size for your house and property. If they're too big your house will look small, and if they're too tiny they won't pull off the visual trick of anchoring the house to the site.

When deciding how large foundation plants should be, use the height of your house's foundation as your first guideline. If the foundation is very low, so that the house almost seems to sink into the ground, use only the most petite of shrubs, or better yet, consider a mass of low groundcover plants that can stretch out horizontally away from the house. A high foundation calls for more vegetation arranged in two to three layers, with taller plants close to the house and smaller ones in the foreground.

Balance and Symmetry

Is your house very formal and symmetrical in style? If so, don't upset the balance with a wild collection of foundation shrubs in odd sizes. Instead, play it safe by having the landscape design on either side match like bookends. Or attain symmetry by closely watching the "weight" of plants located on opposing sides. Shrubs and trees of differing species that are of similar size have comparable weight. For example, a group of three shrub roses on one side of your house would coordinate appropriately with dwarf spiraeas on the other.

Except for the matching shrubs near the entryway, this landscape makes use of a variety of plants selected for color, including pink astilbe, yellow lady's mantle, and violet purple clematis.

The Funnel Effect

Use this design trick to make your foundation plantings spotlight the entryway to your house. At the far corners of your house, manage shrubs so that they grow to a height equal to two-thirds the distance from the ground to the eaves. As they get closer to the entryway, have shrubs gradually get smaller, so that those near the door are no more than one-third the distance from the ground to the eaves. Of course, you can add some upright vertical elements to help maintain interest, but let the size of shrubs funnel the eye toward the entry. Large trees or shrubs to the side of, or behind, your house can further refine the scene by forming a frame.

WONDERING WHY?

The Dead Zone

Over time, elderly evergreens, such as junipers and arborvitae, develop an inner dead zone that is mostly hidden from view by green foliage. Don't try to save time with these shrubs by pruning too aggressively, because the dead zone will never green up, no matter what.

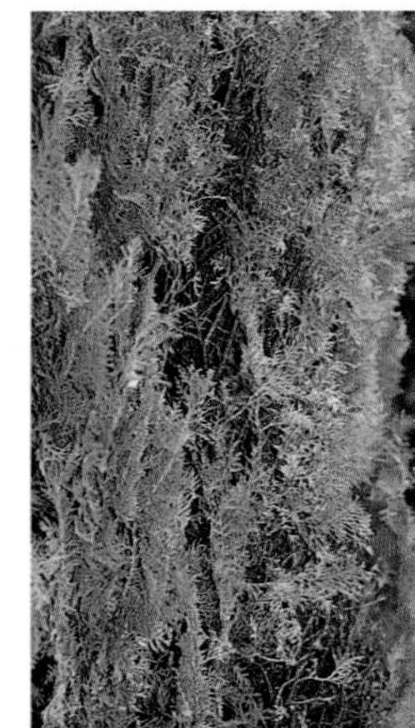

The section close to the main trunk of woody conifers will never sprout new green growth, so use pruning shears with restraint.

When shrubs gradually get smaller as they near the entryway, the house appears larger and the front door becomes the obvious focal point.

Better Foundations with Less Work

Azaleas bloom best when allowed to grow into their natural shapes, so pruning does more harm than good. Azaleas always bloom at the same time as dogwoods.

TOOL TIP

Sharper Shears

If you prune shrubs manually, make sure your hedge clippers are sharp and well oiled. Better yet, invest in electric hedge clippers, which slice through woody stems like butter. Wear gloves when working with hollies or other prickly shrubs.

Sharp pruning shears make a cleaner cut, which makes pruning chores go fast and is easier on plants too. Most deciduous plants are best pruned when they are dormant.

Everyone wants their house to look good, so caring for foundation plantings is mandatory in all but the most natural of landscapes. With a good common-sense design in place, here are ways to keep your foundation looking well dressed and well groomed, *without* tying up too much time.

Paint Your Masonry

A masonry foundation always looks better when it appears clean and refurbished, which is easily accomplished with a fresh coat of paint. Either match the color of your house or go with a contrasting dark color that is already in use elsewhere on your house, such as on your shutters or exterior doors. Or your repainted foundation can bring in a third color, which is often just the thing to bring a house to life. Dark red, dark green and dark charcoal gray are popular and attractive choices.

Replace Overgrown Shrubs

Naturally dwarf shrubs are a modern phenomenon, and it certainly makes sense to get rid of oversized shrubs in favor of smaller ones. Constant pruning is the only way to keep a bush small. And because elderly shrubs have huge root systems, their regrowth after pruning tends to be fast and furious. To get rid of big, overgrown shrubs, you may be able to saw them off a few inches above the ground and then go back after a few months, when the roots have begun to die, and dig out the main root mass. There is usually plenty of room between old shrub stumps to plant new dwarf shrubs. Or you can get professional help from landscapers, who have special heavy equipment for pulling out old shrubs.

Japanese maples and dogwoods bring year-round structure to the foundation of a large upright house. Smaller shrubs and bulbs provide seasonal color.

Keep Them Low

Before truly dwarf shrubs became widely available, it was customary to have shrubs grow as high as the bottom of your windows. However, the more the house is opened to view, the cleaner and larger the house appears. When choosing plants for a new or renovated foundation planting, choose very low growers that will mask the foundation but not the house. Then add vertical interest with strategically placed upright blooming plants such as star magnolias, serviceberries or lilacs.

This house is set so low that there is no need to mask the foundation. Instead, rock-lined beds make the house look settled in its place.

Play by Number

All shrubs need some maintenance such as fertilizing, watering and pruning. To simplify these tasks—and have a landscape with a strong feeling of unity—concentrate on using only three species in your foundation planting, and use at least three plants of each species. In a very large landscape the number of species can be expanded to five, but it's still important to keep things as simple as you can. If you want to collect plants and experiment with new species, do it in a flower bed located in another area of your yard. That way, the plants in your foundation beds will be the constants that carry the landscape from season to season with a minimum of care.

Layered boxwoods and azaleas hide the foundation from view. The small dogwood provides spring color, summer shade, and structure through the winter season.

Allow Elbow Room

Placing shrubs several feet away from the house will help you, your house and your shrubs. You will have better access to exterior walls, the house will benefit from good air circulation, and the shrubs will bask in maximum light. If drips from eaves or gutters muddy up the area behind the shrubs, install a layer of rock or stone against the wall of the house.

Mulch Like Mad

Weeds large and small invade foundation beds, and woody weeds, including tree seedlings, make formidable adversaries. A thick mulch of any organic material, including bark nuggets, pine needles or leaf mold, will discourage invaders and make those that do appear much easier to remove. In very sunny beds, you will probably see many other weeds, including crabgrass.

A thick mulch of pine needles separates this foundation bed from the lawn. Perky pansies provide a welcome ribbon of color.

Herbicides can help, but the best defense is a double mulch in which a layer of roll-out plastic or fabric mulch is covered with more attractive organic mulch. Beware of pebble or stone mulches unless you live in a dry climate. In high rainfall areas, many weeds easily establish themselves in this type of mulch.

Install an Edging

Unless your yard is very shady, a swath of lawn will probably adjoin your foundation bed. To eliminate the need to trim the edge between them, separate the two with some type of edging. In Zones 6 to 8, bands of liriope often serve this purpose, because you can mow right up to liriope without causing damage. Other edging options include a band of mulch, a brick mowing strip, or concrete steppingstones laid end to end. Landscaping timbers seem like a good idea, but you will invariably spend time brandishing a weed trimmer to fight grasses that grow up beneath them, out of reach of your mower blade.

In narrow sideyards, keep foundation plants low so they don't take up space, as has been done here with caladiums (left) and assorted impatiens, torenia, begonia and coleus (right).

Collect Prunings in a Tarp

You'll save a lot of raking, bending and lifting by placing a tarp or old sheet under shrubs before you start pruning them. Then simply gather together the corners and drag the clippings to your compost area. Or get a helper to assist in dumping them from the tarp or sheet into a garbage bag.

Better Gardens in Deep Shade

Do you look at the shadiest parts of your yard and lament the lack of color, long for sprigs of grass, or simply sigh at the bare ground? Instead of feeling frustrated, accept your dark corners for what they are—places where there's not enough light to grow many plants, but perhaps an ideal situation for letting the simple contrast between light and dark work its magic.

Plants need light to grow, and light is often severely limited on the north side of buildings or in the shade of large evergreen trees. These are the two situations that usually define deep or dense shade in home landscapes because they place all-day, year-round limits on light.

White and pink azaleas and variegated hostas light up a shady spot dominated by mature trees. The darker the place, the more you need light-colored plants.

Fortunately, areas in deep shade are usually small, such as narrow sideyards, which can quickly be transformed into more attractive and functional spaces with very little effort. In the process, you may be able to capture and magnify available light by adding light-colored walls, fences, containers or plants. Naturally, any light-colored addition to a dark place also adds contrast.

Indeed, you need substantial shade to fully appreciate the soft glow of white or light-pastel flowers, which tend to fade to nothing in full sun. White impatiens, for example, appear positively luminous in deep shade, as do plants with variegated leaves such as many hostas, ivies and caladiums. But to get the most from the color white, you also need two more things—the contrast provided by varying shades of green and plenty of variety in texture. Don't be afraid to mix lacy ferns with hostas, fill a stone trough with dark green liriope, or make use of white crushed marble mulch. In deep shade, the secret to success is to celebrate the tension between light and dark.

Wondering Why?

White Leaves for Dark Places

Plants with white or heavily variegated leaves look great in deep shade, and sometimes they actually need shade to grow well. For example, all-green English ivies can handle substantial sun, but varieties edged with white will burn if they are not grown in shady spots. And here's a design tip: If you want to use a lot of variegated plants, feature one choice selection, such as a certain variety of hosta or lamium (a mounding groundcover plant). Especially in shade, the effect of mass planting a variegated plant is charming, as if the area was trimmed in lace.

'White Nancy' lamium is a beautiful mounding plant to accent shady places beneath trees. In late spring, tiny white flowers add to the plant's appeal.

The light leaf veins and frilly edges of 'Lime Frill' coleus make it a plant to treasure in shady spots, where it offers refreshing light.

This robust community of bishop's weed, ferns and hostas depends on an excellent foundation of soil for its success. Shade plants need this extra advantage.

Natural Edge: The Case for Moss

Grass won't grow in deep shade, but if the soil is acidic and there is sufficient moisture, you may be able to have moss instead. With encouragement, wild woodland mosses can form a captivating groundcover that cares for itself.

Mosses need moisture, so you may need to use a sprinkler to provide water in dry weather, or to help pieces transplanted to your mossy area gain a foothold. In the fall, it's important to rake away fallen leaves or pine needles so that the moss can get light and fresh air.

Because moss can be slippery and is easily damaged by foot traffic, install steppingstones in pathways. Stones can be purely decorative too. Large, attractive stones "planted" in a moss garden can turn a shady nook into a work of art.

Like a meditation in green, a small gazebo looks out into a wooded glen carpeted with soft mosses and studded with lichen-covered stones.

Deep-Shade Survival Tactics

In addition to limited light, spots in deep shade may have other problems that make gardening difficult, such as extensive tree roots, poor drainage or blocked air circulation. So before you embark on gardening in dark pockets, consider whether you should be dreaming up a hard surface instead. If you paved the area with stone, would you use it as a place to read and relax? If the place is dominated by a large evergreen tree, perhaps it would be best to install a neat frame around the root area and fill it with smooth river stones.

If you opt for plants, you will probably need to add some soil to give their roots plenty of room to spread. Because less light means less photosynthetic energy, even shade-tolerant plants such as hostas and ferns need every advantage, from the ground up. Dig to cultivate the soil if you can, and then add more good quality topsoil to form a raised bed that drains well. To the soil under trees you can safely add up to 3 inches of topsoil without harming the tree's surface roots or trunk. However, adding a deeper bed can invite tree disease problems or suffocate essential tree parts.

And don't forget water. Spots close to your house may be shielded from rain by eaves and gutters, so they tend to stay quite dry. And trees (evergreens in particular) work like big umbrellas that keep rain from reaching the ground below. And the moisture that does make it to the ground is quickly taken up by tree roots and plants. But there is an easy fix. When planting in deep shade, install soaker hoses in beds as soon as your plants are in place. Then hide the hoses from view with a blanket of attractive mulch.

You can always have color in shady spots if you stick with plants that thrive in low light, such as impatiens and caladiums.

Better Grades of Shade

Low-growing azaleas thrive in filtered shade from widely spaced trees, and share the pine straw mulch that paves this napping spot.

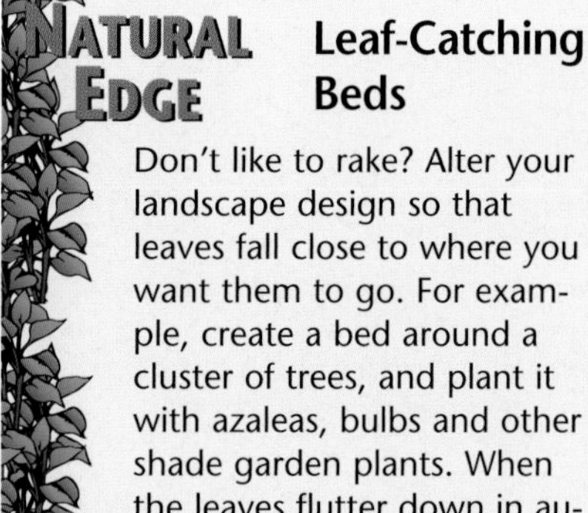

Leaf-Catching Beds

Don't like to rake? Alter your landscape design so that leaves fall close to where you want them to go. For example, create a bed around a cluster of trees, and plant it with azaleas, bulbs and other shade garden plants. When the leaves flutter down in autumn, many will fall right into the bed, and those that don't quite make it can be quickly raked into place.

You can call it light shade, filtered shade or partial shade. Whatever words you choose, we are talking about areas that receive some direct sun each day, but far from a full quota. Eastern exposures get full morning sun and afternoon shade. Places beneath tall, slender trees get dappled or filtered sun all day. There are lots of variations in between.

As far as garden plants are concerned, these are all better grades of shade. A few hours of sun brings out the best in shade-tolerant plants, and sun-tolerant flowers develop better color and hold their blooms a little longer when they get a few hours of relief from the sun.

Partial shade can be such a low-maintenance gardening niche that the more you have of it, the better. Beneficial side effects of partial shade include less watering and weeding, played out in an arena that favors dramatic seasonal changes. Because partial shade is usually created by deciduous trees that shed their leaves in winter, much more sun hits the ground from fall to spring, when the trees are bare. So plants that keep growing through winter (depending where you live) such as pansies, hellebores and most spring flowering bulbs, are especially well suited to these sites. See pages 74-77 to learn more about the many ways you can naturalize a semi-shady area with easy-to-grow bulbs.

Raising Shade

One easy way to combine the benefits of part sun and part shade is to raise the canopy of tree limbs by removing those close to the ground. Pruning off limbs less than 10 feet from the ground allows more light and fresh air to penetrate to the surface and to the plants that are growing there.

Another option is to selectively prune out large tree limbs, particularly any that may have been damaged by violent weather or are so unbalanced that they might break off in heavy winds. But never "top off" a tree by having the limbs shortened all over. This procedure is terrible for trees, looks ugly, and results in weak new growth.

Tall, thin trees that have few low branches admit abundant light in winter, and provide filtered shade from spring until fall.

Gardening among Roots

Some trees are much nicer to garden under than others. Deeply rooted oaks and other hardwoods often spread their roots in wide patterns that make it possible to find plenty of places to plant without chopping into roots. Yet sycamores, beeches and most maples have such fibrous and extensive surface roots that you will be fighting a losing battle if you attempt to keep them in bounds. Dig a fertile planting site beneath one of these species, and within months it will be taken over completely by a woody web of roots.

Consider one of these two solutions to landscaping the area around a problem tree. Cover the surface with flagstones or steppingstones and either fill the crevices between them with pebbles, or stud the area with iron-clad groundcovers such as English ivy or periwinkle. Either approach looks much better than half-bare ground riddled with exposed roots.

Where numerous surface roots make it impossible to dig, try establishing evergreen groundcovers, as has been done here with pachysandra and English ivy.

GREAT COLOR PLANTS FOR SHADE

Azalea	Hydrangea
Begonia	Impatiens
Caladium	Ivy
Clematis	Liriope
Cleome	Pachysandra
Coleus	Pansy
Dogwood	Phlox
Dusty miller	Plumbago
Foxglove	Pulmonaria
Heuchera	Stachys
Honeysuckle	Vinca
Hosta	

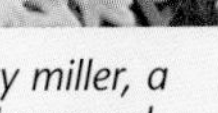

Dusty miller, a hardy annual.

Cleome, also called spider flower.

The color range of impatiens is huge, and includes orange 'Tango'.

Annual phlox in shades of pink.

WATCH OUT!

Slugs and Snails

They're slimy, eat almost anything green, and they come out at night. The pests in question—slugs and snails—are naturally attracted to shady areas, so they are common foes in a shade garden. If you see smooth-edged holes in leaves, perhaps with glistening trails of slime nearby, you will know you are dealing with one of these pests. Don't bother looking for them during the day, though. They are uncannily adept at hiding away in mulch and other bits of cover.

The easiest way to control slugs and snails is to trap them. You can buy commercial slug and snail traps, or make your own and bait them with beer. Slugs and snails love beer, and your traps can be any container the pests will fall into as they attempt to feed. Try clear plastic drink bottles, laid on their sides between plants, with enough beer in them to form a half-inch-deep pool of death. Plastic margarine tubs, with an inch of beer in the bottom and set in mulch or soil up to their rims, also work well.

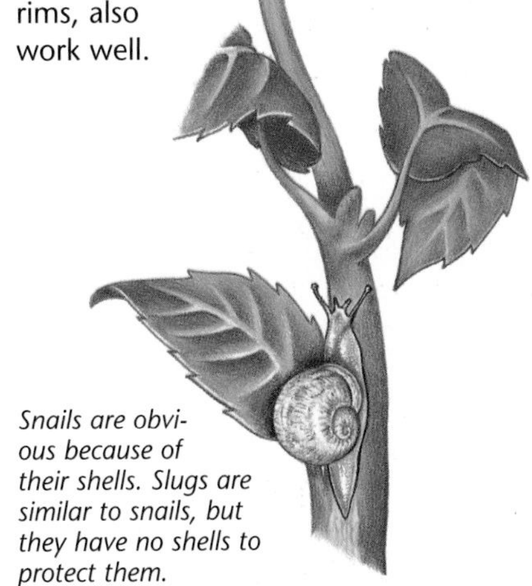

Snails are obvious because of their shells. Slugs are similar to snails, but they have no shells to protect them.

Managing a Sun-Drenched Yard

Rock cotoneaster is a willing spreader that also produces attractive berries for birds. Best of all, this shrub needs little or no pruning.

Plants derive the energy they need to grow from the sun, so it should be no surprise that many of the most colorful and prolific garden plants perform best in full sun. Most lawngrasses thrive in sun too, so you do have a choice between putting your sun-drenched places into garden or lawn. Having it all without committing to weekend after weekend of maintenance means striking some sort of logical balance between garden and lawn. Here are strategies that can help.

Natural Edge

Winter Rains

Short and cool days mean that whatever rain falls in winter stays in the soil longer, so it makes sense to capitalize on winter rains if you live in a climate where summers are hot and dry. Springtime can be extremely colorful if you make use of half-wild annuals that are sown in fall for bloom the following spring, including larkspur, corn poppies and bachelor buttons. Plant in October, and you may need to water only enough to get the seeds to appear out of the ground, and then again in spring when your flowers bloom. Companies that sell wildflower seed often offer seed in bulk, or you can start with packets.

Emphasize Long-Lived Shrubs

Besides the advantage of being able to plant them only once, followed by years of enjoyment, over time shrubs develop huge root systems that sustain them through droughts and reduce their need for supplemental fertilizer. Many of the shrubs featured in this book also need minimal pruning, so they are an easy way to beautify sunny spots. And you'll actually do less work with each passing season.

Leave No Open Spaces

The plants we love thrive in full sun, but so do weeds. Prevent weed problems before they start by mulching between plants and making sure that any open spot of soil is promptly occupied by either plants or mulch.

Mass Iron-Clad Perennials

There is a reason why daylilies (page 109) are found in nearly every sunny garden. Once planted, they prosper and multiply, so you can cover lots of space with them quickly and easily. In addition to daylilies, chrysanthemums (page 104), peonies (page 130) and sedums (page 138) are prime perennials for sun. Make the most of your time and effort by making large plantings, which look great and simplify maintenance chores.

Sedums and Other Succulents

To survive in a desert environment, plants must be able to grab water when it comes and then hold onto it for a long, long time. The leaf type known as succulent, seen in cacti, jade plants, sedums and portulacas, exemplify this talent, which is invaluable in places where the summer sun bakes the moisture out of plants. Prickly pear cactus is hardy to Zone 7, and most sedums go all the way to Zone 3. Plant these or other hardy succulents in hot spots and you can save lots of time not watering thirsty plants.

Prickly pear cactus is usually hardy to Zone 7. Even in severe summer droughts, it rarely suffers.

Daylilies are such vigorous growers that they can be counted upon to multiply. Planted in masses, they are an ideal low-maintenance flower for sun.

NATURAL EDGE

Create Some Shade

Planting trees is the best long-term approach to creating shade, but while you're waiting for trees to grow, harness and use the natural exuberance of vines. Annual vines, which are grown from seed planted each spring, often are happy to entwine themselves on a simple trellis made of string. Morning glories, hyacinth beans and scarlet runner beans die back with the first frost, so they are an easy way to run a single-season test to see if a vine is right for a certain situation.

Perennial vines are definitely in order if you have a fixed structure such as a pergola to clothe in foliage and flowers. Clematis, climbing roses, campsis, Boston ivy and wisteria are all worthy candidates for this job.

Hyacinth beans thrive in hot weather, so they are an ideal vine to plant from seed to put to work as a temporary summer shade screen.

A sunny wildflower meadow provides a parade of color, as seen here with oxeye daisies (white), larkspur (purple), poppies (red) and coreopsis (yellow).

Frame Your Lawn

This lawn design strategy is discussed in more detail in Chapter 5, but it basically means shrinking the lawn so that its edges are defined by a broad band of groundcover (such as liriope or pachysandra) or perhaps a new patio or walkway.

Have Fun with Color

Turn the page for ideas on making the most of what your sunny yard can offer in terms of flowers with unstoppable flower power. The best flowers for sun have vivid, saturated color that holds up well in intense light, so be prepared to see a lot of red. Orange, yellow and fuchsia, played out in contrast with blue or gray, can turn a sunny spot into an exciting oasis of color.

Block Evaporation

The sun takes moisture from the soil, so providing water for plants is a constant challenge in sunny sites. Organic mulches such as chopped leaves, straw or bark are good barriers to slow down the loss of soil moisture, but you can do even better by going to a double mulch. Beneath the organic mulch, lay down a sheet of perforated plastic, roll-out fabric mulch or even old newspapers or pieces of cardboard. In addition to blocking evaporation, double mulches also discourage nasty weeds.

This garden conserves water three ways—drip irrigation, roll-out plastic mulch, and a top layer of organic much that hides the rest from view.

Better Gardens in the Summer Sun

Narrow-leaf zinnias are an ideal low-care flower for sun because they resist both drought and disease.

Most of us can't wait for summer to come so that we can feel the warmth of the sun again. But then the days get long and a little too hot, and every minute spent working outside seems to last for an hour. However, with a little planning, you can find yourself enjoying a boisterously beautiful summer garden without spending long steamy hours keeping it up. After all, you probably have plenty of other ways—that don't involve dirt—to enjoy summer!

Because many annual flowers are such strong bloomers, you will definitely want to devote at least a small space to flowers you can pop into the ground as bedding plants, surround them with mulch and then sit back and enjoy. In most climates petunias can be counted upon to bloom continuously all summer, and they come in so many colors that finding ones you like is easy. See pages 66 and 67 for other planting ideas for annuals that come in six-packs, and tips for helping them grow well in your yard.

It's important not to get carried away with a huge flower bed that will undoubtedly need to be weeded, watered, fertilized and groomed often. Using a thick mulch will reduce how much weeding and watering you will need to do, and you may need to fertilize only once if you use an organic or timed-release fertilizer. How much time you spend removing old blossoms or trimming to control leggy growth depends on which flowers you grow. A few, such as melampodium (page 127), portulaca (page 134) and small-flowered zinnias (page 145) need very little attention, and the same is true of the other hot-weather annuals described in the "Summer Replacements" box (next page).

Wondering Why?

Bracts vs. Petals

If your flowers seem to fade too fast in the summer sun, switch to species that produce tiny flowers surrounded by bracts rather than petals. True petals, such as those found in roses and peonies, are packed with water. In comparison, the "petals" of gomphrena, strawflowers, sunflower and zinnias are dry and papery, so they are slow to wither in hot sun.

The petals of zinnias and many other sun-tolerant flowers hold only a little moisture. Narrow leaf shape gives plants another edge against heat and drought.

Summer Replacements

The first days of spring are so inspirational that we pack them full of gardening, and fill flower beds with flowers that like cool weather such as pansies, sweet alyssum, snapdragons and other spring bloomers. But then summer comes, and these cool-natured flowers slowly melt away. Here are some prime summer replacements that are widely available at garden centers in late spring, especially in warm climates where they are most needed. When grown in good soil with adequate water and fertilizer, they will bloom through the most torrid of summer heat waves.

Gomphrena.

Gomphrena – Also called globe amaranth, available in white and many shades of pink.

Lantana – A butterfly favorite that bears multicolored clusters of blossoms.

Lantana.

Pentas – In red or pink, this garden newcomer thrives in humid heat.

Pentas.

Purple Heart – With bold purple spiking foliage, this tropical survives winter to Zone 7.

Purple heart.

Annual Vinca – Called periwinkle or Madagascar periwinkle, this heat lover hangs tough through torrid summer days.

Annual vinca.

Drip Irrigation

Water is too precious to waste, and the most efficient way to water is also the healthiest for plants. Drip irrigation, in which water slowly drips into the soil from perforated soaker hoses or from drip irrigation lines equipped with little emitters, supplies moisture to the soil while keeping leaves dry, which helps prevent various leafspots and mildews. Plus, you can turn on a drip hose at night and water your garden without competing with the evaporative power of the sun. Water from a drip line goes exactly where it's needed, unlike a sprinkler that often waters your sidewalk, car or driveway in addition to your garden. But best of all, drip irrigation saves hours and hours of time not spent standing at garden's edge with a hose in your hand.

Drip irrigation lines that include emitters can be arranged so that they drip water right where it's needed, as seen here with chrysanthemums and ageratum.

Dress for success when you garden in summer heat. Wear loose-fitting clothing, and don't forget a hat for shade.

Summer Garden Survival Tactics

When summer really gets cooking, you need to take care of yourself before you can take care of your garden. Here are five ways to make summer gardening more enjoyable, and less likely to cause you unneccessary discomfort.

Work Early in the Morning or Late in the Evening

This just makes sense, but it's amazing how many people defy nature by working outside in the heat of the day.

Cover Your Head

A wide-brimmed hat cools your head, and mysteriously discourages gnats and mosquitoes at the same time.

Wear Light Colors

In addition to minimizing solar heating, light colors do not attract bees and other insects. Bright reds, blues and oranges make you a real curiosity to the same critters that visit colorful flowers.

Let Someone Else Mow

It will be worth the cost if you get to spend your time on gardening projects that you truly enjoy.

Sit Back and Smell the Flowers

All work and no play isn't fun. Make time to relax and enjoy the rewards of gardening.

Ways to Redo a Ditch

If part of your property includes a ditch, you already know how difficult it can be to maintain the most troublesome of landscape features. Most ditches are too steep to mow and downright dangerous to clean up with a weed trimmer, so they are often left neglected until nature tames them with floodwaters from heavy rains. Because rainwater does need a travel route, you can't just fill in a ditch and forget it. Short of laying a drainage pipe and covering it with soil—a huge and expensive undertaking—there are several faster fixes for dastardly ditches.

In places where rocks and boulders are a natural part of the terrain, ditches tend to evolve into rock-lined crevices as more and more soil is carried away. Simply adding rock that matches or coordinates with the native stone already showing in the ditch stops the erosion process and looks much better than a mixture of stone, dirt and weeds. Shop around for contractors who sell stone, usually by the ton, and make use of their expertise when deciding how much stone you will need.

If the area just above your ditch is too narrow or steep for any other use, it's wise to extend the lining of stone up over the edges of the ditch so that more stone is visible. Besides looking good, this often eliminates problem areas that are awkward to mow. Once your ditch is lined with stone, maintenance will be limited to hand-pulling weeds or spot-treating them with herbicide once or twice a year.

In place of eroded soil, the bottom and sides of this rock-lined ditch have been furnished with stones. When filled with rainwater, this ditch works like a babbling brook.

Improved drainage can be beautiful, as is shown here with a handsome dry creekbed that meanders through a garden filled with hostas.

WATCH OUT!

Protect Your Digits

Always wear heavy gloves and boots when handling rock or stone. A heavy stone dropped on your toes can leave you limping for weeks, and sharp surfaces of stones will quickly eat up the skin on your hands. Keep an extra pair of gloves nearby in case you need them.

Always respect the weight of heavy stones. Besides protecting the skin on your hands, gloves that fit well ensure a firm grip. Leather is tops.

Places in moist shade that occasionally flood make a fine home for ferns. Stones help anchor plant roots, and support mosses and other tiny plants.

NATURAL EDGE — Going Grassy

If stacking stones isn't your thing, remodel your ditch with grasses that never need mowing. Petite clump-forming ornamental grasses give the sloping sides of a ditch a windblown look, and they can do a good job of stopping erosion too. Various forms of sheep fescue (*Festuca ovina*) work well, or you can try blue fescue (*F. cinerea*), which is very similar. Both are hardy to Zone 4. Tough, maintenance-free species daylilies that bloom orange (*Hemerocallis fulva*) also make a good groundcover for ditch banks, though they tend to become so crowded after a few years that they stop blooming. Still, the foliage makes a fine summer groundcover, and the thick roots hold the soil firm through the winter.

Depending on your climate, you may want to line only the bottom of your ditch with stone, and use the sides for attractive plants. If the site is very damp (or at least does not often dry out completely) the sides of the ditch may be ideal for ferns. Be sure to choose a species widely known to grow well in your area, and then plant the ferns just before your rainy season starts.

Groundcover plants such as English ivy, vinca minor and vinca major need less moisture than ferns, and they also tolerate more sun. Yet lean and stressful growing conditions make establishment of groundcover plants somewhat slow, so be patient. To enhance visual interest of a bank clothed in green, include a few large stones or boulders to provide changes in texture.

Comely Contours

If you buy stone by the ton and simply have it dumped in your ditch, it will take only a few hours of work to correct the placement so that the stones are evenly distributed where they need to be. However, if you want to put more time into the project, you can reshape one or both sides of your ditch and stack the stones so that they look more like a stone wall. In the process, you can fill in the bottom of the ditch a bit so that it is no longer deep or jagged.

Begin by finding a source of stone that you like, but wait to have it delivered until you are ready to start stacking. Meanwhile, use a pick, mattock and spade to sculpt the side or sides of your ditch so that it is slightly sloped away from the center. Even if you want the sides to be perpendicular when you're done, it's important to stack stones at a slight outward tilt. Otherwise, pressure from the surrounding soil can cause the walls to fall inward, undoing all your hard work.

As you shape the sides, let the extra soil fill the bottom of the ditch and make it nearly level. Select your largest, flattest stones and arrange them in the bottom of the ditch, all the way to the edge. Then start stacking stones along the side or sides. Take your time and enjoy the artistry of arranging stones. This is a lasting improvement that will enhance your landscape and look good for years to come.

A curving, rock-lined swale serves as a visual divider between a section of lawn and a mass planting of ornamental grasses.

CHAPTER 4

MORE COLOR WITH LESS WORK

Let easy flowers bring excitement to your landscape.

Any place planted with a flowering plant will draw you like a magnet, which is the whole point of adding color to your landscape. Color always says "look at me," so it's logical to add color to areas where you want to have this kind of energy and power.

Entryways are a natural choice for color accents, but sometimes color is most appreciated when it is used as a surprise factor, enriching a place that would otherwise go unnoticed. When used in well-placed splashes, a little color goes a long way. So keep colors simple and change them from year to year to keep things interesting.

In terms of maintenance, you will get plenty of carefree color with flowering shrubs such as azaleas, lilacs and viburnums. However, these and many other woody plants bloom only in spring, so you also need color plants that wait until summer to strut their stuff. It's a happy coincidence that inexpensive annuals, purchased as bedding plants, often provide the most color for the longest time. Best of all, annuals can be grown in containers that can be easily shifted from place to place—wherever you want to create a little excitement.

Playing with color is fun, so feel free to use your imagination and experiment with new ideas. Numerous tried-and-true guidelines are given on the following pages, but all the rules of using color are flexible and subject to interpretation in keeping with your personal taste and the one-of-a-kind situation in your yard.

ACCENTING WITH COLOR

Entryways are natural sites for high-impact use of color. This house and landscape are united by a knee-high hedge of lemon yellow marigolds.

The smartest low-maintenance strategy for using color in the landscape is to concentrate on accents—small plantings chosen and situated so that they punctuate the landscape so effectively that you think you are seeing much more color than is really there.

Using color accents is easy, especially if you simply emphasize areas where you are prone to look anyway—entryways, scenes viewed through the most frequently used windows (typically the kitchen and family room), or outdoor living areas such as decks or patios. To further help you find prime places in your landscape for color accents, consider the following ways that color accents can energize your yard.

Movement

Because color attracts attention, you can use it to draw people through the landscape. Low edgings along a footpath draw the eye downward and help tell your feet which way to go. A colorful hanging basket stationed near outdoor seating works like a beacon, clearly defining a place intended for active use.

Background

As you will see in the pages to come, maximizing color often involves contrast or the way a color appears when it is combined with other shades and textures. When locating accents, look carefully at the backgrounds involved. Then you will know if a light, bright or dark color will be likely to show up best.

Dainty pansies and other assorted flowers help guide visitors' footsteps, ensuring maximum safety on a long run of stone steps.

WATCH OUT!

Party Clashers

Orange goes with purple, white or brown, but it's usually a disaster with pink. Magenta is similarly limited in its matches, though it's great with gray, white or soft yellow. While orange and magenta are the shades most often named as party clashers, they are also high-energy colors that sizzle with fun when planted in the right places. Either can be gentled down with yellow or blue, or you can make them appear almost elegant by growing them in close company with white.

Vivid 'Calypso Orange' calendulas easily grab attention from afar. Because of the strong color, good complements are limited to gray, white or purple.

NATURAL EDGE

Never Underestimate White

Use white to separate colors that don't quite work together, or to tie a large collection of colors together. White flowers or leaves will light up shade, or you can use white to frame brighter colors in sunny spots. Want to bring an evergreen groundcover to life? Edge it with white pansies and watch it pop.

Use white flowers to bring light to scenes dominated by evergreens, or to separate and blend brighter color combinations.

Height and Position

How will the color accent be viewed—at eye level, from above, close up or from a distance? From afar, a small mass or drift of a single bright color is ideal. For close-up viewing near an entryway, neat, upright plantings that don't sprawl into walking space are preferred. On a deck, a broad and low container—always pleasing when viewed from above—is a nice touch.

Size and Scale

You want to limit how much time is needed to plant and maintain colorful flowers, but you also want to have the right amount of plants, so that your color accents fit the spaces in which they are located. With containers, you can choose between having a single large container (which is easy to keep watered) or several smaller ones that can be quickly rearranged. Edgings can be broad or narrow, and there is a place for both. For example, when edging a walkway, a foot-wide band of well-mulched plants will make the walkway feel wider and more spacious. However, when edging a planting of foundation shrubs, a narrow ribbon of bulbs or flowers is usually highly effective and needs very little of your ongoing attention.

Strive for simplicity in flower beds, and layer two or three flowers together according to height, with the tallest plants in the rear. Layering plants increases the illusion of depth, making a flower bed appear larger than it really is. To make this trick work well, it's important to space plants close enough so that they grow together into a happy mass when they reach mature size.

Mix and match color plants with others that have interesting textures or colorful foliage, as seen here with red geraniums and purple heart.

Warm and Cool Colors

Before you choose specific colors to accent your landscape, you must make a preliminary choice between the two color types—warm and cool. Warm colors include red, hot pinks, oranges and bright yellows. Bold to the point of being almost brazen, warm colors are easily seen from a distance. Warm colors can be money savers, too, because you need only a few boldly colored plants to attract plenty of attention. The disadvantages are that some warm colors tend to be overpowering, and very dark shades of red or pink are poorly seen at night.

Cool colors include soft pastel pinks, blues and yellows, as well as gray and white. Cool colors impart a relaxing mood, and their gentle ambiance is always welcome in shady spots because they reflect so much light. In a high-contrast setting, such as that framed with evergreens or viewed against a dark background, small plantings of cool colors come through as very noble and defined. However, in bright sun or other intense light, cool colors tend to wash out and lose their punch.

Cool blues and pinks create a relaxing mood, and they always go together well. Here blue globes of echinops tower over pink phlox.

Grow flowers in drifts to simplify maintenance and give the colors plenty of punch. Here 'Moonbeam' coreopsis (left) and a double rudbeckia (right) work together in harmony.

Sure-Fire Color Combos

Clean contrast—between white and deep, saturated colors such as magenta (shown), deep pink and red—gives a flower bed a crisp, tailored appearance.

What makes colors really come to life? Sometimes it takes another color that introduces an element of tension or contrast. However, do not jump to the conclusion that you always need to combine colors to make them exciting, because this simply is not true. For example, a single color of impatiens planted in the shade of a tree or building often needs no additional help because of the natural contrast between flowers, foliage and other nearby plants or textures. Evergreen groundcovers and other "texture" plants may actually look less appealing if you try to jazz them up with color.

That much said, let's talk about boosting the intensity of places where you have decided that color is needed, by combining different colors or shades. Because light colors make space seem larger while darker ones make the eye settle on a more concentrated view, decide early on which one will dominate. Also remember that light colors placed in front of brighter ones tend to create more contrast than bright ones set against a light background. However, if the two plants are of the same type and height—for example, fuchsia and white petunias or yellow and red pansies—placement of the two colors is less of an issue.

NATURAL EDGE

Repeating Patterns

The fewer different types of color plants you use, the simpler it will be to keep up with their needs for water, fertilizer and grooming. And it's a happy coincidence that when you repeat plantings of the same plants, it gives the landscape a feeling of unity and wholeness. You can do this with annuals put to work as edgings, as when you plant begonias or pansies in a broad band, repeating a specific color pattern over and over. Or you can create a signature grouping using perennials or shrubs, and repeat this grouping in different parts of your yard. For example, hostas, ferns and pulmonarias work together well in shade, or you might combine peonies, daylilies and caryopteris in sun. And the same shrub groupings you choose for your foundation plantings can be repeated in other parts of your yard.

A round, raised bed of pink and red wax begonias forms an island of color. A color mixture of one type of flower makes a good neighbor for the greens of lawns, shrubs and trees.

TOOL TIP

Color Wheel

Opposites attract. That's the idea behind the color wheel, a handy way to know if colors will match, give good contrast, or clash. Colors directly opposite each other on the color wheel are high contrast, or complementary, colors. If you place a triangle in the center of the wheel and rotate it around, colors at each point of the triangle are a safe three-way combination. It's important to pay attention to subtle differences in hues too. So use the color wheel as a general guide, but let your eyes make the final decision when you choose plants.

Use a color wheel to take the confusion out of choosing colors. Those opposite each other on the wheel always partner well.

Dynamic Duos

If you don't want to guess about color, try these tried-and-true plant combinations.

Red and white always work well together. A few pink begonias share the spotlight with more high-contrast colors.

Red and White

Crisp and neat, red and white always looks clean and manicured, but carries plenty of energy too. Frame a small drift of red geraniums with white petunias, or make the most of partial shade by flanking red salvias with white impatiens.

Red and Blue

Red zinnias may look a little coarse on their own, but not in the company of blue salvia. Ageratum, a common summer bedding plant, is a dependable source of blue for combining with red geraniums. Pair blue pansies with any shade of red for beautiful special effects.

Yellow and Blue

Yellow daffodils and blue pansies are a classic rendition of this combination. In summer beds, edge yellow melampodium with blue ageratum, or use blue sage with yellow zinnias or sunflowers.

Pink and Gray

Pink is never wishy-washy in the company of gray foliage plants such as dusty miller and stachys. Full, bold pinks work best, but gray can bring out the best in baby pink impatiens too, especially in partial shade where natural darkness provides needed contrast.

Pink petunias glow in the company of soft gray foliage plants such as dusty miller or artemisia.

Orange and Purple

Orange is never a problem color when paired with deep purple. In hot summer areas particularly, pair orange zinnias or sulphur cosmos with purple angelonia or Mexican bush sage. In spring, orange tulips look great in the company of blue pansies.

Orange zinnias mingle among the leaves of purple fountain grass. Many of summer's best bloomers are orange.

Terrific Trios

When you get deeper into plant combinations, you will discover that texture is just as important as color. One strategy that works well in many situations is to start with a major color plant, then add a strongly textured plant, and finally a pinch of a minor color—just enough to add interest. This "trio" approach works whether you are playing with shrubs, trees, perennials or annuals. For example, an azalea that blooms pink in spring will become a breathtaking sight with blue vinca minor blooming at its feet, punctuated with a few small yellow daffodils. In more sunny, open spaces, combine daffodils with daylilies and roses for a good mix of textures and bloom times. With annuals, using neutral-texture plants such as dusty miller or white petunias or impatiens makes easy work of three-way plant combinations.

Pink azaleas and blue wood hyacinths get a jolt of excitement from darker and lighter colors in the background.

Color in Containers

You can grow flowers with similar needs together in the same container, as has been done here with coleus and New Guinea impatiens.

Tool Tip: Watering Wand

If you have a number of pots, hanging baskets or window boxes to water, invest in a watering wand—a long-handled metal wand with a nozzle on one end that screws onto your garden hose. The wand makes it easy to reach into containers, resulting in much less mess and wasted water.

Besides saving on mess, a watering wand makes it easy to water container-grown plants without wetting the foliage, which can invite diseases.

If you want color in your yard and the ability to move it around at will, concentrate on growing colorful flowers in containers. They are without peer for enlivening entryways, and small yards in particular benefit from the dense dashes of color you get with containers.

However, because of the high maintenance required for numerous small containers, it is often best to invest your time and energy in a few large containers. All containers demand constant attention to watering, and the more water you provide, the more nutrients leach out of the soil, so you will then need to feed plants frequently too. This is as simple as mixing soluble fertilizer into a watering can, but it's still a repetitious task.

One thing that helps simplify the watering/feeding syndrome is to use a high-quality potting soil. Potting soils are not all alike, and the better brands include a mixture of peat, compost, sand and other light-textured materials that hold moisture well. Some also contain a small amount of timed-release fertilizer. However, you will still need to begin feeding plants after a few weeks, when the fertilizer has been used up or washed away.

In terms of maintenance, it's hard to beat plastic containers, which are lightweight, hold moisture well and now come in a variety of attractive colors and textures. Certainly clay pots are more authentic, but they crack easily, do a poor job of retaining water and can be cumbersome to move. Many other materials are available, including half barrels and large immovable concrete urns. Of course, once any container is filled with damp soil and plants, it will be heavy. Instead of trying to lug awkward containers from place to place, invest in a small wheeled dolly for this job.

Anything that holds soil, yet lets excess water drain away, can be used as a planter. This antique wagon filled with pansies and primroses is a real charmer.

Time-Saving Tip: Comeback Containers

You don't have to discard the potting soil in containers after using it only once, which is good news if you're using very large or heavy pots that are hard to move around. Remove as many roots as you can when pulling out spent plants, because rotting root tissues can host disease. And before filling containers with new plants, refresh the soil by mixing in enough high-quality potting soil to reach the top. Unless you are growing a shrub or tree, which do best when left undisturbed, replace the soil entirely every 3 years.

WATCH OUT!

Drainage Dangers

Containers for plants must have holes in the bottom through which excess water can drain. Otherwise accumulated moisture will cause roots to rot. Check for drainage holes when buying containers; some will have perforated "knock out" holes that you can remove by tapping with a screwdriver and hammer. However, decorative glazed clay pots or brass planters may have no drainage holes at all. In this situation, install your plants in well-drained plastic pots, and then slip them inside the prettier planters.

This wall planting, comprised of numerous containers attached to the rails of a balcony, forms a cascade of color that is awesome to behold.

Matching Plants and Pots

Because their roots are restricted, plants grown in pots tend to be a little smaller than they would be if they were grown in the ground. It's also customary to set plants close together in containers, so that they weave together into a dense mass, and close spacing adds to the dwarfing effect. For example, cleomes that grow 4 feet tall in the garden may not top 2 feet in pots when surrounded by pink begonias. When growing shrubs or trees in containers, it is usually best to begin with a naturally dwarf cultivar that will feel at home in close quarters.

Just as you might do when planning to display flowers in a vase on your dining table, consider the shape of the plants and containers you want to use, as well as how the finished creation will be viewed. Begonias are naturals for broad, low containers that are viewed from above, but it's best to install taller plants seen at eye level in upright urns or pots. Install cascading petunias in hanging baskets, or put them on pedestals so that their elegant growth habit is shown to its best advantage.

Plant a Container Bouquet

Like arranging flowers and greenery in a vase, you can arrange living plants in large pots or window boxes to form container bouquets. The guidelines are simple—use a mixture of plant heights, textures and colors, and crowd plants a little to make the planting appear lush and full. This is a great thing to do with leftover bedding plants, but you can use perennials and groundcovers in the mix too. Rooted pieces of English ivy (page 121) or vinca (page 144) are always welcome additions because of the way they cascade over the edges of containers.

When growing low, spreading plants such as verbena in containers, set the pots on the ground so they can be viewed from above.

Ten Unstoppable Annuals for Pots

- Begonia (page 98)
- Dusty miller (page 111)
- Geraniums
- Impatiens (page 120)
- Lobelia
- Melampodium (page 127)
- Pansy (page 129)
- Petunia (page 131)
- Sweet alyssum
- Verbena (page 142)

Containers are a good place to grow fancy varieties with double flowers such as 'Appleblossom' geraniums or frilly grandiflora petunias.

Quick Color from Six-Packs

Plume celosias create fireworks in a bed that also features red salvia and blue ageratum. All three are easy annuals that thrive with little care in warm summer weather.

If you want to work up a good case of spring fever, visit a garden center in the spring and get lost in the sea of bedding plants offered for sale. It won't take long to conjure up dreamy visions of summer flowers dancing in your yard, and few things are simpler than growing flowers from bedding plants. But even if you grow only the toughest of bedding plants such as begonias or pansies, skipping bed preparation or neglecting basic maintenance can spell trouble. To make sure your summer flowers thrive with little care, it's important to shop carefully, plant right, and give your garden thoughtful care.

In the interest of reduced maintenance, keep your collection small, and try to create concentrated splashes of color rather than sprinkling individual plants here and there throughout your yard. It also greatly simplifies matters if you stick with no more than three different species in a given year. Don't worry. Most bedding flowers are annuals that grow for only one season, so you will have plenty of chances to try different species in future years.

When planting a large area, you may be surprised at how many plants you need. Look on plant tags to see how much space each plant requires.

WATCH OUT!

Rootbound Bedders

If you see tangled roots growing out through the drainage holes of a cellpack, it's a sign that the plants are badly crowded. If possible, opt for younger plants that have not been waiting as long for a home. They will transplant better, and bloom longer and stronger too.

Gently break apart the lowest roots of bedding plants as you transplant them. This step encourages the development of vigorous new roots.

Tips for Easy Transplanting

- Keep bedding plants constantly moist until you get them situated in beds or containers.
- Dig beds at least 12 inches deep, and mix in an organic or timed-release fertilizer according to label directions.
- Squeeze seedling containers from the bottom to free plants rather than trying to pull them out by the stem.
- Untangle the bottom half-inch of roots if they are matted together. If the roots are severely knotted, break them apart with your fingers and set the plant in the ground with its butterflied bottom spread as wide as possible.
- After the planting is done, water thoroughly, and top the bed with a 2-inch-thick blanket of mulch.

A blanket of mulch looks attractive, and plants benefit from the way mulch conserves water and discourages weeds.

The Need to Feed

As summer gets cooking, annual flowers often need a booster feeding to keep them growing strong. You can sprinkle a little organic or granular fertilizer over the soil around plants, or use a plant food that you mix with water. If plants perk up after a booster feeding with a liquid, you will know they were in need of nutrients.

Wondering Why? Pinching and Deadheading

If you pinch or clip off old blossoms when you see them, you will help your flowers set more buds. Inside old flowers are developing seeds, and the less energy plants expend nurturing seeds, the more they have available to send to new flowers.

Fifteen Fine Bedders

Ageratum – Blue or white powderpuff blossoms on low, mound-forming plants. Full sun to partial shade.

Ageratum.

Begonia – Pink, red or white flowers on petite plants, some with bronze leaves. Full sun to partial shade. Also see page 98.

Celosia – Feathery plumes or convoluted crowns in bright reds, yellows and rusty orange tones. Full sun.

Dusty miller – Soft gray foliage goes with everything, and is outstanding with blue or pink flowers. Best in partial shade. Also see page 111.

Geranium – Red or white are most common, but pinks are available too. Needs great drainage, best in almost-full sun.

Impatiens – Huge range of colors and a strong preference for shade make this a sure bet for outdoor living areas. Needs plenty of water. Also see page 120.

Lobelia – Hundreds of deep blue or white flowers on small spreading plants make this a great texture plant or edging. Best in full sun in cool climates.

Marigold, French – These are the small or dwarf marigolds with flowers only 1 to 2 inches across. Nonstop bloomers, best in full sun.

Melampodium – Plants stay covered with dozens of little orange-yellow daisies through the hottest weather. Full sun. Also see page 127.

Pansy – Best color flower for cool weather, with an extremely long bloom time and wide range of colors. Full sun to partial shade. Also see page 129.

Petunia – Versatile, elegant and eager to bloom, petunias are unbeatable for beds, window boxes or other containers in sun or partial shade. Also see page 131.

Celosia.

Salvia – Upstanding and large, bright red salvia spikes can fire up partial shade, or you can use blue species in sunnier sites. Also see page 137.

Verbena – Annual verbenas bear clusters of richly colored flowers, and there are softer hues as well. Best in full sun. Also see page 142.

Vinca, annual – Often called periwinkle or Madagascar periwinkle, this white, pink or purple bloomer thrives in hot weather and full sun.

Zinnia – Always cheery and easy to grow, zinnias are at home in any sunny spot. Check out the different types, which become more numerous every year. Also see page 145.

The Drama of Drifts

If you have a lot of property to maintain, perhaps you can devote part of it to large swaths of space planted with native and imported wildflowers and grasses. Or, if it's a shady spot, make use of spreading groundcovers that never need mowing. Either type of mass planting saves work by using extremely carefree plants that can be managed as self-perpetuating plant communities. They don't have to be mowed constantly in the summer the way lawns do, and they don't require the weeding and watering that flower beds need.

At best, mass plantings should have some size to them, the same way that plant colonies develop in wild places. In a home landscape, mass plantings should be at least 30 feet long and 15 feet wide, with a flowing teardrop shape or other outline that fits the site yet looks natural, as if it might have happened on its own.

Because a low-maintenance wildflower drift will look somewhat unkempt at times, such as when flowers and grasses are shedding seed or when bulb foliage is ripening, they are most appropriate for places other than the front yard and other high-visibility areas. The plan described here brings color to the area by making use of bulbs and wildflowers, but you can simplify even more by being satisfied with the textures of ornamental grasses (in a sunny site) or evergreen groundcovers (in shade).

A large planting of ratibida, a wildflower sometimes called clasping coneflower, becomes a meadow in a side yard formerly devoted to lawn.

Colorful Cover Crops

Although they are most famous for their ability to improve the soil, several cover crops are so pretty that they make great mass plantings Crimson clover is stunning in full bloom, and can be combined with bachelor buttons for an even more colorful display. Planted en masse, buckwheat's white flowers create a frosty vision, and the bold yellow of mustard flowers always gets lots of attention.

Crimson clover.

Ornamental grasses bring a windswept look to a sunny site, and they remain attractive well into winter. Care consists mostly of late-winter pruning.

Corn poppies and bachelor buttons team up to paint an old orchard. The mowed edge at left helps tame the site while making it more approachable.

WATCH OUT!

Cultivate No Weeds

When you are trying to encourage wildflowers and native grasses, it's never a good idea to plow, disc or till before planting. Cultivation invites weeds, which are the natural way the Earth heals over scarred, open places. When you do cultivate a little spot, immediately plant it with seeds, or plug in a plant you want to try.

Romancing Wildflowers

Growing a wildflower meadow is rewarding and fun, but it's very different from growing a garden. The simplest way to begin is to simply stop mowing an area, preferably in the fall, and then see what happens. By spring you will probably be delighted by a number of little wildflowers that sprout—tiny things such as bluets, toadflax or bird's-foot violets that you may need a wildflower book to identify. In places where nothing fun seems to be growing, add to the collection by taking a sharp hoe, scratching up small patches of soil, and seeding them with wildflowers known to grow well in your area.

Some easily grown, widely distributed wildflower species include oxeye daisies, corn poppies, California poppies, purple coneflowers, coreopsis, gaillardia, cosmos and many more. Start with packets of seeds, and try every flower that interests you that might possibly work. Expect some failures and much success too. What you are trying to do is discover wildflowers that are perfect for your climate, your soil, and the level of care you are willing to provide.

While you're fiddling with wildflowers, let nature enrich your meadow with pretty wild grasses. Grasses that grow into clumps help stabilize the site yet won't crowd out wildflowers, so keep the tufting types even if you don't know their names. Most produce interesting seedheads at some point during the growing season, which sway in every breeze, glisten with dew and glow in the evening light. Do keep a close watch for creeping grasses and vining weeds, which you can hoe into submission or spot treat with an all-purpose herbicide. If allowed free reign, weedy plants such as bermuda grass, quackgrass or bindweed can rapidly overtake wildflowers and small native grasses.

Surprisingly, many bulbs will persist in a meadow for years with no attention, as you can see by riding through the countryside when spring daffodils are in bloom. Decades after a house has disappeared, daffodils, grape hyacinths and other bulbs flourish with no human care. In fact, a three-way partnership of small daffodils (which bloom in spring), native and introduced wildflowers (which bloom best from spring through early summer) and uncut wild grasses (which keep their handsome texture well into fall) make a compatible plant guild that looks attractive for months at a time and needs mowing but once a year, in late fall or early winter.

Better Backdrops

All flowers look better with a tall backdrop that helps frame them up nicely. A backdrop will also make a half-wild meadow look more planned. Plant tall sunflowers at the rear of your drift, or perhaps ornamental wheat, which grows about 4 feet tall. Other offbeat possibilities include broom corn or ornamental amaranths such as Joseph's coat or 'Hot Biscuits'—an ornamental form of edible amaranth.

A section of fence is also useful for separating a wildflower meadow from the rest of the landscape, making it look more purposeful and planned.

Old magnolias form a backdrop for millions of grape hyacinth, which persist for years with no attention at all.

COVERING SOME GROUND

Mass plantings made up of a single plant make a clear textural statement, and also lend the feeling of movement to a landscape's design. You can make the most of this special effect by making areas planted with spreading plants long and narrow rather than square or circular. Or, let your mass planting proceed in meandering bands that connect parts of your landscape, define boundaries or frame a lawn that you'd like to keep small.

The most obvious advantage to mass plantings is that whatever maintenance is needed can be done in one session. Daylilies covering a sunny slope can be fertilized in spring and then left to flourish and bloom. In shadier spots, evergreen groundcovers may need occasional weeding and trimming, but they never demand constant attention once they are established.

Several of the plants described in detail in Chapter 6 are good candidates for mass plantings—drifts in which the individual plants grow together to form a sea of foliage (and seasonal flowers too). To help sort through and compare them, the types of sites they prefer and the maintenance needed to grow them well are listed below.

Broad panels of groundcovers such as vinca major can replace lawn areas that you don't want to mow. Include walkways so all parts of your yard are easy to access.

TEN TERRIFIC GROUNDCOVERS

Name	Page	Site	Maintenance
Daylily	109	Full sun to partial shade, in any good soil. Adapts well to slight-to-moderate slopes.	Clip off spent flower stems in late summer; rake off dead debris in winter; fertilize in spring.
Ferns	113	At least a half day of shade, in rich damp soil. Best in open woodlands.	Fertilize lightly in spring; provide water during summer dry spells.
Ornamental Grasses	115	Full sun to partial shade, in any good soil. Adapt well to slight-to-moderate slopes.	Cut back to low mound in late winter; fertilize in spring.
Hosta	118	Partial to predominant shade in any good soil. Great near entryways and formal areas.	Fertilize in spring; clip off flower stems in late summer; rake away dead debris in winter.
Ivy	121	Partial sun to partial shade in any good soil. Ideal for framing lawn, adapts to serious slopes.	Fertilize in spring every year; shear back every few years; trim edges as needed.
Juniper	122	Full sun to partial shade in any soil that is not extremely alkaline. Great for slopes.	Maintain a good mulch over root zones; fertilize in spring.
Liriope	124	Partial shade in any good soil. A fine choice for framing a lawn or as a mass planting in formal areas.	Trimming off old leaves in early spring is optional.
Pachysandra	128	Predominant shade in fertile, well-drained soil. Perfect for manicured places near entryways.	Fertilize in spring; shear back every other year to promote bushy growth.
Plumbago	133	Partial shade in gritty, well-drained soil. Best in open woodlands with high shade.	Rake away debris in winter; fertilize in spring.
Vinca major, V. minor	144	Partial to substantial shade in any soil. Good on slight slopes, great beneath bushes and small trees.	Fertilize in spring; trim edges as needed to control spread.

A beautiful mass planting of hostas edged with pachysandra covers the sloping, wooded parts of this yard, saving its owners many hours of difficult mowing and raking.

WATCH OUT!

Don't Slip Down Your Slope

Steep places that are difficult to mow often are just right for mass planting of groundcovers, but planting and maintaining any plants on a slope can still be tricky. To prevent excessive soil erosion, always mulch between plants. Better yet, lay down a roll-out fabric mulch and set plants in planting holes cut in the fabric. Slopes often are bare because the soil is infertile, so be sure to mix a little fertilizer into each planting hole. After plants are in place, hide the fabric mulch from view with a more attractive material that stays in place well, such as pine needles or wheat straw.

Preparing to Plant

You can use a tiller to cultivate the space you want to devote to a mass planting, which is a good idea if the soil is poor and needs to be enriched with organic matter. But it is often simpler to kill off existing weeds and grasses with herbicide, wait a few weeks, then plug in healthy, well-rooted plants. Weed problems tend to be minimal when space is prepared this way, which is an important consideration. The hardest part of getting a groundcover planting established is keeping the space between plants free of weeds until the groundcover grows together and naturally chokes out weeds—a process that can take 2 to 3 years.

Black-eyed Susans and other vigorous wildflowers often reseed themselves so well that you need only plant them once for years of enjoyment.

Clusters of Color

Groundcovers and grasses alone will bring a spot to life, but if you want to add color don't be afraid to add clusters of flowering shrubs such as caryopteris, forsythia or lilac, which can be grouped together or planted solo as specimen shrubs. In shady spots where you want a bit of relief from a sea of green foliage, station large containers planted with impatiens or other bright annuals. Very large containers that bring color up above ground level often work best.

Pretty pots of daffodils with dwarf snapdragons tucked around their edges punctuate a shady glen. Variegated Vinca minor *is the groundcover.*

THE CHARM OF A COTTAGE GARDEN

A cottage garden teems with flowers that form a tapestry of color and texture. In the center, white iris separate columbine (left) from dianthus (right).

The most irresistible and enduring tradition that has come to us from England is the cottage garden, a style developed by plant lovers of modest means who sought to stuff their small properties with beautiful plants. While more prosperous gardeners were developing intricate semi-formal borders laid out adjacent to large lawns, cottage gardeners created an entirely different look. In a cottage garden, plants are arranged in natural-looking groups so that they billow into soft mounds that appear to have planted themselves.

Spacing is close, so that each cloud of flowers and foliage flows into its neighbors, and the arrangement is so lush that there is hardly room for lawn. Typically, the only features more important than flowers are broad stone walkways that lead to half-hidden patios or sitting areas.

This does not mean that you cannot have a lawn as part of your cottage garden, or that a cottage garden must take up your whole yard. In fact, you should carefully consider the size of this undertaking, because it is not the lowest-maintenance way to manage your landscape. However, turning a smallish space into a wonderland of flowers is great fun, and doing what you love never feels like hard work.

NATURAL EDGE — Easy Reseeders

Most of the plants grown in cottage gardens are perennials, but annuals are welcome additions too, particularly those prone to shed seeds that later pop up as volunteer seedlings. Larkspur, cosmos, coral sage (*Salvia coccinea*), rose campion (*Lychnis coronaria*), chamomile (a fragrant herb with tiny daisy flowers), poppies and sweet alyssum are but a few popular cottage garden annuals with strong talents for making return appearances, year after year.

Rose campion is an old-fashioned reseeding biennial with soft gray foliage. Depending on variety, blooms may be magenta or light pink.

TIME-SAVING TIP — Add a Picket Fence

"Plant" a decorative fence once and it should stand sturdy for years, all the while bringing a feeling of order to the crazy wildness of a cottage garden. The classic design of white picket fencing is affordable and easy to install, and you can even get it in vinyl, which will need cleaning every couple of years but will never need repainting. In a cottage garden, you can even have a gate with no fence attached. If you like poking around flea markets or estate sales, these are great places to pick up old handmade gates that can do the work of art pieces in a cottage garden.

You can temper the exuberance of a cottage garden with a simple picket fence. Let it double as a trellis for vines or tall flowers that need support.

A grassy walkway leads to a garden bench tucked among daylilies and other stalwart perennials. Annuals such as purple lobelia, used as an edging, add to the color quotient.

Cottage Garden Basics

Usually paired with small houses and bungalows, cottage gardens often have an informal style in which plants are arranged logically, by height, but not symmetrically. In keeping with the relaxed mood, the edges of beds are often curved rather than straight. Do try to keep curves as broad as possible, because acute curves quickly become awkward and somewhat difficult to keep nicely groomed.

If you want a cottage garden that occupies only a part of your landscape, the most effective place will be the corridor between where cars are parked and your front door. That way, nothing will be missed by you or your delighted visitors.

There are no hard-and-fast rules on selecting the plants used in a cottage garden, though some plants do seem to be required growing, including fragrant lavender, daisies and at least one old-fashioned rose that smells as good as it looks. Because softness is so important, plants with gray ferny foliage such as dusty miller and artemisia are of great value.

You can choose your own color scheme for a cottage garden, though it is best to stick with quiet pinks, whites, blues and yellows, and use vibrant reds or oranges only as punctuation points. Small trees help give a cottage garden needed structure and year-round appeal. Crabapples, flowering cherries and other blooming trees are especially welcome.

To keep planning simple, just draw up a plan in which you group three to five plants together in clumps or teardrop-shaped drifts. To unify your cottage garden, repeat one plant that blooms in a light neutral color (or produces eye-catching foliage) at least three times. Make sure your repeating plant excels in terms of softness; stachys (page 141), caryopteris (page 102), or dusty miller (page 111) would be excellent choices.

WONDERING WHY?

Defining Daisies

Daisies are charming in the garden and long-lasting in a vase, but it's easy to get confused about them since no two are alike. The daisies that grow wild on roadsides, often called oxeye daisies, are well worth growing in a garden, but why limit yourself to only one type? Shasta daisies are nearly evergreen in mild winter climates, and they have long, stiff stems just right for cutting. Now classified as *Leucanthemum*, these daisies include cultivars that bloom from midsummer onward, such as 'Becky' (hardy to Zone 5) and large-flowered 'Alaska' (hardy to Zone 4). For top performance, Shasta daisies need deep, rich soil, regular fertilizer and water, and prompt deadheading of spent flowers.

Shasta daisies and their wild cousins will charm any garden, and they make great cut flowers too. Plants planted or divided in fall bloom the following spring.

Soft pinks and blues blend together well, as in this bed with tall ageratum and pink dahlias. They're snuggled up against a caryopteris (bluebeard) bush.

Easy Color from Bulbs

Daffodils are dream bulbs for a less-work garden. They bloom beautifully year after year, and even hungry mice leave them alone.

WATCH OUT!

Repel Rodents

Mice and other rodents eat numerous types of bulbs, including crocus and tulips. They leave daffodils alone, so you may have some luck encircling more palatable bulbs with daffodils. Another defensive strategy is to plant bulbs in deep pots, sink the pots in the ground up to their rims, and then cover them with chicken wire. You can also fashion baskets from chicken wire and place them in the planting holes before planting the bulbs. The wire baskets are hidden from view after planting, but tunneling rodents can't get through them to devour your bulbs.

Throughout this book, bulbs are often mentioned as low-maintenance plants that deliver lots of color for their cost, both in terms of time and money. That's because bulbs are essentially little ready-to-bloom horticultural packages. Plant them, give them a few months to root and grow, and you will be rewarded with spectacular flowers year after year.

There are hundreds of species of bulbs, from tiny white snowdrops to huge drumstick alliums. Don't be afraid to try any bulb that interests you, because chances are excellent that they will do well. The most popular bulbs are described on the following pages, but there are many more worth trying. Also see the little bulbs, suitable for growing in a lawn, that are described on pages 88 and 89.

Landscaping with Bulbs

In addition to rich, eye-catching color, bulbs have elegant forms that deserve to be admired up close. Plant bulbs in clusters so that a group of uniform blooms appears in a concentrated space. This usually looks much better than arranging bulbs in straight lines or sprinkling them through a flower bed.

Numerous bulbs fall into the category of spring-flowering bulbs. Daffodils, hyacinths and tulips lead this parade. Plant these bulbs in the fall, because they need the winter season to develop roots. And don't worry if the leaves poke through the soil before the last snow has melted. The bulbs know what they're doing. They will survive and bloom beautifully.

You can plant spring-flowering bulbs by digging a broad, flat-bottomed planting hole and arranging a number of bulbs together in the bottom, or by using a tool called a bulb planter that takes up plugs of soil. Then drop the bulb in the hole, doing your best to get it right side up, and pulverize the soil plug to fill in over the bulb. If you are planting hundreds of bulbs, there are even augers you can use that attach to rechargeable drills—a fast way to speed up the job.

Plant tulips in the fall for an eye-catching display in mid-spring. Tulips naturalize better in cool climates than in places where summers are long and hot.

Hardy gladiolus don't grow as tall as more tender florists' types, but they can be left in the ground year-round to Zone 6.

NATURAL EDGE

Made for Shade

Daffodils are a cinch for naturalizing in sun, but there's also a great perennial bulb for shade. Although little known, wood hyacinths (variously classified as *Scilla campanulata, Hyacinthoides hispanica* and *Endymion hispanicus*) will produce beautiful blue blooms for years when planted in partial shade. Native to Spain, wood hyacinths become dormant in summer, when the soil is dry, and reappear in early spring. They are outstanding grown at the base of tall trees.

If part of your garden receives summer shade from tall trees, let wood hyacinths bring their blue spikes to the scene in late spring.

Summer bulbs such as lilies or gladiolus need a proper flower bed to grow their best, so take some time preparing a suitable planting hole for them, well amended with compost or other organic matter. Add mulch to keep the soil moist, and you have every reason to expect success.

Tips for Better Bulbs

Bulbs come with the basic equipment to grow themselves, but there are a few pointers to keep in mind to get the most out of these miraculous little packages.

Plant Plenty

A dozen tulips grouped together is not too many. You may be able to use fifty little crocuses that bloom close to the ground.

Drainage Counts

Bulbs can rot when grown in low places where the soil does not drain well. But because most bulbs need to be planted deeply, rotting is a constant risk in high rainfall areas. One approach that works well and looks great is to encircle a planting space with large stones, place bulbs in the bottom of the enclosure, and then fill in over them with several inches of soil.

Chill Before Planting

In Zones 8 and 9, it's important to refrigerate spring-flowering bulbs for up to 6 weeks before planting them in early winter. Warm soil causes them to start growing soon after planting, which can be a disaster.

Leave Skins Intact

Never peel bulbs before planting them. The skins help protect them from pests and diseases.

Calculate Planting Depth

Cover bulbs with soil twice as deep as the size of the bulb. Plant a 1-inch-diameter bulb 3 inches deep (1 inch of bulb, 2 inches of soil on top), a 2-inch bulb 6 inches deep, and so forth. Mix a little compost into the soil under the bulb so that when the roots emerge they find some nutrition waiting for them.

Let the Leaves Mature

The green season for bulb plants is when they store up supplies for the next season's bloom, so neither mow, tie, bend nor smother the leaves after the flowers are gone. Instead be patient and wait until the leaves naturally turn yellow to clean up behind your bulbs.

The skins that cover tulips and other bulbs deter rodents and keep the bulbs from sprouting until the time is right.

Eight Great, Easy Bulbs

These are the bulbs you will find so temptingly displayed at garden centers and discount stores, usually in the right season for planting. Look for spring-flowering bulbs in the fall, but wait until spring to plant those that bloom in summer, such as lilies and gladiolus. Choose bulbs that not only feel hard when you gently squeeze them, but also show few signs of sprouting. If you won't be planting them right away, store dormant bulbs in a cool place where they won't dry out too much.

Caladiums are perfect for pots kept in warm shade. Depending on the cultivar, leaves may be heart shaped or lance-leaf types, which are a little smaller but equally easy to grow.

Caladium (*Caladium* hybrids)

Once the weather turns hot, there's no stopping tropical caladiums. Colorful heart or lance-shaped leaves bring excitement to shade, and some varieties also tolerate sun. Grow the corms in containers, and fertilize them every other time you water. Caladiums work well in container bouquets combined with impatiens and other shade-tolerant summer annuals. Store the dormant corms indoors, in dry pots, through the winter. Never expose caladium corms to temperatures below 55°F.

Snow crocus are among the first flowers to bloom in spring, so they are always a cheerful sight. Hybrid crocus come in a range of pure colors, and some have striped blooms.

Crocus (*Crocus* species)

Beautiful cup-shaped blossoms in white, yellow, lilac and purple announce spring. They are fine for perennializing beneath large trees or along walkways. Also grow lavender fall crocus, which are among the few flowers that bloom reliably when winter is on the way. Spring-blooming crocus are hardy to Zone 3; fall bloomers are good in Zones 5 to 8.

Daffodil (*Narcissus* species)

Yellow, white and many shades in between, species and cultivars are so numerous that you can have a parade of varieties in bloom from early spring to midsummer. Some are fragrant, and all make fine cut flowers. All are rodent resistant, and many perennialize well in Zones 4 to 8. Dainty and fragrant miniature varieties are indestructible.

Even fancy daffodils such as double-flowered 'Ascot' are easily grown in a wide range of climates.

Gladiolus (*Gladiolus* hybrids)

Winter hardy to Zone 7, gladiolus corms are so inexpensive that these dramatic flowers are often grown as annuals. Their upright posture makes them perfect for planting along fences, and the color range is huge. They thrive in full sun and make great cut flowers too. Expect blooms about 2 months after planting. Plant some corms late, in early summer, to extend bloom time.

Gladiolus last a long time as cut flowers because the buds open gradually up the stem. The lowers blossoms wither as those near the top unfurl.

Grape hyacinths form lovely clumps when planted in open woodlands, or you can use them to edge sunny beds or even plant them in a casual lawn.

Lilies always bring a regal presence to the garden. Great drainage is mandatory for success with fragrant Orientals like these.

Grape Hyacinth (*Muscari* species)

Usually blue, but white cultivars are available. Tremendous for naturalizing in sun or shade. Excellent beneath trees and shrubs, or scattered in the lawn. Foliage of most species appears in the fall and remains green through winter. Bloom time is mid spring. Tolerant of weather extremes, these little bulbs grow in Zones 2 to 9.

Iris (*Iris* species)

Irises produce beautiful flowers in spring and their spiking foliage remains in the garden through summer, where its texture offers welcome contrast. Tall bearded iris produce huge, showy blooms, and most cultivars are hardy to Zone 3. Dutch iris, hardy to Zone 5 or 6, offer more understated elegance with orchid-like blooms that make long-lasting cut flowers.

Lily (*Lilium* species and hybrids)

Lilies of many species are stars of the summer garden. Bushy Asiatic hybrids bloom reliably in early summer in less-than-ideal conditions, but if you have a deep, fertile spot with super drainage, you can grow dramatic Orientals. All lilies are fine for cutting, and will persist for years with little maintenance beyond spring feeding and mulching in Zones 3 to 9.

Bearded iris have few problems, and the exotic blooms are one of the things that make spring worth waiting for.

Tulip (*Tulipa* species)

Available in every color and size, tulips are always a regal presence in the spring landscape, and they are easily grown in Zones 3 to 8. Tulips often bloom well for only a year or two, though some species will naturalize. Full sun is essential. Otherwise expect the blooms to turn toward the south or west, looking for stronger light. Grow some extras especially for cutting.

Tulips gradually open wide as the blossoms age. Cool weather helps them hold their classic bud shape longer.

CHAPTER 5

Better Lawns, Less Work

Create a living carpet that fits your site and your life, and won't break your back with work.

At its best, a lawn is a healthy swath of turfgrass that benefits the environment by filtering rainwater, manufacturing oxygen and providing a lovely place for play and relaxation. At its worst, a lawn is a mixture of struggling grasses and weeds that requires constant mowing and never looks quite right.

Just as with gardens, good lawns require planning and some work up front. Chronic neglect just won't work. But before launching into a campaign to improve your lawn, think about these matters:

Is the site suitable for a traditional turfgrass lawn? The best lawngrasses need at least a half day of full sun, along with decent drainage and moderately fertile soil. Lawn size is also within your control, and you may find that only certain sections of your landscape have what it takes to support a good lawn. Just as you want garden areas that are easy to maintain, your goal with your lawn should be to have a grass-covered space that fits the site in which it is planted so that it practically grows itself.

Keep an open mind as you think of ways to make your lawn (or un-lawn) a working part of your landscape. In addition to information on better ways to grow grass, this chapter includes ideas for lawn alternatives that may be just what you need. But first we'll see if good grass is a worthy goal for your climate, site and soil.

Getting Lucky with Your Lawn

There's an old saying that says, "You make your own luck." And so it is with lawns. If your climate, soil and site match the needs of certain lawngrasses, having a beautiful lawn is easy. In the United States, the luckiest of all lawn lovers will have one of the situations described. Pages 82 and 83 reveal more information on the turfgrasses named, and how to grow them.

Lawns composed of cool-season blends reach their full green glory early in the spring, just in time to help show off the splendor of spring-flowering shrubs and trees.

A lawn need not be large to do its job. When it comes to lawn, quality is often more important than quantity.

Cool Climate, Full Sun, Deep Topsoil

The upper Midwest, much of the Northeast and the Pacific Northwest are blessed with the exact conditions to grow cool-season grasses such as bluegrass, perennial ryegrass and creeping fescues. If the site is sunny with a very slight slope to foster good drainage, you need only to fine-tune with routine maintenance (pages 84 and 85), and your lawn should be healthy and green from early spring until winter.

Bluegrass is the leading grass for lawns in cool climates because it's both beautiful and dependable, with excellent texture and color.

Mild Climate, Dappled Shade, Regular Rainfall

Although it is classified as a cool-season grass that grows best in cool weather, modern varieties of tall fescue will stay green and vibrant year-round if conditions are right. The country's midsection, from New Jersey to Virginia westward through Missouri, is just right for turf-type fescues. Where the soil is deep and fertile, with a near-neutral pH, bluegrass is a good bet too.

Warm Climate, Full Sun, Good Drainage

Any of the warm-season grasses will grow well in Zones 8 and 9, but none is as easy to maintain as centipede. Millions of homeowners in the Sun Belt have replaced bermuda and zoysia with this creeping grass, which resents heavy fertilizer and thrives on heat.

In the Upper South and Mid-Atlantic regions, improved tall fescue, sometimes called turf-type fescue, is a dependable lawngrass with good shade tolerance.

Making Do

So, what if you don't live in a great zone for grass? Many areas are not great grass zones, and the explanations are clearer than most lawn care professionals care to admit. Increasingly, water is a problem since lawngrasses (other than buffalograss) pretty much collapse when the soil becomes dry. Deep-rooted tall fescue will stage a comeback, but other turfgrasses can be seriously damaged by drought when accompanied by stringent watering restrictions.

Weed control is a problem in the upper South and Great Plains, where summers are hot enough for warm-season grasses like bermuda and zoysia. Yet these grasses become dormant in winter, and winter weeds move in with a vengeance. Tall fescue becomes drab in summer heat, so it is but a partial solution.

The truth is that there is no complete solution. Modern turfgrasses are good, but it's important to realize that there is nothing natural about a velveteen lawn. Unless you live in a lucky lawn region, having such a lawn will require constant infusions of fertilizer, water, weed control and labor.

Maybe it's time you shrunk your lawn or considered alternative approaches that will make lawnkeeping more rewarding and fun.

The fine texture of a good lawn makes everything around it look better. A lawn adjoining a walkway makes an entryway feel more open and spacious.

WONDERING WHY?

What's Thatch?

When creeping grasses grow very vigorously, over a period of time the stems layer over one another at the soil's surface. The topmost stems have healthy green grass blades, but the ones closest to the soil may be dead. As more and more dead stems accumulate, a layer of "thatch" forms between the healthy green grass and the soil. Thatch can be a breeding ground for diseases, and forms a barrier that keeps water and fertilizer from reaching grass roots.

Removing thatch is best done with a piece of heavy equipment called a power rake, which you can rent. However, this is only necessary if the problem is so serious that the layer of thatch is more than an inch thick. And there's more good news. To prevent thatch, cut back on watering and fertilizing. Pushing lawns to grow too well is the leading cause of thatch.

Thatch keeps grass roots from reaching deep into the soil, and can be a breeding ground for fungal diseases.

Understanding Turfgrass

This planet supports thousands of species of grass, but very few are willing to grow into large colonies that form a carpet underfoot. These select few grasses have been improved and hybridized to form modern turfgrasses—a process that began thousands of years ago and has made huge advances thanks to sophisticated breeding methods.

A turfgrass forms a tough, resilient turf that persists over time and withstands a reasonable amount of wear. The most wear-resistant turfgrasses have a creeping habit in which stems, stolons or runners wander about at the soil's surface, gradually knitting the grass plants together into a living carpet. Yet some excellent turfgrasses, such as tall fescue and perennial ryegrass, grow into tufts instead of creeping about. However, the tufts are so upright, that when they are closely spaced, the resulting turf has the appearance of a creeping grass.

On purpose or by accident, many lawns are made up of a mixture of species. Grasses that are well adapted naturally move into hospitable sites, which is how fescue emerges beneath trees in lawns planted with bermuda. Yet diversity is always a good thing, which is why blends of several species are often a smart choice if you have the luxury of choosing seed or sod for a new lawn.

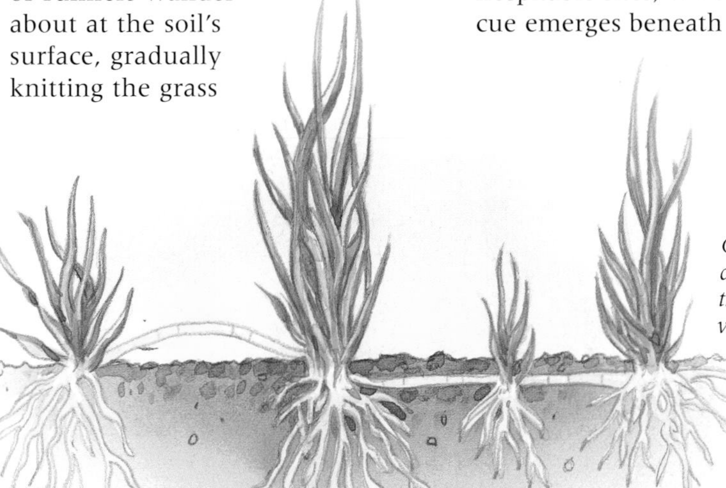

Creeping grasses constantly renew themselves by developing runners at or just below the soil's surface.

Tufting grasses such as turf-type fescues, buffalograss and perennial ryegrass spread very little, but they create a tight turf by growing close together.

Best Lawngrasses

When it first greens up in spring, bluegrass usually shows strong, deep green color. If you don't mind them, a few dandelions and a sprinkling of white clover add seasonal color.

If low maintenance is your priority, choose your lawngrass carefully. Make use of the updated lawngrass varieties that tolerate trouble and are bred to grow in your climate. Here is a quick guide to the leading species for less-work landscapes.

Cool-Season Grasses

These grasses begin to show vigorous growth when soil temperatures rise above 45°F, and remain in good condition as long as summer days are not too hot. They are the grasses of choice in Zones 2 to 6 and higher elevations of Zone 7. Fertilize cool-season grasses in early spring, just as they show vigorous new growth. Set your mower blade at a 2-inch cutting height, and mow when the grass is 3 inches tall.

Bluegrass

Long known as Kentucky bluegrass, this creeping grass has very thin, dark green blades that give the lawn a beautiful texture. Loam or fertile clay soil with good drainage and a pH of 6.5 to 7.0 is ideal. Bluegrass grows best in full sun but can tolerate light shade, especially in Zones 6 and 7. A well-established bluegrass lawn is moderately tolerant of drought.

Bluegrass can be grown from seed or from sod. There are dozens of named varieties, and it is customary to grow three different varieties together to create a lawn with maximum tolerance of stress and pests. You will also find bluegrass seed blended with seed of other cool-season grasses such as perennial ryegrass, which helps the lawn withstand heavy wear, and fine fescue, an outstanding cool-season grass for shade.

The lush look of a bluegrass lawn comes from its numerous thin blades, which have a deep green color when the lawn is properly fed.

Perennial Ryegrass

Only a few cool-season lawns are made up of this grass, which grows into low tufts that spread ever so slightly. However, perennial ryegrass has great color and texture, and it can bounce back from injury very quickly. In sites where bluegrass struggles on its own, try overseeding lightly with perennial ryegrass in early fall. In warm climates, this grass is used as a "wintergreen" grass in dormant bermuda. It has a finer texture and requires much less mowing than less expensive annual ryegrass, which is often used for the same purpose.

Fine Fescue

Creeping fescues are the shade lovers of cool-season grasses, though they also grow in sun. Patches become dormant in hot weather, and green up when cool conditions return. Fine fescue is most often used in cool-season blends that include bluegrass and perennial ryegrass. In yards that include areas of dappled shade, fine fescue is a tremendous asset to the lawn.

Transitional Zone Turf

The central states are often called the transitional zone because there is enough cool weather to grow cool-season grasses, and enough warm weather to grow species that need hot summers. Neither type of grass is perfect for these climates, but one grass, tall fescue, comes closest to being a good fit.

Tall Fescue

Often called turf-type fescue, this tufting grass greens up in the fall and remains green through winter, spring and into early summer. Hot summer weather gives it trouble, so tall fescue lawns often look their worst in July and August. Tall fescue is planted from seed, adapts to many types of soil, and grows in both sun and shade. Numerous named varieties are available, which are far superior to outdated Kentucky 31, which is best dismissed as a pasture grass. Plant seed in early fall or early spring, and mow high, at 3 inches.

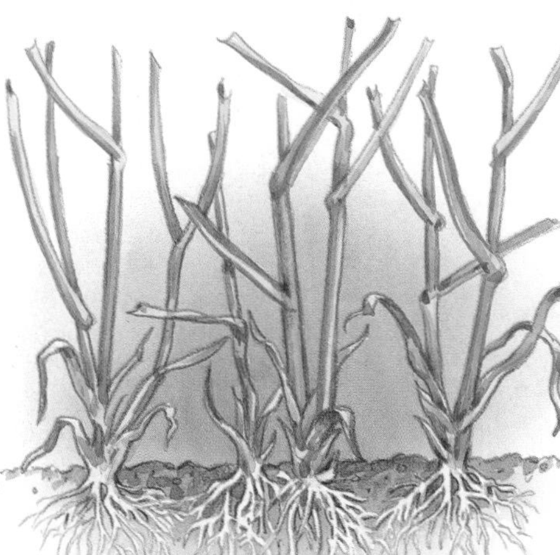

The blades of tall fescue are wider than those of bluegrass so it has a slightly coarser look, but its deep roots make it much more tolerant of drought.

Warm-Season Grasses

These grasses begin to green up when nighttime temperatures rise above 55°F, and have a talent for withstanding heat. They become dormant in cold weather, but provide fine texture even when they are buff-colored rather than green. Fertilize warm-season grasses in early summer, when vigorous new growth appears. Preventive control of crabgrass is often needed as well (see pages 84 and 85).

In warm climates where centipede is hardy, another low-maintenance grass called St. Augustine is often grown in places where there's more shade than sun.

Buffalograss spreads slowly, and depends on its height to shade out weeds. Once established, it can handle extreme drought with ease.

Hybrid Bermuda

This is not a low-maintenance grass, because a good bermuda lawn needs attentive fertilizing and frequent close mowing at 1½ inches. Grooming the lawn's edges is also mandatory if the lawn adjoins sidewalks or curbs. Fine-textured hybrid bermuda is planted from sod, so initial installation is often quite costly. Do not confuse hybrid bermuda with open-pollinated bermuda that is grown from seed. The latter is extremely invasive, and almost impossible to keep out of flower beds and other places where it is not wanted.

Buffalograss

A newcomer to American lawns, this native grass of the Great Plains is a fine choice in places where summers are hot and dry. It tolerates drought better than most weeds, and grows into a deep carpet that should always be mowed very high, at 3 to 4 inches. Buffalograss has an upright growth habit, though it also creeps sufficiently to form a tight turf. This grass can adapt to alkaline clay, but it suffers when subjected to heavy foot traffic. The best varieties of buffalograss are not grown from seed, so you will need to plant a new buffalograss lawn from sod or plugs.

Centipede

If you live in the lower South and want a low-maintenance lawn, centipede is the obvious choice. Although centipede is winter hardy only through Zone 8, it is so vigorous and easy to grow that most lawns in Zones 8 and 9 are now of this species. It is important not to fertilize this grass too much. A single feeding in spring is almost always sufficient. Special fertilizers labeled for use on centipede often include iron, which is a special nutritional need of this grass. Mow centipede at about 2 inches, and repair injured or bare spots with rooted sprigs taken from other parts of your yard.

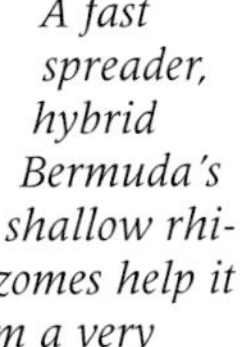

A fast spreader, hybrid Bermuda's shallow rhizomes help it form a very tight turf. Full sun is required.

Centipede grows very rapidly in warm weather, so it can be planted from sprigs. It is happiest with very light applications of fertilizer.

Making a Good Lawn Better

If your home came to you outfitted with a pretty lawn, it is usually simple to keep it green and growing without making it your life's work. Or perhaps your lawn is good, but you want to make it just a little bit better and easier to manage. These strategies will bring out the best in any lawn and will not eat up a lot of time.

Variegated liriope planted as a band around this rose bed's edge separates them visually and makes the lawn's edges easy to maintain.

Frame the Edges

Any lawn will look more handsome and refined if it has clean edges. The edges need not be created with a power edger or string trimmer. Instead, consider installing a permanent frame of brick. Brick or stone edgings, installed at the same height at which you cut your grass, are called mowing strips because the wheels of your mower ride on the bricks and give a clean-cut edge every time. And, a mowing strip can often do double duty by retaining mulch in flower beds placed on the side opposite from the one that borders the lawn.

Any level surface upon which your mower's wheels can roll will work as a mowing strip. This one is made of molded concrete.

Where liriope and other evergreen groundcovers are hardy, plant them in a broad band around your lawn. The shift in color and texture looks great, and eliminates the need for mechanical edging.

Use a Controlled-Release Fertilizer

Some lawn fertilizers' granules are coated. These fertilizers gradually release their nutrients into the soil, so you need to fertilize only once or twice a season. They cost more than uncoated products, but are worth it. Invest in a fertilizer spreader to get an even application and make the job go fast.

> **Time-Saving Tip**
>
> ### Mow High
>
> The ideal mowing height varies with grass species, but it's always wise to err on the high side. Mowing high discourages weeds and insulates the root zone from changes in temperature and moisture. The rule of thumb is to mow off one-third of the length of grass blades at each mowing, which should leave behind a thick, trouble-tolerant turf.

The coated granules of fertilizer will feed plants long after the smallest uncoated ones have dissolved. Controlled-release fertilizers sold at discount stores are often a good buy.

Lawns require ample water, especially in spring when they make most of their new growth. Water so that water goes deep into the soil, where you want new roots to develop.

TOOL TIP: Get Out the Bagger

So you went on vacation and came home to an ankle-high lawn? Get out the bagger and collect your clippings to use as mulch or mix into compost. A too-thick layer of clippings left on the lawn to rot will smother the grass below, leaving yellow (or even dead) patches. But for routine mowing, in which fine clippings are left behind, let them lie. As they decompose, the clippings will enrich the soil with organic matter.

Besides using a bagger to collect excessive clippings, you can use your bagger to chop and collect leaves in the fall. Then mix them into your compost heap.

Water Deeply

When conditions become so dry that you feel you must water your lawn to save it from certain demise, make sure you do it right. Keeping in mind that it takes time for water to percolate deep into the soil, set sprinklers to run for no more than 20 minutes at a time in any given location. Then go back for a repeat watering session after a few hours. A thorough deep watering every week to 10 days will do a drought-stricken lawn much more good than shallow waterings every few days.

Prevent Weeds

Crabgrass is a big, rangy annual grass that sprouts in spring and persists in thin lawns all summer. It is easily prevented by applying a fertilizer with crabgrass preventer in spring at about the time that forsythias or dogwoods bloom. The chemical inhibits the germination of crabgrass seeds, but it can prevent germination of turfgrass seeds too. Do not use crabgrass preventers on newly planted lawns or in areas where you plan to sow seeds in the next 8 weeks.

If weeds are already present, the best offense is to remove them by hand, preferably when the soil is moist. Pull them out, roots and all, and patch bare places with grass seed or plugs taken from other parts of your yard.

Post-emergent herbicides, which kill weeds that are already up and growing, must be handled very carefully. Check the label to make sure the product is appropriate for the type of grass you have, and follow application directions precisely. These herbicides do not always work quickly in cool weather or when weeds are quite mature. And, after the weeds are gone you must promptly repair bare spots.

Of course, the best approach to weed management in lawns is to keep your grass as healthy and vigorous as possible. Tight turf naturally chokes out weeds.

Crabgrass spreads by seeds, and once a seedling becomes established it quickly crowds out less vigorous grasses nearby. Never let crabgrass shed seeds in your lawn.

Apply fertilizer and other lawn chemicals with a spreader to ensure even distribution. Apply half by walking north to south across your lawn, and the other half by walking east to west.

Keep a Sharp Blade

Every spring when mowing season begins, either replace your mower blade or have it professionally sharpened. A clean cutting edge is good for your grass, and a lawn cut with a sharp blade looks better too. You can replace or sharpen a blade yourself, though sharpening is really best done at a mower shop. The challenge in sharpening old blades is keeping them properly balanced. Besides, if you go to the trouble of hauling your mower to a shop, you can also have the spark plug and oil replaced—the best way to make sure your mower starts fast every time and runs as it should.

Create a Casual Lawn

Many of us have lawns that look nothing like the ones in magazines. There's some grass there, but there are also weeds and assorted unknown plants. We mow these casual lawns in the summer so that they look like regular lawns, but we seldom go to the trouble of feeding, seeding and weeding.

Such lawns need a name, and the term "casual lawn" seems to fit. If you like the idea of a casual lawn, keep reading. As long as you don't insist on the monocrop situation of a finished swath of turf, there are endless ways to make such a lawn colorful and interesting by studding it with pretty plants that grow less than 6 inches tall.

In many ways, embracing a casual lawn is similar to bringing back the meadow lawns of times past. These were the types of lawns that existed before the invention of the gas-powered lawn mower in 1902. Meadow lawns consisted mostly of grasses, but also made use of clovers and little bulbs. Any low-growing plants were welcome to the plant community. Fragrance was a plus, too, since these lawns existed before people took for granted deodorant, hot baths and indoor toilets.

There's plenty of white clover in this lawn, which helps form a tight turf. A legume, white clover can convert nitrogen from the air to nutrients it can use.

Contemporary casual lawns have another dimension that comforts our awareness of ecological issues. The concept of diversity, in which different plants grow in close proximity as a compatible community, mimics the planting plans fostered in nature. Diverse plant communities support a diversity of other life forms such as earthworms, birds and butterflies, which are the essence of any healthy biosystem. Chemical inputs are unnecessary because the community governs itself.

Yet a casual lawn need not be wild or created with native plants. That notion is best played out in an enriched prairie, a special type of plant community (pages 90 and 91) for areas that would be prairies if not for man-made alterations. Rather, you might think of an enriched casual lawn as a special kind of garden. Anything that grows goes, and the prettier the better. Growing a casual lawn is a simple matter of plugging in plants that fit and getting rid of those that don't, all the while trying to keep the area looking like a lawn. These plants can be bulbs, herbs and diminutive blooming plants, along with a broad palette of grasses. Growing an enriched casual lawn is fun and requires less work than a traditional one.

WATCH OUT!

Wily Weeds

As you do with your party guests, you should be selective about which plants you allow to make themselves at home in your lawn. Hoe out vining weeds such as bindweed or honeysuckle, and use a crabgrass preventer in spring if crabgrass is your main reason for mowing during the hottest part of summer. Make up your own mind about dandelions. They are both pretty and edible, but they shed so many seeds that they can quickly overtake your yard and make you unpopular with your neighbors too.

After a few years, a lawn usually settles in, matures and becomes much easier to manage. When a lawn suits its site, routine mowing and feeding are all that are needed.

Even in a casual lawn, plant seed in areas that are very thin. Tall fescue, perennial ryegrass, and bluegrass seed can be planted in early fall or first thing in spring.

NATURAL EDGE

Johnny Jump-Ups

You can call them mini-pansies, violas or Johnny jump-ups. By any name, these modern hybrids of an old favorite have retained their ancestors' ability to shed thousands of seeds. Grow these vigorous annuals in flower beds near your lawn, and you will probably see numerous small seedlings popping up in the grass. They won't grow very high before being mowed down, but each little bloom will likely bring a smile to your face.

Johnny jump-ups reseed with great enthusiasm. Plants from flower beds often shed seeds that end up in the lawn. Delay spring mowing slightly to enjoy the colors!

Getting Started

You don't need to wait for a certain season to begin adding comely plants to a ho-hum lawn. But if your lawngrass is thin, do sow seed of a tufting grass, such as perennial ryegrass or tall fescue, in either fall or spring. To promote good germination, mow and rake the area to expose as much bare soil as possible before planting, and create crevices where the seed can settle in and germinate. Then set up a sprinkler to keep the area constantly moist until the seeds sprout, usually about 10 days.

Little spring-flowering bulbs can turn a casual lawn into a fairyland, and fall is the best time to plant them. Fragrant herbs such as thyme or Roman chamomile can be added in the spring, along with bits of creeping phlox. Meanwhile, be on the lookout for "un-grasses" that you might want to add to yours. Some of these, such as violets and cinquefoil, are often regarded as weeds. But in a casual lawn, they may be welcome flowers.

The next two pages describe numerous cultivated plants that you might want to adopt in your lawn. To showcase each one, plant them in widely spaced groups, so that they look like they scattered themselves about naturally. Few sights are more lovely than a legion of bright crocuses, peeking their heads above a sleeping lawn first thing in spring.

To grow a naturalized mass planting of crocus in a grassy area, let the foliage stay after the flowers fade. When handled this way, flowers will return for many seasons.

To plant little bulbs, stab a sharp hand trowel into damp soil, pull open a crevice, and drop the bulb in the hole. Then press the turf back in place.

Coloring Up a Casual Lawn

Grape hyacinths will naturalize in any type of lawn, though they're best in cool-season grasses where the green foliage is hardly noticed during the winter.

Clovers and other widely distributed plants will find your lawn sooner or later, but there are a number of beautiful plants that take to life in a casual lawn so well that you may want to plant them on purpose. Use these as a starting point, but also be on the lookout for others that may be unique to your climate. Where winters are mild, various shamrocks make fine lawn plants. In cold climates, little alpine plants may grow as well in your lawn as in a rock garden.

Spring Surprises

The seven "little bulbs" described here are available from bulb dealers from late summer to fall, and you can often find packets at retail stores too. Use your imagination, but do try to locate like-bulbs together so that they look natural. Be sure to place some close to sidewalks, because passersby will invariably stop to admire the show.

Greek windflower (*Anemone blanda*) produces white or pink daisy-like flowers in early spring atop tufts of ferny foliage. They grow only 6 inches tall and naturalize well in Zones 5 to 9. Soak the dry corms in water overnight before planting them in the fall.

Snowdrops (*Galanthus* species) always delight with their nodding white blossoms on 4- to 6-inch stems. Plant bulbs in the fall, as a slightly taller backdrop to winter aconites or crocus. Snowdrops grow best in Zones 5 to 8 and resist rodent damage.

Grape hyacinth (*Muscari* species) produce clusters of rounded, balloon-shaped blossoms that resemble clusters of grapes. Traditionally blue in color but also available in white, these tough little bulbs prosper in Zones 4 to 9. In most climates, the grass-like foliage appears in fall and persists through winter.

Squill or bluebells (*Scilla siberica*) pop open like riveting blue stars atop dainty 4-inch stems. Foliage is grasslike and rodents ignore the bulbs, so squill is always a sure thing in Zones 4 to 8.

Squill make a lawn look like it has been visited by flower fairies. Both the flowers and the foliage are long gone by early summer.

Winter aconites (*Eranthis hyemalis*) bring a touch of yellow to the spring palette. Keep the tiny bulbs moist, stored in your refrigerator, before planting them in the fall. Winter aconites are hardy to Zone 4 and grow best in cool-summer climates.

Crocus (*Crocus* species) have earned the devotion of gardeners everywhere through their fine performance year after year. Stunning colors include white, yellow, purple and stripes, all with bold orange stamens. Adapted in Zones 3 to 9, crocus bulbs must be planted in fall if they are to bloom in the spring.

Glory-of-the-snow (*Chionodoxa* species) is one of the first flowers of the year, producing 5-inch-tall stalks studded with lilac-blue blossoms. The foliage blends well with grasses, and the tiny bulbs are hardy to Zone 4. Plant in fall, and expect to see new seedlings popping up each year.

Before winter has ended, clusters of glory-of-the-snow make it hard to go back indoors once you have been touched by their promise of spring.

Moss pink endures between rocks and on slopes, or you can use it to paint your lawn pink or edge your driveway in lilac.

Clusters of Color

Let these low-growing perennials flourish in a casual lawn. They are especially welcome on slopes that are infrequently mowed.

Moss Pink (*Phlox subulata*), often called thrift, forms broad mounds that bloom in spring, in pink, white, blue and many shades in between. The less you mow over it, the better. Stop mowing altogether from fall until early summer. Adapted in Zones 3 to 9.

English daisy (*Bellis perennis*) is regarded as a weed by some but not by people who want pretty little daisies blooming in the lawn in late spring. Allow to grow uncut from fall to spring. This willing reseeder likes full sun. It grows as a perennial in Zones 4 to 6, and as a hardy annual in Zones 7 to 9.

English daisies are coming back into style as color plants in lawns. In warm climates, they are sometimes used as fall-to-spring bed partners with pansies.

Cinquefoil (*Potentilla tridentata*) grows like a weed but is much prettier. Small yellow flowers that appear in early summer have a satiny finish. Likes acid soil and full sun to partial shade in Zones 2 to 7.

Golden star (*Chrysogonum virginianum*) is a 4-inch-tall native that features starry yellow blooms off and on all summer. Needs rich soil and partial shade, so it's great for damp edges of the lawn in Zones 5 to 9.

Golden star prefers places that resemble its natural home in the woods, complete with acidic soil rich in organic matter and part-day shade.

Creeping thymes are edible, but you will love the way they smell when you crush them underfoot too. Several cultivars produce bright pink flowers.

Fragrance Underfoot

You would not want to make a habit of walking on these low-growing fragrant herbs, but if you do you will be delighted with the aroma of the crushed leaves. Expect a few flowers too, especially if you locate these plants at the lawn's edge, where they can be passed over by the lawn mower.

Roman chamomile (*Chamaemelum nobile*) needs sun and good drainage, and though it is adapted in Zones 5 to 8, humid heat gives it trouble. Tiny daisy flowers can be used for tea.

Creeping thymes (*Thymus serpyllum, T. praecox*) grow only 4 inches tall, but they need sun and fast-draining, gritty soil. Adapted in Zones 4 to 9, thymes make lovely meandering ribbons in a casual lawn, or grow them between steppingstones.

Sweet woodruff (*Galium odoratum*) is the perfect finishing touch for shady spots where the soil stays moist. The soft, finely cut foliage grows 8 inches tall and is lightly fragrant underfoot. Adapted in Zones 4 to 8.

Sweet woodruff blankets the ground beneath an elderly rhododendron. Woodruff spreads by shedding seeds and sending out rooted stems along the soil's surface.

An Enriched Native Prairie

To have a lot of color in a wildflower meadow, you will probably want to include some non-natives such as bachelor buttons (purple) and Siberian wallflower (orange).

Much of the Midwest was once a grass-covered prairie, a special climate-specific ecosystem that evolved over millions of years. Native prairie plants have deep roots that enable them to thrive with no fertilizer or supplemental water. And the diverse plant community that exists in a native prairie supports exactly the kinds of wildlife we like to watch, namely birds and butterflies.

So it is no surprise that there is a sizeable landscaping movement taking place that promotes the use of native prairie plants as lawn alternatives. Specialized nurseries have sprung up all across Illinois, Wisconsin and Minnesota to meet the demand for appropriate plants.

Make no mistake: a native prairie planting does not look like a lawn. More often, it is comprised of numerous grasses of varying sizes accompanied by perennial wildflowers and small shrubs. In the wild, fire is the natural force that perpetuates prairies. Without fire, larger shrubs and trees would soon begin to grow.

But you can grow a piece of prairie in your yard without striking a match. Mowing down the vegetation once a year (or having it done with a brush cutter or bushhog) has the same renewal effect on a prairie planting as burning. Whether you mow in late summer, fall or early spring is up to you. Because mowing at different times of the year favors different plants, you can increase the diversity of the plants in your prairie by mowing different parts of it at different times of the year.

Going Native

Native prairie grasses and "forbs"—the name native-plant people use for flowers and other non-grasses—have what it takes to stand up to the stresses nature throws their way, but they are easily crowded out by more aggressive imported plants. For this reason it is wise to get rid of lawngrasses in any space being converted to prairie, either by cutting it off with a sod cutter (which you can rent) or by killing it with herbicide. Both are radical measures, so you will probably want to start small and let your prairie increase in size gradually. Indeed, it is wise to keep a band of turf alongside a prairie planting to make your house look well-groomed and to have a refined open space from which to enjoy your prairie.

Instead of cultivating the soil, which will turn up millions of weed seeds, mulch over it with a 3-inch-thick layer of clean straw. This mulch will prevent erosion and give you unlimited opportunities for setting out seedlings whenever you like. If you want to sow seeds, simply rake back a patch of mulch, score the soil ½ inch deep with a hoe, and seed away.

The first and second seasons will be quite educational as you learn to identify the natives you have planted, which will no doubt be accompanied by others that spontaneously appear, as well as by weeds and aggressive imported plants that insist on staging a comeback.

You can hoe out plants you don't want, or squirt them with an all-purpose herbicide (such as glyphosate). Herbicides are more effective than hoeing to control weeds that grow from root buds, such as bindweed, Canada thistle and quackgrass.

Use prairie dropseed along the front edges of a prairie planting. The clumps have a refined shape and texture.

*Blazing star (*Liatris spicata*), also called gayfeather, is a top perennial for wildflower meadows or prairie plantings. The spikes make lasting cut flowers too.*

Red switchgrass is usually a strong reseeder, and the plants grow into large masses that become even more colorful in early fall, when days become shorter.

Purple coneflower is pretty enough for a garden yet tough enough for a meadow or prairie. Plants grow slowly for the first year or two, and become bushier with age.

Prairie Plants

Soil moisture is the biggest factor to consider in choosing plants for your prairie. Dry land supports numerous grasses and wildflowers, while wetlands host rushes, sedges and lowland wildflowers such as Joe-Pye weed. Check with local native-plant nurseries, conservation agencies or wildflower societies for lists of plants known to grow particularly well in your area. Remember, you are not trying to invent something new as much as you are to restore something very, very old.

Because most houses are situated on dry land, several plant species are favored time and again in prairie plantings. Use this short list as a starting point, but keep a very open mind. An acre of native prairie can contain hundreds of different plant species, and it may take a lifetime to learn to recognize and appreciate them all.

Grasses

Big bluestem, little bluestem, sideoats grama, switchgrass, Indian grass, prairie dropseed, prairie cord grass, porcupine grass.

Flowers

Silky aster, cream wild indigo, sand coreopsis, pale purple coneflower, western sunflower, bush clover, blazing star, spiked lobelia, gray goldenrod, black-eyed Susan.

*The petals of black-eyed Susans (*Rudbeckias*) often include bands of brown or mahogany. Seed-sown species offer the greatest variability in flower color.*

Porcupine grass is big and showy, so it's a good choice to place near entryways to a meadow area. Or use it as part of a backdrop combined with larger shrubs and trees.

WATCH OUT!

Be Aware of Weed Laws

Is it legal to have a little piece of prairie in place of your lawn? Before you launch into this project, make a few calls to check on "weed laws" that govern how tall the vegetation in your yard can be allowed to grow. Some communities are heavily pro-lawn, others have embraced natural landscaping because of its environmental benefits, and some have taken the middle ground, allowing prairie plantings as long as there is a buffer strip between the tallish plants and public roads and walkways.

Going Lawnless with Mulch and Moss

No grass grows in this woodland garden, but stones, moss and mulch cover bare soil. Spring-flowering bulbs make the most of late-winter sun.

Some sites just were not meant to grow grass. Shade, extreme soil and too little or too much moisture set the stage for a lawnless yard—a fact to be celebrated rather than bemoaned. There is no rule that says that a home must have a lawn to be beautiful. In a glen of pines or other conifers, the fallen needles that naturally carpet the ground have the same fine texture as grass, and they require no maintenance at all! Where fuzzy mosses colonize compacted soil that refuses to support other plants, why not encourage the moss and let it take over? Battles with nature always require lots of time and effort, and most of the time you lose anyway.

Woodland Wonders

If your yard is thick with trees, then it is a woodland. Turf does not grow in this environment, but many other plants do. In addition to the thousands of native plants that need a woodland environment, beautiful ornamentals such as azaleas (page 96), hostas (page 118) and pulmonarias (page 135) naturally thrive in the shade of trees and the soil that is created when fallen leaves and needles decompose into humus.

You may want to remove badly placed trees to improve your view or to protect your house from falling limbs, but it is never a sound idea to remove trees so that you can grow grass. A thinned woodland will try to regenerate itself by sprouting numerous small shrubs, brambles and other plants that naturally precede trees in the forest-birthing process called natural succession. So you will be challenged by grass, have a whole new legion of prickly plants to battle, and you will probably miss the shade. Worst of all, you will have to start raking and cleaning up after your trees—an unnecessary burden on your leisure time.

Give in to the notion of letting your woodland go natural. Open up well-defined pathways, install steppingstones if needed to ensure safe footing, and let leaves and little limbs rest where they fall. Maintenance of a woodland yard is limited to sweeping walkways, cleaning up big limbs and unwanted underbrush once or twice a year, and perhaps studding in a few color plants for extra interest.

In arid climates, landscapes that require little or no supplemental water simply make sense. You can have a landscape that is attractive and interesting using very few plants.

You can coax the thin layer of acid soil over barely-covered rocks and tree roots into supporting a soft green garden of moss. The key: sufficient moisture.

Capitalizing on Moss

For years, homeowners in high-rainfall climates have lamented the persistence of moss in their lawns. They were told it was a problem to be remedied by lightening up shade and improving the soil and changing its pH—all radical, laborious processes. It's so much better to embrace your moss and help it grow. Few scenes are as cool and serene as a shady yard paved with soft green moss.

The right conditions for moss include shade from mature shade trees, compacted soil with an acidic pH (which you already have if you have moss), and plenty of moisture. Northern exposures that receive substantial shade from buildings and trees often work best.

Nurturing a native stand of moss is easy. Every few months go through by hand and pull out weeds or grasses, which are usually few since the conditions that are good for moss are too dark and harsh for most other plants. Moss is delicate, so go barefoot or wear smooth-soled shoes when weeding your moss.

To discourage non-mosses, patch holes with clumps of moss taken from nearby woods, set them in firm contact with the soil, and water well. Incidentally, you cannot buy moss that is likely to adapt well to hospitable parts of your yard. You just have to take it, preferably from private land with the owner's permission. When taking moss from wild places, take up small pieces, less than 6 inches square, and the native stand should quickly recover.

You will probably need to water your moss frequently during unusually dry weather, especially the dry heat of late summer and early fall. Because moss grows right at the surface, you can water it a little at a time, so that it is nicely dampened to about 2 inches below the surface. Using a sprinkler, you can probably accomplish this in less than 10 minutes.

When the leaves start falling, plan to sweep or blow them off your moss lawn so it will get needed light. Allow no cleats, kids on bikes or other violent encounters to threaten the area. If people are drawn to admire the beauty of your moss, provide steppingstones so that you can share the beauty without squashing it.

NATURAL EDGE

Moss-Covered Stones

The texture of hard stone marries beautifully with soft moss, and there's an easy way to inoculate stone with starter colonies of moss. In fall or spring, when the weather is cool, take two handfuls of moss and a quart of buttermilk and pulse them in a blender a few times. Then use a large paint brush to slather the mixture onto large stones or stone walls. Be sure to get good coverage on north-facing surfaces, the first places that moss is likely to establish itself. Sprinkle water on the inoculated surfaces frequently to maintain moisture.

Over time, lichens and a wide range of mosses will appear on rocks in damp places. Colonies usually begin on the sides of stones that slowly dry after morning dew.

CHAPTER 6

50 Less-Work Plants

Backbone plants for better gardens with less work.

Whether you are looking for annual flowers that will give you a summer of satisfaction or a tree that will beautify your yard for years to come, the plants listed here are a logical starting place. They have been chosen based on their propensity to thrive in a wide range of climates with little need for exacting care. Most are inexpensive as well, simplifying the task of making landscape improvements on a limited budget.

Especially if you are new to gardening, it is often challenging to decide precisely where to place plants that have captured your attention or your heart. Each entry here begins with an overview of how the plant is best used in home landscapes, along with particular needs the plant may have for soil or exposure. Then leading species or cultivars are discussed, followed by tips for successful planting.

As you shop for plants for your landscape, make a habit of carefully reading plant tags. In addition to the species and cultivar names, you should find information on the plant's mature size and how much sun and water it needs for good growth. This is particularly important with shrubs and trees, which vary tremendously from one cultivar to the next.

If you find that you truly enjoy gardening, discovering rewarding plants will likely become a lifelong adventure. Just be sure to always keep a plant's maintenance needs in mind before you bring it home. Remember: The goal with less-work landscaping is for you to run your garden rather than having it run you!

Azalea

Shrub
Rhododendron species and hybrids

In Northern areas, most azaleas shed their leaves in fall. New leaves, along with lovely blossoms, arrive again in mid-spring.

The most colorful of all spring-flowering shrubs, azaleas do a good job of taking care of themselves if you plant them in precisely the type of niche they require. Azaleas struggle in spots that get too much sun, and they are almost as stressed by too much shade. However, if you have a spot that gets dappled shade during most of the day, or is sunny in the morning and shaded in the afternoon, you have a sweet spot for azaleas.

Azaleas also need moderately acid soil (with a pH between 4.5 and 6.0) that stays moist close to the surface, where many of the roots are found. In many areas of the Eastern U.S. the soil is naturally acidic, so you need only remember to never lime azaleas, and you can expect them to thrive. Alkaline soils high in dissolved salts simply will not do. In Western areas where these conditions prevail, grow azaleas in large pots kept on a shady deck or patio.

Choosing Azaleas

Depending on the cultivar, azaleas may be either evergreen or deciduous. Most evergreen azaleas are hardy only to Zone 7, while some deciduous species are hardy to Zone 4.

Evergreen azaleas are available in a huge color range, and because they make such a strong color statement, it is often practical to buy plants in bloom so you will know exactly what color you are getting. Plant deciduous azaleas in early spring, before they break dormancy, because the growth of new roots usually accompanies the emergence of leaves and flower buds.

Evergreen azaleas bloom so profusely that the foliage is completely hidden from view. Some new varieties bloom in the fall as well.

Growing Azaleas

When you buy your plants, also buy a block of peat moss, the perfect soil amendment for this particular shrub. Alternatively, you can work a 3-inch layer of rotted leaf mold into the soil. Dig a broad planting hole, twice as wide as it is deep, and thoroughly mix in the peat moss or leaf mold. Set plants so that the cultivated soil forms a slightly raised mound, with the plant sitting slightly high compared to surrounding soil, but at the same depth that it grew in its container. As the soil settles, the mound will gradually flatten out.

Water thoroughly, and mulch around the plant with 2 inches of shredded bark, pine needles or other mulch. Water as often as needed to keep the soil from drying out for the first year after azaleas are planted.

Feed established azaleas each spring with a fertilizer formulated for plants that prefer acid soil. Water weekly during serious droughts. Let azaleas shape themselves as they grow, and prune only to remove dead or damaged limbs.

Barberry

Shrub
Berberis species and hybrids

Barberries are slow-growing shrubs that you can basically plant and then forget, except when they get your attention with their spring flowers, vibrant summer foliage and berries that persist into winter. Birds often nest in barberry bushes, though people and other animals are deterred by their thorns. You can use barberries as foundation shrubs, put them to work to create a hedge that never needs pruning, or locate large cultivars where they will form a backdrop for smaller plants.

Barberries grow in Zones 5 to 9. In cold climates they are decidous shrubs best adapted in full sun or partial shade, but evergreen types (which are not as cold hardy) can handle more shade. With most barberries, new leaves emerge pinkish red in spring, ripen to green, and then turn bright-orange to yellow in fall. Yellow spring flowers are followed by berries in late summer that may be red, purple or black, depending on species.

A few barberry cultivars have variegated leaves, which are interesting in the garden and can also be used in cut-flower arrangements.

Choosing Barberries

Hardy and dependable, Japanese barberry (*B. thunbergii*) is the most common type sold in nurseries. Cultivars vary greatly in size, and many have reddish leaves. 'Crimson Pygmy' grows only 2 feet high and 3 feet across, so it is often used in foundation groupings. Korean barberry (*B. koreana*) is taller, often reaching 6 feet, and it is an excellent producer of red berries. Wintergreen barberry (*B. julianae*) holds its leaves through winter even in cold climates, though they turn bronze as the weather becomes more frigid. Mature bushes are 8 feet tall. An interesting hybrid called 'Mentor' barberry grows to 6 feet tall and wide, with low stems that sweep the ground, giving a hedge a nice, full appearance.

There are numerous other named cultivars which vary in height from 3 to 7 feet. Shop carefully and read plant tags to make sure you get a barberry to fit the place and use you have in mind.

Growing Barberries

Barberries are flexible when it comes to sunlight, and they do not demand rich soil. Their one requirement is neutral to slightly alkaline soil with a pH between 6.0 and 8.0. If your soil is acidic, mix lime into the soil as you prepare the planting hole. Dig a hole three times as wide as the root ball or container, mix in lime if needed, and set the plant at the same depth it grew in its container. Water well, and weekly thereafter if dry conditions prevail. After the first year, barberries usually need no supplemental water or other special care.

Many barberries are famous for their fall color, which is always a rich crimson red. Naturally, unclipped barberry hedges make a strong statement in autumn.

Begonia

Annual Flower
Begonia x semperflorens-cultorum

There are begonias to grow as houseplants and others to tuck into hanging baskets kept on a shady porch. But the easiest, toughest, most long-flowering of them all are annual begonias, variously known as wax-leaf begonias, fibrous begonias and bedding begonias. The dainty flowers can be white, pink or red, and leaf color varies between green, green tinged with red, or bronze-red from stem to tip. Truly low-care plants, annual begonias grow 10 to 12 inches tall, bloom continuously all summer, are self cleaning, and adapt to full sun or partial shade.

Begonias grow beautifully in window boxes or pots, especially large containers that can hold three or more plants. They are also a good choice for edging beds, and because they are so uniform you can make a patterned edging by repeating color patterns (such as two pinks, one white) down the sides of a walkway or drive. In terms of size and staying power, begonias work well with ageratum, a compact blue annual that grows especially well in warm weather. Begonias also are great for planting in small masses near mailboxes or other focal points.

Although they are most often grown in low-maintenance beds, try growing wax begonias in containers. Keep the containers at eye level so you can admire the blooms up close.

A low window box filled with pink wax begonias looks good in all types of weather. These plants are self-cleaning, so they rarely need pinching or grooming.

Choosing Begonias

Don't worry about variety names in begonias. When you shop for bedding plants, simply choose flower and foliage colors you like. Plants with larger flowers tend to produce fewer of them, and may not stay as neat and uniform as those with smaller blooms.

Growing Begonias

These annuals grow from very tiny seeds, so it is best to begin with bedding plants, which are inexpensive and widely available in spring. Keep the seedlings moist, and feed them with a liquid fertilizer mixed at half strength just before planting. Work an organic or timed-release all-purpose plant food into the soil at the rate recommended on the label before setting plants out. If roots have completely filled the containers, gently break apart the bottom half-inch of roots as you set out the plants.

Water newly planted begonias as needed for a month to keep the soil lightly moist. A mulch looks nice, discourages weeds, and helps retain soil moisture. Begonias rarely have problems with pests, but they may need a light trimming in late summer to help stimulate new growth. In addition, a late-summer drench with a water-soluble fertilizer will help keep begonias blooming all the way until frost arrives.

Birch

Tree
Betula species

Historically, birch bark has been used to make items ranging from shoes to paper to canoes. Today we value the year-round drama of birch trees' peeling multicolored bark, their small leaves that let light pass through, and manageable size that makes them good fits in suburban yards. Birches do need moisture, so they are not the best choices for arid climates, but otherwise they have few requirements, need no pruning, and seldom are bothered by pests or diseases.

Birches grow quite rapidly when young, especially when planted in full sun and given ample moisture. When deciding where to plant birches, allow room for surface roots, which can be extensive. In a low-maintenance landscape, a great scheme is to plant a trio of birches in an island bed in the sun, and then install a flowing bed of groundcover beneath the trees. The groundcover will benefit from full sun as it matures and fills in, and later on it will hide the birch's surface roots from view. A soaker hose snaked among the groundcover plants can be used to water the trees and the groundcover in times of severe drought.

Choosing Birches

Large and lovely, paper birch (*B. papyrifera*) is the white birch of canoe-making fame. A Northern native adapted in Zones 2 to 7, paper birch features white bark striped with gray and black, yellow fall foliage, and a mature height ranging from 50 to 70 feet.

The shaggy bark of river birch gives it year-round interest. Plan ahead for a young tree's surface roots by planting a groundcover or a group of low shrubs around its base.

A favorite of landscape designers, Eastern native river birch (*B. nigra*) grows to only 30 feet tall, so it fits easily into most yards. River birch often develops multiple trunks that fork near the ground, and the 'Heritage' cultivar in particular shows several colors of brown and white in its peeling bark. Adapted in Zones 4 to 9, river birch is resistant to bronze birch borer, an insect that causes serious injury to many other birches.

The 'Hertitage' cultivar has bark that constantly peels in layers as the tree grows. Shedding is heaviest in spring, and slows down in summer and fall.

Where alkaline soil conditions predominate, try European white birch, also known as weeping birch (*B. pendula*). This popular, delicate-looking tree grows to 40 feet tall and features white bark, glossy green leaves and a strong tendency to develop arching side branches that draw down into a weeping posture as they reach maturity.

Growing Birches

Native American birch species prefer slightly acidic soil, while European birch will adapt to more alkaline soils of the West. Moist sites are ideal, especially for river birch, which is a lowland tree. Set out new trees in spring, and keep well watered during their first year. Should you want to prune limbs from any birch, do so in early summer, after the leaves have reached full size. Winter pruning often causes the trees to "bleed" sap in spring.

Blueberry

Shrub
Northern highbush type: *Vaccinium corymbosum*
Southern rabbiteye type: *Vaccinium ashei*

If you like the idea of being able to pick delicious berries from shrubs that can easily pass for ornamentals, you will love blueberries. Distantly related to azaleas and rhododendrons, blueberries grow into 5- to 6-foot-tall shrubs with small green leaves that turn red in the fall. Because they set fruit better if more than one variety is grown, consider planting a trio of bushes and letting them grow into an informal hedge. Blueberries require sun and moist, acidic soil, and if these needs are met, they will thrive with little care.

Especially if you live in the West, where many soils are alkaline, check your soil's pH before forging ahead with blueberries. Their preferred pH range is 4.5 to 5.2, which is moderately acidic. Attempting to grow blueberries or any other acid-loving plant in alkaline soil is fighting against nature, and sooner or later you will lose.

Your biggest challenge in growing blueberries is gathering the fruits before they are discovered by hungry birds. Bird netting may keep birds at bay.

Choosing Blueberries

There are three types of blueberries. The two most common ones, highbush and rabbiteye blueberries, grow into head-high rounded shrubs, and produce large crops of berries in early summer. The highbush types are hardy to Zone 3, and are widely grown as far south as Zone 7. However, from Zones 7 to 9, rabbiteye types are preferred because they are much more tolerant of high heat. Named varieties of both types are numerous. Check with your extension service for pamphlets that list the best cultivars for your area.

A third type, lowbush blueberries, grow to only about 1 foot tall, and they are extremely hardy, surviving Zone 2 winters. The small berries have great flavor, but because of the bushes' petite size, lowbush blueberries are not as useful as landscape shrubs.

Blueberries grow into open, rounded shrubs that almost always produce yearly crops. Pale, white early-spring flowers give way to clusters of flavorful berries.

Growing Blueberries

Set out container-grown plants in early spring, in soil that contains acidic soil amendments such as peat moss, leaf mold or compost. Buy big 2-year-old plants, because blueberries grow slowly and do not reach full size until they are at least 6 years old. Plan ahead to water young blueberries, perhaps using leaky jugs (see page 43). Blueberries have shallow roots that dry out quickly, though their drought tolerance improves as the plants develop more extensive roots. Mulch with 4 inches of straw, rotted leaves, shredded bark or another organic material to help retain soil moisture.

Blueberries need little or no pruning—just enough to trim off dead or damaged branches. Fertilizing once a year is usually sufficient. Spread an organic or controlled-release fertilizer around the plants first thing in spring, and follow up with a fresh supply of organic mulch.

Boxwood

Evergreen Shrub
Buxus species

Dwarf boxwoods grow slowly and keep their shape with only light pruning. Be careful not to damage boxwood roots, and you can partner them with flowers like primroses.

Any less-work landscape in Zones 5 to 9 should not be without this indestructible and versatile shrub. Boxwood's glossy green leaves and stocky shape make it a superb backdrop for other plantings. You can use boxwood to enclose "rooms" in the outdoor landscape, to screen out unwanted views, to mask a foundation, to outline a terrace, walk or flower bed, to fill planter boxes or large containers, or to accent a formal spot such as a piece of living sculpture.

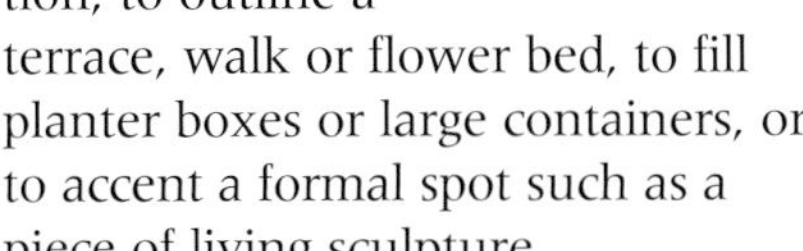

Choosing Boxwoods

Boxwood owes its versatility in the landscape to the fact that it comes in so many forms, from prostrate, globe and half-erect, to weeping, columnar and pyramidal. Some boxwoods are slow growing, while others are relatively fast. Your choice will depend on where you would like to situate a boxwood and what sort of design effect you desire.

Most commonly grown boxwoods are cultivars of two species, *B. sempervirens* (Common boxwood) and *B. microphylla* (Littleleaf boxwood). Littleleaf boxwood is fairly heat tolerant, rarely gets more than 3 feet tall, and features bright green leaves less than an inch long. It is usually used as an edging, low hedge, accent or rock garden plant. Common boxwood is a cold-tolerant, wide-spreading shrub or small tree with very dense, evergreen foliage. Although very old plants may reach 20 feet, it usually grows to a height of 5 to 10 feet. It is usually used as a foundation shrub near corners of buildings, or as a screening plant.

Growing Boxwoods

Site boxwood in well-drained soil in part shade. Avoid areas that remain wet, such as near a downspout. Dig a hole twice as wide as the root ball but only as deep, so the plant will sit in the hole at the same level it was growing at the nursery. Fill the hole with good topsoil, gently firm the soil around the roots, and water deeply. Continue to give the shrub good, deep waterings until it takes root, usually about three months. Spread 2 to 3 inches of mulch around the plant to protect its shallow root system, and never cultivate around a boxwood at the risk of damaging those roots.

You can let boxwoods go unpruned for an informal look, or use electric pruning shears to train them to a specific shape. Dwarf cultivars need very little trimming. Prune larger boxwoods in late spring and again in midsummer. Stop pruning by late summer, because new growth that appears in the fall is easily damaged by cold winter weather.

Littleleaf boxwoods such as 'Green Pillow' have a slightly different texture that is softer and less stiff than common boxwood, but littleleafs are not as tolerant of winter cold.

CARYOPTERIS

Shrub
Caryopteris x *clandonensis*

The 'Longwood Blue' cultivar produces numerous long, blossom-laden branches that bees love to visit. Light pruning in late summer stimulates reblooming in the fall.

True to its common names of blue-mist and bluebeard, this shrub will provide a billow of blue flowers in the summer landscape. Such a true shade of blue is hard to come by in the perennial world at that time of year, and caryopteris provides soft contrast with the abundant yellows and reds of other summer flowers. With lightly fragrant leaves, stems and flowers, caryopteris is hardy from Zones 6 to 9. Plant a small group of these shrubs in any sunny site, or use them to fill space in summer flower beds, where their gray-green foliage will go well with all types of annuals and perennials.

Choosing Caryopteris

The caryopteris sold in nurseries resulted from a cross between *C. incana* and *C. mongholica* made in England back in 1930. On this side of the Atlantic, breeders have improved upon the original with varieties such as 'Heavenly Blue', which has darker green leaves, deeper blue flowers, and is altogether a superior plant to the original hybrid. 'Heavenly Blue' gave birth to both 'Blue Mist', with gray-green foliage and light blue flowers, and 'Dark Knight', which bears the darkest blue flowers of any other cultivars. 'Longwood Blue' was selected at Longwood Gardens in Pennsylvania, and has silvery foliage and sky blue flowers. 'Worcester Gold' is easy to spot because it has yellow-gold foliage that contrasts nicely with its blue flowers. The foliage is less attractive in climates with hot summers, but it still looks wonderful in the spring and early summer.

Growing Caryopteris

The easiest way to begin growing this shrub is to pick up a few plants at the nursery. Give caryopteris a spot in well-drained, loose soil and full sun, and it will prosper for years to come—reaching 36 to 48 inches wide and up to 48 inches tall. Although caryopteris is known as a shrub, it really is treated like a "sub-shrub" which means it is cut down almost to the ground in late winter. Or you can simply snip off branches killed back by cold winter weather. After pruning, feed plants with an organic or timed-release fertilizer applied around the base. Flowers are formed on the new growth of the season, so you will not harm the plant by cutting it back. In fact, you will be helping it to keep flowering at its maximum potential. When flower production slows down in late summer, lightly prune the tops of the stems for an increase in late-season blooms.

It's easy to see how this shrub earned the name of 'Blue Mist'. Flowers are produced continuously all summer, even when winter cold kills plants back to the ground.

Cherry, Flowering

Flowering Tree
Prunus species

No doubt about it—ornamental cherries are among the most beautiful of all flowering trees. Covered with blossoms of pink or white that are sometimes fragrant, flowering cherries will steal the show in a spring landscape. They are related to the regular cherries that produce those delectable summer fruits, but unlike their edible counterparts, flowering cherries are specifically bred to put on a grand floral display. Any fruits they may produce are fairly inconspicuous.

If you have enough room in your landscape, choose a special spot for this tree so it can be viewed in all its glory. A flowering cherry will look fantastic in island beds in the front yard, surrounded by evergreens such as dwarf Alberta spruces and low-growing blue junipers. You don't have to have acreage to grow a cherry tree though. Flowering cherries will even succeed in city plantings as long as they have a little room to spread and good growing conditions.

A flowery springtime show of white and pink blossoms is the hallmark of flowering cherry trees. This variety is P. lannesia.

Choosing Flowering Cherries

The Yoshino cherry (*P. yedoensis*) is the famous flowering cherry that encircles the Tidal Basin in Washington, D.C. It bears single, fragrant, light pink blossoms that fade to white. Hardy from Zones 5 to 8, Yoshino cherries are fast-growing and may reach 40 to 50 feet tall. Japanese flowering cherry (*P. serrulata*) is among the best of the flowering cherries. The *P. serrulata* cultivar 'Kwanzan' can be found in numerous city plantings, and with good reason. It has large clusters of double pink flowers and dark green leaves that turn orange-red in fall. 'Kwanzan' tops out around 30 feet, and is hardy from Zones 5 to 9. There are also many not-so-tall cultivars of *P. serrulata* worth seeking out. To identify them, look for varieties with decidedly Japanese sounding names. For something more unusual, the weeping Higan cherry (*P. subhirtella* var. *pendula*) adds a lovely cascading effect to a garden design with its waterfall of single pink flowers.

Ornamental cherries in the Kwanzan group have a beautiful form that will turn your yard into a park. When the petals fall in mid-spring, the ground is carpeted in pink.

Growing Flowering Cherries

Plant your cherry in full sun in a spot where its natural open-vase shape can reach its fullest grace. Cherries thrive near water because they like to have their roots moist (but not sopping wet, of course). Plant either container-grown or balled-and-burlapped specimens in spring. If you need to prune off broken branches or cut selected branches to shape your tree, wait until after the tree blooms in spring to do your snipping.

When growing a cherry in open lawn, be careful not to damage its trunk with mowers or string trimmers. The bark is thin, and offers little natural protection from these types of injuries.

Chrysanthemum

Perennial Flower
Dendranthema species

The leading flowers of fall, chrysanthemums can be bought in pots, or you can grow them as dependable garden perennials.

Most gardeners know chrysanthemums as the flowers you buy in pots in late summer, which promptly burst into bloom. These are great flowers for adding instant color to porches, patios and other high-visibility spots. Keep them well watered and you are practically guaranteed a vibrant show of color for several weeks.

Yet there is another category of chrysanthemum, the garden mum, that is among the most reliable perennials you can grow. Locate garden mums in full sun in a spot that can use strong color in late summer and fall, and you will be amazed at how easy they are to grow. Whether potted or perennial, mums wait for the lengthening nights of fall to flower, though a few also bloom in spring in some areas. One of the secrets to success with mums in the landscape is to key your selections to your climate. Northern gardeners need extra-hardy early mums, while mid-season mums work best in Zones 5 to 7. In the far South, choose late mums for color that lasts until Thanksgiving or beyond.

Choosing Chrysanthemums

To ensure their winter hardiness, order perennial garden mums in spring and get them planted by early summer. In Zones 4 and 5, look for *D. rubellum* 'Clara Curtis' (a pretty pink) or 'Mary Stoker' (yellow), both with daisy-type flowers. Cultivars for Zones 6 to 7 are numerous and include apricot strains under various names including 'Single Apricot' and super-dependable 'Mei Kyo', which produces pink button-shaped blooms. In Zones 7 and 8 'Yellow Jacket' covers itself with yellow flowers year after year. There are many others cultivars from which to choose, and the best places to look may be your neighbors' yards.

Growing Chrysanthemums

Prolonging the color show from potted mums is a piece of cake. Keep them lightly moist, and if they dry out, stick the pots in a bucket of water until they have absorbed all they can hold—usually about an hour. The pots are usually so packed with roots that keeping them watered is the biggest challenge.

Perennial garden mums practically grow themselves. It is important to leave the dead plants intact after winter's first freeze turns them brown, because the skeletons help protect the crowns from winter damage. Clip the plant off when new green growth shows in spring and the last freeze has passed. Pinch back the new growing tips in early summer to encourage branching, and then feed plants with an organic or timed-release fertilizer according to the rate given on the label. Mulch to discourage weeds, and keep the soil moist.

The 'Clara Curtis' variety survives Zone 4 winters, and blooms reliably in early fall. Here it is accompanied by the seedpods of lunaria, a hardy biennial often called money plant.

CLEMATIS

Flowering Vine
Clematis species

Clematis is a gentle vine that is easily grown on low pillars or mailboxes. It also can be trained on a string, wire or chain trellis to frame a window or porch.

If you want an elegant, restrained vine that will delight you in spring with beautiful flowers and perhaps put on a second show later in the season, clematis is the first vine to consider. Like many other vines, clematis has a special penchant for sites in which its roots will be shaded while its foliage grows upward into the sun. You will likely find such a spot in a gap between shrubs, near the edge of a wooded area, or perhaps at a corner of a porch, deck or patio. Clematis vines cling to support by curling their leaf stems around string, wire, lattice or any other structure you provide.

Choosing Clematis

Most gardeners like what are called large-flowered clematis—cultivars such as rich purple *C.* x *jackmanii* or pure white 'Henryi'. Many more are available in shades of pink, red and blue, in a range of flower forms. The soft blue flowers of 'Betty Corning' nod like backswept bells, while many newer varieties have double flowers packed with petals.

Sweet autumn clematis is more vigorous than the large-flowered types, and it forms a thicker vine to cover chainlink fences or similar structures. Extremely easy to grow, autumn clematis blooms in fall by covering itself with tiny fragrant white blossoms.

Growing Clematis

Clematis will grow in Zones 4 to 9, but they are at their best in Zones 5 to 7. The warmer and sunnier the site, the more they appreciate a little afternoon shade. Clematis also need soil that is rich in organic matter so that it holds moisture well, with the pH adjusted to near neutral. You can create such a spot by digging a 4-inch blanket of compost into the planting hole and adding a liberal dusting of lime if your soil is naturally acidic.

Set out new vines in early spring, and handle the plants gently as you remove them from their containers. Keep the root zone lightly moist throughout the first growing season, which is much easier if you cover the ground with a 3-inch-deep blanket of organic mulch.

Each spring, rake back the old mulch and fertilize the vine with a 1-inch-deep layer of rotted manure. Then renew the mulch. Most large-flowered clematis bloom on new growth, so they can be pruned back to 12 inches or so in early spring. However, you may find that leaving more old growth intact enhances flowering. Even when winter weather kills vines down to the ground, clematis bounce back and become larger and stronger every year. Most reach peak bloom after three or four seasons.

Flower size is always on the rise in newer varieties of clematis. The best way to display cut blossoms is to float them in a glass bowl or large brandy glass.

Cleome

Annual flower
Cleome hasslerana

After the blossoms fall, long bean-like seed capsules ripen along cleome's stems. Ripe seeds plant themselves and are ready to sprout when the soil warms in spring.

This native of Argentina is a wonderfully heat- and drought-tolerant flower that provides much-needed height for the back of a bed. Where summers are long, cleome can reach shrub-like proportions of over 4 feet tall, and will bloom from early summer until frost.

Plants are striking—they resemble fireworks with branches topped in eye-catching shades of purple, pink and white. True to its common name of "spider flower," the airy flower clusters of cleome have stamens that look like spider legs coming out in all directions. Adaptable to either full sun or partial shade, cleome's blooms draw hummingbirds and all sorts of happily buzzing bees to the garden. Cleome also makes excellent cut flowers for large arrangements. Be careful when you are handling a bunch of cleome, however, because there are spiky thorns on the stems.

Choosing Cleome

Garden-variety cleome bears blooms of soft pink, or pink and white bicolor. If you prefer a different color scheme, try 'Violet Queen', a rich purple strain, or 'Cherry Queen', a shocking carmine variety. Mix in a little white with 'White Queen' or 'Helen Campbell' for a stunning display. If it's a multicolor display that you're after, 'Color Fountain Mixed' will deliver.

Growing Cleome

This annual will grow in any reasonably fertile soil, and often does best with a few hours of afternoon shade. Cleome also needs ample water to become established, but once plants are about 6 weeks old, they can withstand the toughest conditions summer can dish out—heat, humidity and dryness—and still bloom in cheery abundance.

You can begin with bedding plants, or simply start your spider flowers from seed that's been chilled for 5 days in the refrigerator before planting. Because cleome is such a willing sprouter, don't be afraid to plant seeds ¼ inch deep around the time of last frost, planting them in the garden right where you want them to grow.

Unless the plants are spindly and weak, do not fertilize cleome or you could get huge plants and no flowers. Cleome responds to a mid- to late-summer shearing in long-summer areas such as the South. This will spur the plants on to more blooms. Simply lop off the tops of the plants to redirect their energy into producing more flowers instead of ripening seed.

After you've grown cleome once, look for seedlings in the spot you planted them this year, because this flower is a prolific self-seeder. Dig up these volunteers and transplant them where you can use happy dashes of color for practically no work at all.

Because new blossoms open gradually at the stem tips, cleome stays in bloom for many weeks. If flowering stops, light pruning often stimulates a resurgence of blooms.

Cotoneaster

Shrub
Cotoneaster species

This large and varied group of shrubs comes in many shapes and sizes, from sprawling groundcovers to big bushes. Every one of them is tough, pest-resistant and able to withstand drought and wind. Some even do well in seaside conditions. And all provide a big bang in the landscape for very little buck (or maintenance). Dainty white or pinkish flowers in spring and summer give way to small red or orange fruits, often followed by brightly colored foliage in the fall. Cotoneasters are popular with the feathered set too. Birds love the fruits, and bluebirds, cedar waxwings, mockingbirds, robins, sparrows and thrushes seek cover and nesting sites in tangled thickets of cotoneaster branches.

The more cold-hardy species tend to lose their leaves in winter, while the evergreen types are preferred in warmer regions. Cotoneasters thrive in a wide range of soil types, in either full sun or part shade. Creeping groundcover types are excellent on erodable banks or gentler slopes, or you can mass them for their texture, or grow them along the foundation of your house. Tall cultivars are perfect for informal hedges and borders.

In parts of Zones 6 and 7 where winters are mild, bearberry cotoneaster often grows as an evergreen. Many varieties have leaves that turn bronze-red in cool weather.

Hardy and dependable, rock cotoneaster produces a big colorful crop of berries that persists through fall, after the leaves have been shed.

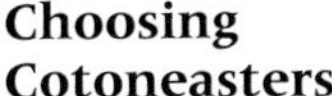

Choosing Cotoneasters

With so many species and cultivars to choose from, you must first decide where you want to put cotoneaster to work. Then you'll know whether you want something small or something tall. In the small department, look for cultivars of creeping cotoneaster (*C. adpressus*), cranberry cotoneaster (*C. apiculatus*), bearberry cotoneaster (*C. dammeri*), littleleaf cotoneaster (*C. microphyllus*) or rock cotoneaster (*C. horizontalis*). All grow well in Zones 4 to 7, and offer a range of variations in leaf color. Except for bearberry cotoneaster, the small species usually shed their leaves in winter. If it's a hedge you want, your choices include excellent selections of spreading cotoneaster (*C. divaricatus*) and many-flowered cotoneaster (*C. multiflorus*), adapted in Zones 4 to 7.

Growing Cotoneasters

Because cotoneaster has a relatively sparse root system, transplant balled-and-burlapped or potted plants in early spring to give them enough time to get established before the rigors of summer hit. Be sure they get regular watering until they become established. Once they take hold, cotoneasters are very vigorous landscape plants. The only pruning you'll need to do is to cut out any broken or dead branches, or snip out ones that are getting in the way of a walkway or driveway. Other than that, cotoneaster does not require regular maintenance. Branches of the low-growing types will often root wherever they come in contact with the soil, thus helping the plants cover the ground quickly.

CRABAPPLE

Flowering Tree
Malus species

The 'Royalty' cultivar produces deep pink blossoms, and leaves that start out green and age to reddish bronze.

Tough and dependable, crabapples cover themselves with fragrant blossoms in spring, then produce thousands of berry-sized fruits that often hang on the trees until they are eaten by birds in late fall. You can gather the tart fruits of some varieties for making jelly, but the main reason to add a crabapple or two to your yard is to enjoy their majestic beauty.

Crabapples also come in compact packages; most varieties grow to less than 15 feet tall. They are fine trees to plant in a lawn, or to use to emphasize a property line or dress up a low fence. You can plant daffodils or other bulbs beneath crabapples to add even more drama to their beautiful spring display.

Choosing Crabapples

Like regular apples, crabapple varieties vary in how much winter chilling they need, their disease resistance, and other characteristics such as height, width and flower color. Check with your local extension service or a knowledgeable nursery expert to find the best cultivars for your area, especially if you live in the Northwest or Southeast, where disease resistance is a high priority. Most cultivars grow well in Zones 4 to 8, and a few very hardy types, such as Siberian crabapple, are hardy to Zone 2. Some varieties also have purple leaves. Fruit color may be red, yellow or a blush of both colors. One of the best all-round selections, *M. sargentii*, commonly called Sargent crabapple, grows only 10 to 15 feet tall and 20 feet wide, and bears tiny red fruits following a thick cloud of fragrant white flowers.

Growing Crabapples

Choose a sunny, well-drained site with at least average soil. If the spot you need to fill is compacted or rocky, dig a planting hole 18 inches deep and 24 inches wide, and mix in two 40-pound bags of compost. Crabapples prefer near-neutral soil, but will tolerate slight acidity or alkalinity if they have otherwise decent soil. Plant trees in late winter or early spring, and water well after planting and thereafter during very dry spells for the first two growing seasons. After that, the trees should have extensive roots and be able to take care of themselves.

Prune crabapples to shape the young trees and to remove damaged wood. Otherwise there is no need to spend time trimming these easy-to-please trees. Healthy trees usually fend off serious insects and disease problems, and recover quickly from these types of natural challenges.

A trio of early-blooming 'Liset' crabapples glow in spring above a lush green lawn. Later, fruits will offer bird-attracting treats.

DAYLILY

Perennial Flower
Hemerocallis species

These tough beauties grow with practically no effort at all, and are impervious to pests, diseases and drought. Daylilies make a fantastic addition to perennial beds—even when they are not blooming, their foliage adds a solid mass of green with a flowing, spiky texture. Depending on variety, plants can range in height from 12 inches up to 4 feet, and by growing different varieties you can have daylilies in bloom from early summer to frost.

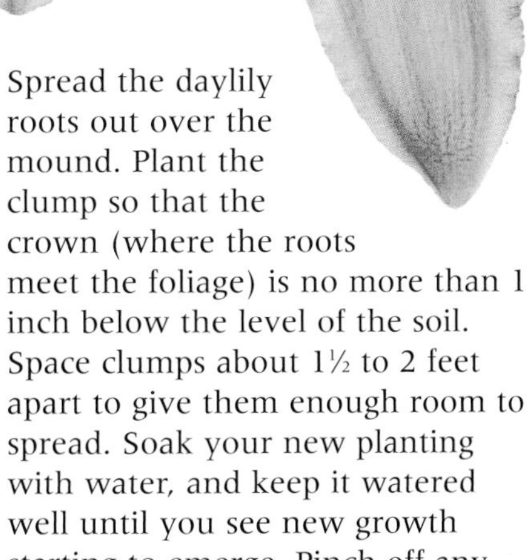

Daylily blossoms often are blushed with contrasting colors. Most varieties are not fragrant, but they make up for it with the sheer beauty of their blooms.

Choosing Daylilies

Daylilies come in just about every color of the rainbow except blue (and flower breeders are working to remedy that). The flowers vary in form too, from the skinny petals of "spiders" to the wide ruffled petals of "tetraploids." When shopping for daylilies, don't worry about variety name. Look for a flower shape that pleases you in a color that will complement your landscape. Big lemon-yellow daylilies go with everything, and most yellow varieties are vigorous and dependable.

Growing Daylilies

Start in spring with healthy plants from a nursery, or plant divisions shared by a generous gardening friend. Choose a planting site that gets at least 6 hours of sun a day. The ideal spot should have rich, well-drained soil with lots of organic matter, but daylilies are basically easy to please. To ensure peak performance of your new daylilies, amend clay soil or sandy soil with compost before setting out plants.

To plant, dig a hole larger than the root mass, then make a mound of soil in the center of the hole. Spread the daylily roots out over the mound. Plant the clump so that the crown (where the roots meet the foliage) is no more than 1 inch below the level of the soil. Space clumps about 1½ to 2 feet apart to give them enough room to spread. Soak your new planting with water, and keep it watered well until you see new growth starting to emerge. Pinch off any seed pods to encourage the plant to form more flower buds.

If you crave a tidy appearance, cut off the flower scapes, too, when the plant has finished blooming.

Clean up any dead foliage from around your daylilies in winter, clipping rather than pulling it away from the plants' crowns. Spread an organic or timed-release fertilizer on the soil around plants to give them a spring boost. To keep daylilies blooming strong, dig and divide them every 3 to 5 years. Dig up your plants, gently split them apart into smaller clumps, and plant the divisions throughout your garden or share them with special friends.

Willing multipliers, daylilies planted 2 feet apart quickly grow into large clumps that form a solid mass of foliage and flowers.

Dogwood

Flowering Tree
Cornus species

Whether white or pink, dogwood blossoms are beautiful in your landscape. They are unsurpassed for structuring large flower arrangements as well.

If you want a yard-sized tree that is pretty to look at year-round, then look no further than dogwoods. Dogwoods are covered with white or pink flowers in spring, red fruits and leaves in fall, and a lovely graceful branching structure to gaze at during winter. All that comes in a package that stays under 20 to 30 feet tall, so you can enjoy a dogwood even if your space is limited. Dogwoods are attractive as specimen plants in flower borders and in foundation plantings at the corner of your house, though they are at their best in open woodland settings. Near buildings, dogwood's natural horizontal form breaks up large expanses of blank walls and contrasts nicely with the vertical lines of a house. They are perfect partners for azaleas.

Dogwood blossoms often are used as signs of spring. To fishermen, they mean that fish start biting. To gardeners, they remind us to apply crabgrass preventer to our lawns.

Choosing Dogwoods

The best known and most beloved dogwood, simply called flowering dogwood (*C. florida*), is native to the woods of the eastern United States. Adapted in Zones 5 to 9, cultivars may bloom either white or pink, and they vary in their tolerance of common diseases. However, good cultural practices, such as providing a semi-shady site and watering during droughts, will go a long way toward keeping trees healthy.

Although its flowers do not appear until after the branches leaf out in spring, Chinese or Kousa dogwood (*C. kousa* var. *chinensis*) is much more tolerant of disease. 'Milky Way', with its creamy white flowers, is probably the most familiar of the Chinese dogwoods.

Whatever you do, do not dig dogwoods from the wild and attempt to grow them in your yard. Only very small specimens would be likely to survive such a move. Nursery-grown trees have bigger, healthier root systems, as well as a lineage that guarantees strong blooming.

Growing Dogwoods

Take a cue from where dogwoods grow in the wild: They thrive in open woods, in the company of taller trees. Full sun can stress dogwoods, especially in warm climates, so much so that trees planted in hot sun actually grow more slowly than those given a shadier location. And, just as in the forest, dogwoods prefer acidic, well-drained soil. Avoid compact or shallow soils, and any site where the soil is normally quite dry.

After planting, spread a 2- to 3-inch-deep layer of mulch around the base of the tree to conserve moisture and to prevent damage from lawn mowers and string trimmers. Mulch should extend all the way out to the tree's drip line, but should not be right against the trunk. Use a soaker hose to water trees thoroughly once a week during severe summer droughts.

Feature dogwoods and azaleas in your yard and you will enjoy all the beauty spring has to offer ... right outside your door.

Dusty Miller

Annual Flower
Senecio cineraria

The frosty felted leaves of dusty miller work magic in the garden, amplifying the colors of nearby flowers and illuminating any site with their unique texture. Although dusty miller is classed as an annual flower, it usually does not bloom at all unless plants are left in the ground and manage to survive winter, which is not unusual in Zones 7 and 8. Two-year-old plants do produce small yellow flowers, but with dusty miller, the leaves are really the show.

Have fun experimenting with the endless versatility of these plants. They are unbeatable when teamed with blue or pink flowers, particularly pansies or petunias, but it's hard to imagine a plant that does not partner well with dusty miller. And although the plants thrive in sun, they also adapt to partial shade, especially in warmer climates. A small mass of dusty miller or even an edging in a place that gets morning sun and afternoon shade is simply stunning. Because dusty miller goes with everything, it also makes a fine addition to large containers planted with a variety of annuals.

Choosing Dusty Miller

You can grow dusty miller from bedding plants, from seedlings you grow yourself, or you can take 4-inch-long stem cuttings from large plants and root them in moist soil. Bedding plants are the fastest and easiest way to go, though you may get little choice as to variety. By using seed, you can grow 'Cirrus', which has flat leaves with wavy edges, or much more feathery 'Silverdust'. Several other look-alike plants go by the common name of dusty miller, including 'Silver Feather', a form of tansy, and various artemisias. However, the inexpensive annual forms are without peer for holding their good looks throughout the summer.

Growing Dusty Miller

These plants ask for little beyond well-drained soil and good air circulation. Keep seedlings moist until you plant them, and be sure to gently break apart the lowest half-inch of roots if you find that they have wound themselves together into a tight mass. Water well, after setting plants at least 10 inches apart, and mulch to retain soil moisture and prevent dirt from splashing up onto the leaves. In very humid climates, take care to keep dusty miller from being crowded by larger plants. The longer the downy leaves remain damp, the greater their risk of melting away due to fungal diseases.

The numerous white hairs on dusty miller leaves make them look and feel like soft gray felt. Their light color and unusual texture make them a go-everywhere annual.

Although color plants usually command the most attention, dusty miller deserves equal billing in this partnership with ageratum.

EUONYMUS

Shrub or Groundcover
Euonymus species

Variegated forms of wintercreeper such as 'Emerald Surprise' bring light to shady spots, and the stems make good filler for flower arrangements.

Adaptable to many soils, tolerant of drought and willing to grow in full sun or partial shade, euonymus are true workhorse plants for a low-maintenance landscape. The euonymus name includes a huge group of plants that range from deciduous shrubs with riveting fall color to stalwart evergreens for foundation plantings. And then there is wintercreeper, a ground-hugging form that can be put to work as a groundcover or woody evergreen vine.

Euonymus flowers are not showy, but their fragrance in spring is often quite noticeable. Many cultivars produce colorful red or yellow seed capsules in late summer that add to their interest. Yet euonymus are basically foliage plants. Year after year, they can be counted upon to provide texture and structure for very little effort.

Choosing Euonymus

A great shrub to use as a specimen or informal hedge, winged euonymus (*E. alatus*) is adapted in Zones 4 to 8. Winged euonymus's green leaves of summer turn bright red in fall, and little pruning is needed to keep the plants shapely. Cultivars vary in size from 3 to 10 feet or more, so always check plant tags to be sure the plants fit the places you have in mind for them.

Not as hardy as winged euonymus, evergreen euonymus (*E. japonicus*) is a popular foundation shrub in Zones 6 to 9. Plants can grow to 10 feet tall, but modern-named cultivars are usually smaller. Many older landscapes include green-leaved cultivars, but variegated varieties are increasingly popular for mixing with darker evergreen shrubs.

Wintercreeper (*E. fortunei*) is a low-growing species often used as a groundcover or vine. Hardy to Zone 4, it is evergreen farther north than other groundcovers. And, in dry climates, wintercreeper tolerates sun better than ivies.

Growing Euonymus

Set out container-grown plants in early spring, and water them regularly through their first growing season. Prune young plants only as needed to keep them shapely. If you need to control the size of mature plants, or if you want to remove old growth and stimulate the production of fresh new stems and leaves, prune plants hard in late winter, cutting them back by half their size or more.

Scale and other small sucking insects can be a problem with all euonymus, so it's important to ask for resistant cultivars when purchasing plants, and to check plants for problems a few times a year. Prune off small infested sections, or spray plants with an all-purpose insecticide labeled for use on evergreen shrubs. Powdery mildew can be a problem too, particularly with plants that receive substantial shade. Cut back diseased plants, because healthy new growth is more resistant to disease than tired old foliage.

Winged euonymus is sometimes called burning bush because of its rich, red fall color. Even after they turn red, the leaves persist for several weeks.

FERNS

Perennial
Numerous species

Hay-scented ferns get their name from the fresh fragrance released when the fronds are cut. This deciduous species spreads into broad colonies via creeping stems.

The sheer delicacy of fern fronds suggests that ferns are finicky plants, but they are not. Rather, ferns are niche plants that thrive with little care as long as they are grown in the right types of sites. For most ferns, good sites are the moist shady spots often found at the bases of buildings, walls, fences or trees. True, there are ferns that grow in brighter, drier exposures, but these are unusual cases. In your yard, you will probably find that ferns are happiest on the shady north side of your house, or in a shade garden cooled by a high canopy of leafy branches.

In addition to shade, ferns greatly appreciate soft humusy soil that stays constantly moist. Slightly acidic conditions are good too, so it's a good idea to lavish peat moss, compost or leaf mold on soil where ferns will be planted. Indeed, planting is the most challenging aspect of growing ferns. Once the plants are established, they practically grow themselves.

Choosing Ferns

Dependable ferns for your garden may include species that are native to nearby woods, and also tried-and-true cultivated varieties. The toughest ferns are deciduous, meaning they die back to the ground each winter and reappear in spring. That reappearance is often a show in itself, as dainty fiddleheads slowly unfurl into finely cut fronds. Visit local botanical gardens to see ferns that are likely to grow well in your area, or simply try your luck with any ferns that have acceptable hardiness ratings for your region. Finding the right fern for a certain spot sometimes takes a couple of tries, but once the right one settles in, it will be as persistent as a weed.

Southern shield fern is a large, vigorous fern that grows well in Zones 6 to 8. It tolerates more sun than most ferns, but still prefers partial shade.

Growing Ferns

Plant ferns in late winter or early spring, just as new growth begins. Dig the site prior to planting and mix in a 4-inch layer of peat moss, compost or leaf mold to boost the soil's humus content. Set plants shallow, so that their roots are barely covered, and install a sprinkler to use as often as needed to keep the soil constantly moist. You can use more efficient soaker hoses, but sprinklers are especially good for ferns because they create the wet, humid conditions that ferns crave.

For the first and second summers after planting, feed ferns with a diluted mixture of fish emulsion fertilizer every four to six weeks. Avoid using harsh chemical fertilizers, which can damage both leaves and roots. After the second year, ferns may need little, if any, fertilizer. In early winter, mow over dormant ferns and rake the bed clean before piling on a nice mulch of shredded leaves.

FORSYTHIA

Flowering Shrub
Forsythia species

First thing in spring, forsythia blossoms line up on bare stems and announce the changing of the seasons. Stems with mature buds can be brought into bloom indoors.

Nothing quite lifts the winter-weary spirit when the earth is still bare like the eye-popping yellow shower of flowers of forsythias. But the sunny bell-shaped blooms aren't the only reason to grow forsythias. These shrubs have earned a place in the low-maintenance landscape because they are practically indestructible.

With a mature size of 8 to 10 feet high and 10 to 12 feet wide, forsythias are really impressive-looking shrubs. Because they are so massive, they seldom work well in foundation plantings around a house. Forsythias are better suited to shrub borders, hedges, plantings on a bank, or masses in parts of the landscape where their flowing form can be appreciated. Plant forsythias with spring-blooming bulbs and small evergreen shrubs to further celebrate them in the landscape.

Choosing Forsythia

There are several species of forsythia in cultivation, but most of the plants available are *F.* x *intermedia.* The names of forsythia cultivars are often confused in the marketplace, so be cautious about what you buy and be particular about the nursery where you buy if you are after a specific cultivar.

Many cultivars are hardy to Zone 4, although flower buds are often killed by late freezes in Zones 4 and 5. 'Meadowlark', 'Northern Gold', 'Vermont Sun', 'Northern Sun' and 'New Hampshire Gold' are reputed to have flower buds that can resist cold better than most. For regions where cold is not as much of a concern, old standard 'Lynwood Gold' is still one of the best flowering forsythias. For a fast-growing groundcover for a slope or to control erosion, consider 'Arnold Dwarf' forsythia. It only reaches about 3 feet high but will spread at least 5 feet wide because its graceful branches root wherever they touch the soil.

Growing Forsythia

Forsythia is really a low-maintenance plant that always looks best when left unpruned. Site plants in full sun; they're not fussy as to moisture. As you space your plantings, keep in mind that they are very fast growing. And even if your neighbors whack away at their forsythias, resist the impulse to trim yours into little meatballs. In fact, pruning is the worst thing you can do to these born-to-be-wild shrubs—they will flower less and less the more they are extensively "sculpted." The only pruning you might want to consider is to snip a few long branches with flower buds and bring them indoors to force for a bouquet to welcome spring.

Here, a boundary planting of forsythias matches a single large specimen grown near the house. In cold climates, forsythias and lilacs often bloom together.

Grasses, Ornamental

Perennial
Various species

It's hard to beat ornamental grasses for durability, low maintenance and subtle beauty. They offer a graceful vertical form and fine texture that contrasts nicely with broad-leaved perennials and even lawns. And there's no better way to make a landscape look more natural. Grasses are among the most disease-resistant and pest-free plants you can welcome into your garden, and they rarely need extra water or fertilizer after they have been in the ground for at least a year and are well rooted.

The foliage of ornamental grasses looks great almost year-round. Even in winter, when the leaves and seed heads have turned a tawny brown, the clumps add interest to an otherwise barren landscape, and look especially lovely when glazed with ice. Grasses are a real boon for birds, who appreciate the seed heads as well as the refuge that the tufts of foliage offer. The size of the species you choose will dictate where to plant it, but most ornamental grasses do need full sun. Grasses look great when massed together for a wild effect, or when a single clump is the focal point of a low-maintenance bed.

The dramatic curled fronds of miscanthus, commonly called maiden grass, last well into winter and adorn the landscape when little else is in bloom.

Choosing Grasses

The selection is limitless, from diminutive blue fescue that stands only 6 to 8 inches tall, all the way up to pampas grass, which can reach 12 feet high in warm, wet climates. Ornamental grasses vary in their winter hardiness, and some can be invasive. Before buying any grasses that are not typically seen in yards in your area, check with your local extension office to find out if a particular grass is considered invasive in your region.

Blue-green sheep's fescue, often called blue fescue, is an excellent texture plant for rocky slopes or dry areas of the garden.

Some of the most popular and best behaved grasses include members of the *Miscanthus* tribe, such as reddish orange 'Flame' miscanthus, and maiden grass, with lovely curled fronds atop upright 4-foot-tall clumps of slender blades. There are also ankle-high fescues (*Festuca* sp.) such as 'Elijah Blue', renowned for its drought tolerance and lovely blue-gray color. Fountain grass (*Pennisetum* sp.) forms fuzzy caterpillar-like fronds, while switchgrass (*Panicum* sp.) resembles a billowy cloud when it blooms.

Growing Grasses

Ornamental grasses will establish quickly and reliably from plants that you can purchase at a nursery or obtain from gardening friends who are dividing some of their own grasses. Many species will grow to full size in their first or second year. It is usually best to cut grasses to about 6 inches from the ground once a year in late winter, before new growth begins. Most grasses will grow best in full sun or slight afternoon shade, and prefer soils of average fertility.

Rose fountain grass keeps its pink color all summer, and holds its furry seed heads well into winter. Small annuals can be grown at the base of large clumps.

Heuchera

Perennial Flower
Heuchera species

A long-time favorite in gardens that receive partial shade, coral bells produce bright flower spikes in summer. In mild climates the leafy crowns are evergreen.

Many members of this large group of foliage plants are native to the United States and make fantastic additions to a partially shaded landscape. The evergreen leaves of heuchera are large and rounded, and come in shades of silvery green, bronze or purple. As an added bonus, some heucheras also send up airy, upright flower stalks in white, pink or red. The blossoms attract hummingbirds and bees to the garden, and make lovely cut flowers as well.

Made for partial shade, heucheras can range anywhere from 12 to 30 inches tall and as wide, depending on the variety. They are ideal for edging beds, mixing with gray-foliage plants, or planting along a woodland edge.

Choosing Heucheras

When shopping at the nursery, keep in mind that plants in this family sometimes go by the common name of coral bells, alumroot or rock geranium. There are many super cultivars to choose from that are hardy in Zones 3 to 9. One of the most popular is 'Palace Purple', with deep purple foliage that fades to bronze in mid-summer in warm zones. 'Veil' is attached to the name of several excellent choices such as 'Chocolate Veil', with purple leaves with light silvering between the veins; 'Emerald Veil', with silvery foliage that has a green edge and green veins; 'Pewter Veil', which has silver netting on the pewter-purple foliage; 'Ruby Veil', with ruby purple leaves and silvery gray veins; and 'Silver Veil', which is silver netted and bears cerise-rose flowers. 'Bressingham Hybrids' can be started from seed, and have coral, red and pink flowers, while 'Bressingham Blaze' has intense salmon-scarlet blooms. 'Chatterbox' is another popular cultivar with large pink flowers.

Growing Heucheras

You can start some heuchera from seed sown indoors or outdoors, but to grow many of the hybrids you have to start with plants. Plant heucheras in moist but well-drained, humusy soil in partial shade, or full sun in the North. In Zones 7 and 8, make sure plants are completely shaded from hot afternoon sun, which can badly scorch the leaves. Keep well watered for a few weeks, and then water only during serious droughts.

Heuchera is very shallow rooted and will heave out of the ground due to the freezing and thawing that occurs in many parts of the country. In order to prevent heaving, plant crowns 1 inch below the soil level, and mulch to insulate them. As clumps of heuchera grow, the centers of the plants become woody. Every 3 years or so, dig up the plants, remove the oldest and woodiest parts, then replant the younger rooted tufts, called rosettes.

Many newer heuchera cultivars feature showy leaves rather than flowers. A good example is 'Cathedral Windows'.

Honeysuckle

Flowering Vine
Lonicera species

Often called everblooming honeysuckle, cultivars of L. heckrotii *have everything this species is famous for—vining habit, long bloom time and fragrant flowers.*

The same regions in which cultivated honeysuckles grow well also have been invaded by rampant Japanese honeysuckle, so the first obstacle you may need to overcome is fear. Unlike the unstoppable weedy version, well-behaved honeysuckles are among the most endearing vines for Zones 5 to 9. Plant them near an entryway so you and your visitors can enjoy the sweet fragrance of the flowers. Or use one of these low-care vines to adorn a lamppost or mailbox. Honeysuckles ramble over fences with no help at all, and you can use them to cover a wall if you provide a wire trellis or framework in which the vines can entwine themselves. Planted so that they wind themselves through an overhead trellis, honeysuckles have the allure of climbing roses without all the fuss.

The ideal site for honeysuckle has a cool, shaded root area that gives way to more sunlight a few feet above the ground. Semi-evergreen in mild climates, honeysuckles shed their leaves in fall in Zones 5 to 7.

Native honeysuckles are big, vigorous plants ideal for covering a wall or fence. Their fragrance is weak, but they are rarely bothered by pests of any kind.

Choosing Honeysuckles

Native to the Eastern U.S., trumpet honeysuckle (*L. sempervirens*) can grow more than 40 feet long. You can keep it much smaller with regular pruning. However, it is not very fragrant, which most people think is the whole point of growing honeysuckles. For fragrance and long bloom time, cultivars of European honeysuckle (*L. periclymenum*) or various hybrids lumped together as *L. heckrotii* are the best bets.

Growing Honeysuckles

Purchase cutting-grown plants in the spring. To give your plants the best possible start, dig a roomy planting hole twice as large as the root mass of the plant, and mix in at least two generous shovelfuls of compost or rotted manure. Set the vine in the prepared hole at the same depth that it grew in its container, and water well. Especially in summer, keep the root zones of cultivated honeysuckles well mulched to help keep the soil cool and moist. The first season, guide new stems as needed to help them find their support.

The main reason to prune established plants is to control their size, and you will need to get to know your plant's blooming inclinations before you establish a seasonal routine. Pruning in summer, after the big bloom period passes, is often best, but you can prune a little here and a little there if your vine shows a willingness to bloom intermittently all summer. Winter or spring pruning delays bloom, and often reduces the number of blossoms as well.

European honeysuckle has the fragrance of wild Japanese strains, but it will only grow to a monstrous size if you encourage it to do so.

HOSTA

Perennial Flower
Hosta species and cultivars

No shady garden is complete without easy-to-grow hostas, which feature leaves that may be green, blue-green, chartreuse or variegated with white or gold. Valued primarily for their handsome foliage, most hostas also produce lavender or white blossoms in early summer. Bees and hummingbirds always appreciate the nodding flowers, and some varieties have excellent evening fragrance. Still, some gardeners clip off the blossoms to make the plants channel their energy toward the development of leaves, but this is up to you.

Hostas grow in Zones 3 to 9, in a wide range of soil types, but they all require some shade. In cool climates, especially sun-tolerant varieties can handle a half-day of sun, but in warm climates more than two hours of sun will make hostas struggle. In all climates, filtered shade from an overhead canopy of trees is just about right.

Chartreuse hostas are especially useful for lighting up dark shade. This variety, 'Solar Flare', has large leaves that help amplify limited light.

Create a garden at the base of a large tree: Plant a collection of hostas possessing different colors and leaf markings. It's easy!

Choosing Hostas

With hundreds of varieties to choose from, it's easy to get confused. Base your choices first on size. Large hostas need a roomy root run, unobstructed by big tree roots, while small to medium varieties are better competitors with trees. Leaf color and variegation patterns can be balanced with cost. Older, well-known varieties are usually inexpensive, while very new and rare hostas cost much more. Of course, hostas that are offered to you free for the digging are definintely a best buy. Plus, the fact that a certain hosta thrived in a friend's or neighbor's yard to the point where they are ready to give some away is a fine recommendation for its value in a less-work landscape.

Growing Hostas

Plant or divide hostas in spring, just as new leaves are emerging. Amend the planting holes with compost or other organic matter to improve the soil's ability to retain moisture, and fertilize newly planted hostas with an organic or timed-release fertilizer. Thereafter, you may not need to fertilize established hostas, but feeding them each spring is a good idea. Never fertilize hostas after midsummer, or you can compromise their winter hardiness. Do provide water during prolonged droughts that cause hosta leaves to become limp and wilted.

Slugs and snails like the same moist, shady conditions as hostas. These pests feed at night, leaving smooth-edged holes in the leaves. It's easy to collect slugs or snails in shallow containers baited with beer, nestled into the mulch between the plants almost up to the rims. The hapless creatures go after the yeasty mixture and fall in and drown. A mixture of water, baking yeast and a little sugar makes a good substitute for beer.

You will not want to clip off the blossoms of fragrant hosta varieties such as 'Royal Standard'.

Hydrangea

Flowering Shrub
Hydrangea species

These low-maintenance plants have long been an old-fashioned staple of the home landscape. Hydrangeas deserve a place in the modern landscape too, because they put on a great display, require little attention and make themselves at home in either sun or partial shade.

Choosing Hydrangeas

If it's color you want, then go with bigleaf hydrangea (*H. macrophylla*). Bigleafs are hardy to Zone 5, grow 2 to 6 feet tall and 3 to 6 feet wide, and bear blooms in pink, blue or white. Blooms may be round and made up of large-petaled flowers (otherwise known as "mopheads") or flat and made up of tiny flowers surrounded by a ring of larger-petaled flowers ("lacecaps"). And, true to their name, bigleaf hydrangeas have huge (5 to 6 inches across), eye-catching leaves.

Oakleaf hydrangeas (*H. quercifolia*) have dark green leaves that are 10 to 12 inches long and 6 to 7 inches wide. In autumn they turn a mix of red, purple and brown. Oakleafs bear elongated clusters of white flowers, are hardy to Zone 5, grow 8 to 15 feet tall, and display peeling orange bark in winter.

For colder climes, there's the panicle hydrangea (*H. paniculata*) and the smooth hydrangea (*H. arborescens*), both hardy to Zone 4. Panicles typically reach about 6 feet tall and bear creamy white flowers that fade to pink. Smooth hydrangea tops out around 4 feet tall, and its blooms begin green, then turn creamy white.

Romantic and much loved as cut flowers, bigleaf hydrangeas are deep blue in acid soil, and become lilac or pink in soil that has a higher pH.

Oakleaf hydrangeas hold their reddish leaves and long flower panicles well into winter. They are ideal for planting as a boundary along a woodland edge.

Growing Hydrangeas

Plant hydrangeas in early spring after danger of heavy frost has passed. You can also plant in the fall, but be sure to allow enough time for plants to establish (at least four weeks) before the ground freezes.

Choose a site in full sun or partial shade. Dig a hole about twice the size of the root ball, and backfill the hole so that the root ball will sit about 1 inch above the original soil level. This will prevent water from standing around the base of the hydrangea, which they do not like. Water the plant well and mulch with shredded pine bark to keep the soil moist around the hydrangea. To prune, just remove dead branches.

As for the color of bigleaf hydrangeas, the rule of thumb is: the more acidic your soil, the bluer the blooms. If your soil is closer to neutral, expect blooms of pink or lilac. Alkaline soil, whether natural or created by adding lots of lime, leads to pink flowers.

Cold hardy and dependable, hydrangeas such as 'Annabelle' produce large white flower clusters that can be dried and used in winter flower arrangements.

Impatiens

Annual Flower
Impatiens species

For brightening up a shady spot, nothing beats this easy-to-grow flower. Impatiens come in so many colors—such as white, pale pink, fuchsia, lilac, red, salmon and orange—there's bound to be a choice that complements your landscape. And if you're bored with the solid colors, single flowers or green foliage of impatiens, try varieties with starry bicolored petals, double flowers that look like miniature roses, or some New Guinea types featuring foliage streaked with bronze.

New Guinea impatiens bear extra large flowers and often have dark variegated foliage. These plants are good choices for large containers set in shady spots.

Choosing Impatiens

Your basic impatiens fall under *I. walleriana*; you can't go wrong with any that have 'Accent', 'Super Elfin', 'Tempo', or 'Deco' in their names. New Guinea impatiens (*I. hawkeri*) have larger flowers than regular impatiens (up to 2½ inches across), colorful variegated or dark green foliage, and they are slightly more tolerant of sun than regular impatiens. 'Tango', 'Little Tango' and 'Spectra' are all popular series of New Guinea varieties. Although rare at garden centers, African impatiens (*I. auricoma*) tolerate deeper shade than most impatiens, and reach up to 1½ feet high, so they can be planted behind other shorter flowers.

Plantings of multicolored impatiens always bring a festive look to shady beds. The color range in impatiens is extensive, so there's always the perfect hue for any location.

Growing Impatiens

The easiest way to grow this cheery flower is to purchase bedding plants at a garden center. Try to purchase impatiens that are just on the brink of first bloom, or have only one flower already showing. That's because impatiens that have flowered quite a bit already may stall when transplanted from small pots to the garden. Be sure that the plants are not overgrown, tall, spindly or wilted, and that the leaves are intact.

Impatiens are also quite simple to start from seed. Sow seed indoors at least six to eight weeks before your last frost date. Put a very finely textured growing mix into six-packs, moisten it, then scatter the seed on the surface and sprinkle a dusting of soil over the top. Cover the six-packs with plastic wrap and put them in a warm place until the seeds sprout. Remove the plastic wrap and place the seedlings under a fluorescent light until it is time to move them outside (after your last frost).

Plant impatiens in shady spots or in pots throughout the landscape. They flower best when situated in light shade. Give them a balanced organic or timed-release fertilizer to start out. Keep them well watered, especially in the South—impatiens need more water than most garden plants. If the plants get overgrown, as they are apt to do in very warm climates, the only other maintenance that's needed is a mid-summer shearing to bring them back into bounds.

Ivy

Perennial Vine
Hedera and *Parthenocissus* species

Algerian ivy is the tropical counterpart of English ivy. It is the best ivy to grow in the Coastal South and other warm, humid regions.

If you want a vine to cover a brick or stucco wall, or perhaps to work as a groundcover on a slope, you will want to look into ivies. Ivies cling to their support with root-like structures that have sticky "feet," and because of this they are not good vines to grow on wood structures. However, in the right place with the right underpinnings, ivies enrich any landscape with elegance and grace, and maintenance is limited to periodic pruning.

Choosing Ivies

There are four major species, each with a special talent. Boston ivy (*P. tricuspidata*) is the hardiest, and will grow as far north as Zone 4. Although it is not evergreen, it shows beautiful green foliage all summer, turning scarlet red in the fall.

English ivy (*H. helix*) is evergreen, adapted in Zones 5 to 9, and extremely vigorous. You can use it as a groundcover (the job it does best), let it grow up trees, or train it to creep up a brick or stone wall. Varieties with variegated leaves need substantial shade, while green-leaved varieties will tolerate a half-day of sun. But established plants need discipline, so don't make the mistake of thinking you can get English ivy going on the exterior walls of your house and then forget about it. At least twice a year, you will need to climb a ladder and trim back stems that approach windows and wood trim.

The softly textured leaves of Persian ivy (*H. colchica*), adapted in Zones 6 to 9, make it an outstanding climber for covering the trunks of stately old trees or weathered stone fences. The tropical temperament of Algerian ivy (*H. canariensis*) makes it the best choice for Zones 9 and 10.

Growing Ivies

All ivies make most of their new growth in early spring, so that is the best time to plant them. Although ivies are very vigorous and long-lived vines, it often takes them a few years to really get going. The first season they need plenty of moisture because their root systems are skimpy. But plants more than three years old seldom need supplemental water.

The ivy that clothes stone walls in the North is usually Boston ivy, a deciduous vine known for its lush green foliage that turns bright red in the fall.

Prune ivies to control their size using plain old pruning shears. When growing English ivy as a groundcover, you will need to weed regularly for a year or so, or you can use an herbicide labeled for use with ivy. To rejuvenate an old planting, mow over it in late winter with your mower blade set at its highest setting. Then rake out the debris, fertilize with an organic or timed-release fertilizer, and stand back.

As a groundcover in temperate climates, English ivy is persistent and long-lived, and looks attractive year-round. If neglected, it can take over old buildings.

JUNIPER

Evergreen Shrub
Juniperus species and hybrids

Creeping juniper covers a gentle slope near an entryway, where it holds the soil yet requires little water. Only a few plants are needed to cover several square feet of space.

Tremendously tolerant of winter cold and willing to grow in almost any soil, junipers are staple shrubs in any low-maintenance landscape. They come in a huge selection of shapes and sizes, from slender columns to broad, spreading fountains to 3-inch-high groundcovers. Choose a cultivar that fits the space in which you want it to grow, and you may never need to prune a single limb. Junipers also vary in color. Depending on cultivar, the foliage may be pine green, gray-green, blue-green or golden chartreuse. Full sun is needed to bring out the best foliage color in junipers. Junipers usually look best when several are planted together to form a rich splash of evergreen texture.

Chinese junipers come in many different forms, so you can select tall-and-slender plants or varieties that grow into broad angular mounds.

Choosing Junipers

Every nursery offers several types of junipers. Because there are so many types, check the plant tags carefully for information about the mature size of the plant. And don't forget that with shrub-type junipers, mature width is often greater than height. Check hardiness too, as most (but not all) junipers can handle winter in Zones 3 and 4.

Cultivars that grow to about 2 feet tall are outstanding when put to work covering gentle slopes, while very low-growing groundcover junipers do best in sites that are only slightly sloped. Use larger shrub-type junipers to help structure groups of foundation shrubs or for defining boundaries. The surprising form of upright columnar junipers make them perfect for punctuating areas of the landscape that can benefit from a strong vertical accent, such as the corners of your house or near a gate that leads to another area of your landscape.

Growing Junipers

Most nurseries sell container-grown plants, which can be planted year-round in Zones 7 to 9. In colder climates, plant junipers from spring to early summer so they will be well rooted before winter comes. Most junipers like acidic soil, so do not add lime to the planting site. It is usually sufficient to dig roomy planting holes, set the plants at the same depth they grew in their containers, refill the holes and water well.

When planting groundcover junipers or covering a slope with spreading forms, install a roll-out weed barrier between plants, and then cover it with at least 3 inches of mulch. You also may need to hand weed for a year or two. By the third year after planting, the lush juniper foliage should shade out any weeds that attempt to make themselves at home among your junipers.

The species commonly called blue rug juniper never grows more than 3 inches tall, and has the appropriate botanical name of J. horizontalis.

LILAC

Flowering Shrub
Syringa species

In the North, where lilacs grow best, they become huge, stately shrubs that can almost pass for bushy trees. Free-blooming and fragrant, lilacs will grow in Zones 3 to 8, though they are at their best from Zone 7 northward. You can use lilacs as lone accents in a lawn, or group them with forsythias or other spring bloomers in a larger bed. In addition to the traditional lilac color, some selections bloom white, pink, dark purple or even yellow. Mature-plant size varies too, from less than 6 feet tall to 15 feet tall and almost as wide. Lilacs need full sun and good air circulation, and thrive in soil that is fertile with a near-neutral pH.

Choosing Lilacs

All lilacs are slow growers that often do not bloom until several years after planting. Old-fashioned lilacs, sometimes called French lilacs (*S. vulgaris*) include dozens of named cultivars in a range of colors, all of which are highly fragrant.

Where winters are cold, this species is always a winner. In Zones 7 and 8, 'Miss Kim' Korean lilac often withstands more heat, as does 'Lavender Lady', an old strain of common lilac that blooms heavily in a wide range of climates. Where a smaller plant is needed, mildew-resistant cultivars of *S. myeri* may be worth their considerable cost.

Gather lilac clusters to enjoy indoors. Lilacs flower so profusely that the blossoms you cut will never be missed in the landscape!

Growing Lilacs

Most lilacs are sold in containers, though mail-order companies occasionally ship plants as bare-rooted specimens. Plant lilacs in early spring, when new leaf buds are just beginning to show, in broad planting holes to which several spadefuls of compost or humus have been added. Also work a half-cup of lime into soil that is naturally acidic, and water plants well, after planting.

French lilacs are mainstays in cold-climate landscapes, where they help celebrate spring with their color and fragrance.

Mulch around lilacs to maintain soil moisture and eliminate weeds. If plants are grown in good soil and kept mulched with bark, straw or shredded leaves, they may never hunger for supplemental fertilizer. However, where soil conditions are lean, it's a good idea to topdress the root zone with composted manure each spring, or to feed plants yearly with a controlled-release fertilizer for shrubs. Where acidic soil conditions prevail, topdress lilacs with lime every three to four years.

Prune away suckers that grow from the base of plants, particularly if you are growing a grafted cultivar. Also prune dead blooms from plants that are small enough to manage this way. Besides making the plants look better, trimming helps expose leaves to sunshine and fresh air, which is an important defense against powdery mildew.

Liriope

Evergreen Groundcover
Liriope muscari, L. spicata

'Royal Blue' is but one of many varieties of L. muscari. *The blue-blossomed spikes are often followed by black berries in early fall.*

Hardy in Zones 5 to 10, liriope is perhaps the most versatile of all small evergreen plants, and it practically grows itself. You can use liriope as an edging, as a foliage plant to mix among flowers, or as a grasslike groundcover in shady spots where little else will grow.

Common liriope has dark green leaves, which makes it great for framing beds filled with light-colored flowers. And, because liriope is willing to grow in either sun or shade, it is a popular edging for long driveways or walkways with varying sun exposures. Variegated forms, in which the leaves are edged with creamy gold or white, make fine "rhythmic" plants to place near the front of beds, alternated with small shrubs, perennials or long-blooming annuals such as petunias or impatiens.

Choosing Liriope

After several years, plantings of liriope become thick enough to dig and divide, so don't be afraid to ask well-endowed friends or neighbors for starter plants. But before you dig (or buy plants from a nursery), examine the roots and crowns to see if they spread by stolons—underground stems that tie plants together—or by simply expanding into tightly packed clumps. Liriope that spreads via stolons (*L. spicata*) makes a great groundcover, but is not the best choice for edging. Cultivars of clump-forming *L. muscari*, sometimes called big blue liriope, are much slower to spread. Almost all variegated strains are clump-forming plants.

Growing Liriope

You can plant liriope anytime except the middle of winter. Early spring is the best season for planting, but you can successfully transplant small clumps until early fall, provided you keep them well watered. Cut or pull large clumps apart so that the ones you set out have only 3 to 5 crowns, and set these small clumps about 4 inches apart. Mulch between plants to retain soil moisture and control weeds. New colonies need 2 to 3 years to form robust bands or fill in as a groundcover.

In late winter, remove old damaged leaves by either mowing over the plants with the mower blade set high, or trimming them to within about 2 inches of the ground with a weed trimmer, or, in the case of small clumps of variegated liriope, cutting off the old leaves by hand with pruning shears. This maintenance is optional, however, and is done mostly to keep the planting looking neat. Left alone, new leaves will push out from the middle of each crown, quickly hiding from view the old withered leaves from the previous season.

Creeping liriope spreads by stolons, so the plants become an even mass rather than a collection of clumps—just the effect you want when covering a large area.

Magnolia

Tree or Shrub
Magnolia species

Like other star magnolias, 'Centennial' blooms in early spring on bare branches, long before larger trees have leafed out. It makes a fine specimen tree in open lawns.

When most people think of magnolias, they envision the huge majestic trees that thrive in the high-rainfall areas of the Deep South. Adding such a tree to your yard is a possibility in humid sections of Zones 7 to 9, where a magnolia's glossy green evergreen leaves and fragrant flowers will make it an instant landscape feature. In colder areas, including protected sites in Zone 5, a different type of magnolia can charm your yard as a large blooming shrub. Growing to 15 feet tall, deciduous star magnolias produce hundreds of white or pink blossoms on bare limbs first thing in spring. Their size makes them ideal for planting near the corners of houses as upright accents in foundation beds, or you can plant them in partially shaded spots in an open lawn.

The broad leaves of magnolia trees shade the ground so thoroughly that neither grasses nor groundcovers will grow beneath them. Plan to maintain a year-round mulch beneath both tree and shrub-type magnolias. The mulch will clothe the bare ground under magnolia trees and benefit magnolia shrubs by keeping the soil moist during dry spells.

Choosing Magnolias

The revered Southern magnolia (*M. grandiflora*) comes in numerous forms, many of which are much smaller than the ancient, 100-foot-tall trees seen around historic homes. The 'Little Gem' cultivar grows to only 20 feet tall, and it also reblooms sporadically through the summer. The leaves of 'Little Gem' and other smallish cultivars are small as well, making them much easier to clean up after when old leaves make way for new ones.

Most star magnolias (*M. stellata*) found at nurseries bloom white, including the 'Royal Star' cultivar, which blooms a little later than the species, so that the blossoms are less likely to be damaged by late frosts. There are also a number of cultivars selected at the National Arboretum that bloom pink or lavender, such as 'Susan', 'Betty' and 'June'.

Growing Magnolias

Buy both tree and shrub-type magnolias in 3-gallon or larger containers, because they can be finicky about transplanting. Dig planting holes twice as wide as the root ball of the plant, and amend the soil with a liberal dose of compost, peat moss or other slightly acidic form of organic matter. Carefully set the plant at the same depth it grew in its container. Water thoroughly after planting and mulch with at least 3 inches of shredded leaves, pine needles or bark nuggets. Provide water during droughts for the first two years after planting. Prune magnolias only to remove limbs damaged by ice or wind.

The blossoms of star magnolia are slightly shaggy, but they have the vanilla white color of other magnolias, and a light fragrance to match.

Maple, Japanese

Tree
Acer palmatum

Full-sized Japanese maples are strong architectural trees, ideal for planting near entryways. Those with bronze foliage bring inspiring color to mostly green landscapes.

If you want a small tree to preside over your patio or adorn an entryway, the first candidates to consider should be Japanese maples. Sizes range from diminutive dwarfs, suitable for growing in pots, to more stately trees that reach 20 feet in height. Width varies with cultivar too, so it is not difficult to find a Japanese maple in exactly the right size for the space you want it to fill.

Truly trees for all seasons, Japanese maples feature handsome layered branches through winter, followed by green, red-blushed or deep red leaves through summer, and finally bright autumn color. Japanese maple leaves are small and finely cut, making these very fine-textured trees worthy of sites where they can be admired up close.

All Japanese maples are winter hardy to Zone 5, though some cultivars have trouble with leaf scorch in the warm conditions of Zones 8 and 9. Locating them where they will get partial shade, especially in the afternoon, often helps solve this problem.

Varieties with very finely cut foliage (such as 'Dissectum') beg to be admired up close. Plant them in areas often used for outdoor fun or relaxation.

Choosing Japanese Maples

Japanese maples with green leaves are easy to work into the landscape, and have the most natural effect. Trees sold by their species name grow into graceful 25-foot-tall trees that turn gold and then bronze in the fall. Low, broad and weeping in habit, specimens of the award-winning 'Waterfall' cultivar are ideal for planting near water gardens or other places used for outdoor relaxation.

Numerous named cultivars have red leaves, or green leaves delicately edged in red. Because their foliage color commands so much attention, it is usually best to plant red-leafed trees together in small groups, or to use them singly, as accent plants. Either way, it is usually best to give them center stage by having no other red-leafed plants nearby.

Growing Japanese Maples

Japanese maples grow best in fertile, well-drained soil that is slightly acidic. Because the trees are often costly, it pays to give them the best possible start, preferably in early spring. Amend a planting hole twice as wide as the root ball of the tree with compost or other organic matter. Plant the tree at the same depth it grew in its container, and stake it to help it grow straight and true. You can remove the stake after the first season, but continue to water as needed to keep the soil lightly moist, particularly during the hottest part of summer. Prune low branches if you like, as well as limbs damaged by ice or wind. Japanese maples' natural shape is so elegant that they are always beautiful with a minimum of attention from you.

Dwarf Japanese maples make fine container plants, which can be left outdoors year-round. In cold climates, keep them in a protected spot in the winter.

Melampodium

Annual Flower
Melampodium paludosum

A nonstop bloomer through the hottest weather that summer can dish out, melampodium has gone from being a virtual unknown to a star in less than a decade. Sometimes called medallion flower or butter daisy, melampodium produces hundreds of small yellow flowers on well-branched bushes, so that full-grown plants look almost like small shrubs. The flowers fall away cleanly as they fade, so there's no need to pinch them off. Faded blooms give way to numerous black seeds, which the plants shed so abundantly that it's typical to find a bumper crop of volunteer seedlings in late spring. These are easy to dig and move to where you want to have mounds of summer color.

Melampodium flowers are small, but they just keep on coming. This annual is also a strong reseeder, and the seedlings are easy to dig and transplant.

Give melampodium full sun in all but the hottest climates, where it can adapt to a half-day of shade. The plants grow best in fertile, slightly acidic soil, but they will thrive in any well-drained site. Melampodium combines well with any type of zinnia or evergreen shrub, or you can plant them at the feet of upright sunflowers. Dwarf varieties make good accent plants for sunny entryways or the front edges of a flower garden.

An outstanding annual for warm climates, melampodium varieties such as 'Million Gold' combine well with marigolds, tithonia (torch flower) and broad-leafed cannas.

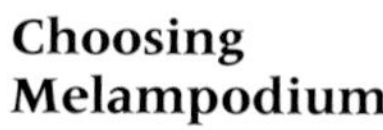

Choosing Melampodium

Leading varieties differ mostly in terms of size, which tends to be larger than is given on plant tags and seed packets. For example, the full-sized 'Medallion' variety is supposed to grow to 24 inches tall, but it will top 30 inches in warm weather with ample water. Dwarf 'Derby' is rated at 8 to 10 inches, but it often branches to 16 inches tall and wide. In between, 'Million Gold' quickly reaches knee height unless it is grown in containers, where it stays a little smaller.

Growing Melampodium

Bedding plants are widely available in spring, or you can simply sow seeds where you want the plants to grow. Either way, don't bother to plant melampodium until the last frost is history and the soil is warm. This is a warm-natured flower that will refuse to grow under cold conditions.

If the soil is lean, work in an organic or timed-release fertilizer before planting. Set plants at least 1 foot apart to allow for their spread, though you can keep them a little closer if you desire a strong mounding effect. Mulch between plants to retain soil moisture and discourage weeds. Once established, melampodium needs water only during very hot, dry weather.

The same blister beetles that devour tomatoes in some areas can damage melampodium, but otherwise this flower has no serious insect or disease problems.

Pachysandra

Evergreen Groundcover
Pachysandra terminalis

Variegated pachysandra is an excellent groundcover to plant near entryways, where its delicately edged leaves are easily noticed and appreciated.

Sometimes known by the unflattering common name of Japanese spurge, pachysandra is the premier groundcover for shade in Zones 5 to 9. Growing to about 8 inches tall, pachysandra forms a sea of glossy green leaves held on uniform, upright stems. Pachysandra enriches the landscape with its captivating texture. Once established, it needs little attention to look handsome year after year. Its flowers that form in spring are barely noticeable, and the same goes for its small berries in the fall.

This groundcover must have shade, and will melt or burn in too much sun. Pachysandra also struggles under trees with extensive surface roots unless a slightly raised bed is created to accommodate its needs. Where the soil is very lean and riddled with roots, English ivy may do better as a groundcover. In comparison, pachysandra excels in sites where the soil is rich, loamy and cooled by a canopy of tree branches.

Choosing Pachysandra

In late spring, check with nurseries for bundles of rooted cuttings. This is an economical way to start if you have a lot of ground to cover; you will need 100 plants to fill 25 square feet. The big three of named pachysandra varieties are 'Green Sheen', with extra gloss in its leaves, 'Kingwood', which has deeply serrated leaves, and white-edged 'Silver Edge', a comparatively slow grower that looks great in high-visibility beds. In addition to these, nurseries often sell varieties that have earned strong local reputations for good performance.

Growing Pachysandra

Pachysandra makes most of its new growth in spring, so it's best to start new plantings at about the time of your last spring frost. Cultivate the soil to loosen it, and mix in a 2-inch blanket of peat moss, compost or other form of organic matter. Set plants 6 inches apart and keep them constantly moist for three weeks. Hand weed the first season. After that, the spreading stolons should choke out most weeds.

Fertilize pachysandra each spring with an organic or timed-release fertilizer. Annually, or at least every other year, top back plants in early spring by cutting them 3 to 4 inches above the soil line. You can do this with pruning shears, a string trimmer or a lawn mower with the blade set at its highest cutting height. This trimming helps the plants develop numerous branches, which look good and help discourage weeds.

To increase the bounty, use a hand trowel to harvest rooted plants and transplant them to other parts of your yard. Pots of pachysandra also make neat low-maintenance accents for shady entryways.

Where winters are mild, pachysandra will hold its rich green color year-round. Harsh winters can damage pachysandra, but the plants quickly recover in the spring.

Use pachysandra to mask the base of a large tree. Mowing around the edges easily keeps plantings in bounds.

Pansy and Viola

Annual Flowers
Viola hybrids

The premier flowers of early spring, pansies begin blooming before winter's end and then produce a continuous parade of cheery flowers for several months. The color range is so huge that you can have lots of fun playing with contrasting colors such as blue and yellow or red and white. Pansies and violas (also called mini-pansies) make fine edgings for walkways and perform beautifully in containers as well.

Many pansies handle cold weather so well that they can be planted in the fall, though they usually do not bloom well until the weather moderates in spring. The plants decline when hot weather comes, though they will hold up admirably in climates where cool nights give them a break from summer heat. But in Zones 7 to 9, pansies are best grown as winter annuals that are planted in fall, enjoyed through spring, and replaced with more heat-tolerant flowers when summer begins.

Choosing Pansies and Violas

For fall planting in Zones 4 and 5, choose very hardy varieties such as 'Delta' or 'Bingo'. All pansies can be planted in fall from Zone 6 southward, or you can set them out first thing in spring.

Pansies come in numerous colors, including varieties without markings or faces. Varieties with medium-sized blooms flower continuously in cool weather.

Hybrid violas are also called minipansies and 'panolas'—a cross between pansy and viola. Varieties such as 'Blueberry Sorbet' cover themselves with perky blossoms.

Violas are a modern invention though their ancestors, Johnny-jump-ups, have been around for centuries. The new hybrid violas are very heavy bloomers, covering themselves with hundreds of 1-inch-wide blossoms so that the plants become wide mounds of color. Violas are more willing to bloom in cold weather than are pansies, so they are increasingly popular as winter annuals in Zones 6 to 8. They are also strong reseeders, often giving rise to pretty surprises in lawns or even in cracks in a concrete driveway.

Growing Pansies and Violas

When shopping for bedding plants, choose young seedlings that have just begun to produce buds. Overgrown plants that are leggy and rootbound never recover their vigor after transplanting.

In fall, set out plants early enough so that they can develop roots before soil temperatures drop below 45°F. In cold climates, lightly mulch over plants after the soil freezes to keep freezing and thawing from pushing plants up out of the ground.

Pansies and violas grown in cold soil benefit from fertilizer. The natural processes that make soil-borne nutrients available to plants proceed slowly when the soil is cold, so you should keep plants satisfied by dousing them with a liquid fertilizer at least once a month. Varieties that produce very large blossoms also benefit from regular pinching off of old blossoms—a sure way to keep new buds and flowers coming for many colorful weeks.

The dark blotches that mark the petals are often called faces. Although the stems are short, intricately marked pansies are worthy of display in small vases.

Peony

Perennial Flower
Paeonia species

You can't beat the bang for the buck you get with this long-lived perennial. Simply stick a few dormant clumps in the ground, and a year or two later you will have a beautiful 3-foot-tall bouquet of blooms to leave in the garden or cut and bring indoors. Nothing in the garden compares to the visual "wow" and the sniff power of the large, soft, frilly blooms of peonies.

Choosing Peonies

There are over 800 peony varieties to choose from, with flower colors ranging from creamy white to deep burgundy. Blooms may have a row of single petals around a central cluster of stamens (known as "single" or "Japanese" types), or have rows and rows of petals ("doubles"), or fall somewhere in between ("semi-doubles"). Some are wonderfully fragrant. The deciding factor in choosing a peony, though, will be where you live.

Peonies that die back to the ground each year are known as herbaceous types. Phenomenally cold hardy, they generally do well no farther south than Zone 7, because they won't flower well unless they receive a thorough winter chilling. If you wish to grow herbaceous peonies south of Zone 7, then choose early- to mid-season cultivars, which will bloom before the weather gets too hot. As extra insurance in hot climes, select single or Japanese flower forms, which can tolerate more heat.

Southern gardeners may also want to consider tree peonies (*P. suffruticosa*), which grow well in Zones 3 to 8. Tree peonies aren't really trees, but actually shrubs with woody stems that reach about 3 to 5 feet high. They produce blooms up to 15 inches across, and can take more heat and do not require as much cold as herbaceous peonies.

Large-flowered peonies are usually fragrant, a trait that has historically linked them to romance and love. Some people call these varieties peony roses.

The single flowers of 'Little Red Gem' are framed by finely cut foliage—an unusual feature in peonies, which usually have broad, glossy leaves.

Growing Peonies

In general, both herbaceous and tree peonies prefer full sun, well-drained soil and abundant water, especially when they are growing vigorously in the spring. Plant peony crowns in fall so that the buds (eyes) on the rootstock are 2 inches below the soil surface. In Zone 7, set plants so that the buds are right at the surface where they will be frozen several times in winter. In colder climates, mulch fall-planted peonies to protect them during their first winter.

Before flower buds form in mid-spring, it is often helpful to stake taller selections or plants with double flowers to keep the heavy blooms from dipping to the ground. With tree peonies, maintenance is limited to snipping off any suckers that pop up from the rootstock (the leaves will look distinctly different), and providing winter protection (such as a loose wrapping of burlap) of above-ground plant parts.

Petunia

Annual Flower
Petunia hybrids

Pretty petunias are so well known that we tend to take them for granted, but it would be a mistake to dismiss these excellent annuals. Available in a huge range of colors, many petunias also emit a pleasing fragrance at night. Petunias bloom best in full sun, but they will adapt to partial shade in most climates. Shade makes the plants stretch out a bit, but this can be an asset if you are growing petunias in pots or hanging baskets. Petunias thrive in a wide range of temperatures, so they often bloom for months before dying of exhaustion (in warm climates) or from exposure to winter's first serious blast of cold.

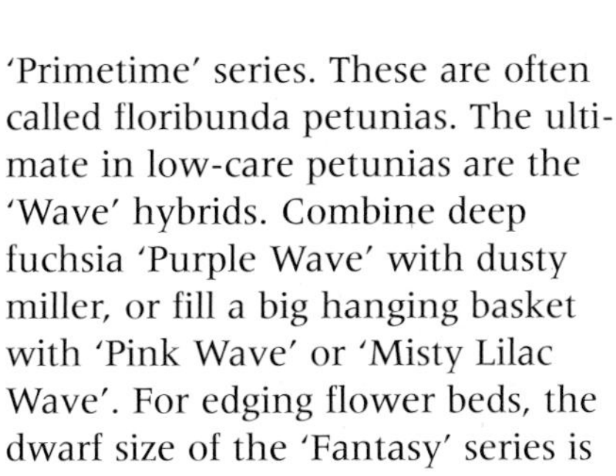

Many petunias—such as 'Primetime Pink Morn'—have contrasting color in their throats. This makes them great for viewing up close.

Choosing Petunias

There are numerous types of petunias from which to choose, each with its own special talents. If low maintenance is your goal, avoid very large-flowered grandiflora types, many of which have huge ruffled blossoms. These do not bloom as long or as strong as petunias with smaller flowers, such as the 'Madness', 'Celebrity' or 'Primetime' series. These are often called floribunda petunias. The ultimate in low-care petunias are the 'Wave' hybrids. Combine deep fuchsia 'Purple Wave' with dusty miller, or fill a big hanging basket with 'Pink Wave' or 'Misty Lilac Wave'. For edging flower beds, the dwarf size of the 'Fantasy' series is just right.

Old-fashioned reseeding petunias, which grow into leggy 18-inch-tall plants covered with blooms in varying shades of pink, will reappear year after year in hospitable places. All you need to do is weed and water, and you can enjoy the beauty of petunias that have the vigor of wildflowers.

Growing Petunias

To provide petunias with the energy they need to bloom for months on end, mix an organic or timed-release fertilizer into the soil before setting out bedding plants in the spring. Buy young plants that have barely begun to bloom, and gently spread the roots as you set the plants in place. Thoroughly water after planting, and mulch between plants to control weeds and to keep the soil moist.

In mid to late summer, rejuvenate tired petunias by cutting them back by about half their size, fertilizing with a liquid or granular fertilizer, and renewing the mulch to keep the soil cool. Fertilize petunias in containers more often, perhaps every 10 days or so if you are using a liquid plant food.

Prolonged dampness can lead to root or stem rot, so it's a good idea to install a soaker hose when you plant a new bed. That way you can provide water as needed without wetting the petunia leaves or flowers.

Old-fashioned reseeding petunias grow taller than modern hybrids, but they typically reseed themselves year after year, and often feature strong evening fragrance.

Petunias are excellent flowers to grow in containers, but they require regular feeding to keep them growing and blooming strong.

PINE

Evergreen Tree *Pinus* species

Fast growth, evergreen presence and willingness to grow in dry soils make pines fine choices for home landscapes. All pines are evergreens, yet they do shed some needles every fall. Do not be alarmed that your tree is dying. Most species produce needles that last about two years, so each autumn you can expect about half of the needles to turn brown and fall to the ground. New needles appear in spring along with shoots of new growth, called candles. If you want to shape a pine into a bonsai pattern, cutting or bending the new candles is how this is done.

Pines grow best in full sun, in soil that becomes dry between heavy rains. Pines prefer acidic soil with a pH below 6.0, and will show yellowish color if the soil becomes too alkaline. Avoid planting pines near busy roadways where they will be exposed to air pollution and winter salt spray. Like people, pines crave clean air.

Loblolly pines are choice trees for the Deep South. Numerous flowers are happy when grown beneath the high shade of pine trees.

White pines make excellent specimen trees in the landscape, though it's important to consider their mature size and avoid planting them near power lines.

Choosing Pines

If you live in an extreme climate, it is often safest to plant species that are native to your area, such as loblolly pines in the Deep South or Coulter pines in the high deserts of the West. White pine (*P. strobus*), native to the Eastern U.S., is one of the most popular and widely available pines. Fast-growing and tall (to 80 feet at maturity), white pines are adapted in Zones 2 to 8. Sometimes you can purchase them as Christmas trees with their heavy root balls tightly wrapped in burlap. From Zone 7 southward such trees can be enjoyed through the holiday season and then planted in the yard. In Northern areas, hold trees in a protected place outdoors and plant them first thing in spring.

Several comparatively slow-growing pines from other continents make good specimen trees in home landscapes. Lacebark pine (*P. bungeana*) is a multistemmed tree that develops mottled bark as it matures. Adapted in Zones 4 to 8, lacebark pine seldom grows taller than 40 feet, and the canopy has a strong tulip shape. Swiss stone pine (*P. cembra*) is hardy, upright and slow-growing, with short, dark green needles.

Growing Pines

To be assured of successful transplanting, set out container-grown trees in late winter or early spring. Pines planted in fall or winter may have problems holding up to cold, drying winds. An antidesiccant spray, applied to the leaves in early winter, can reduce stress on young pine trees during their first winter in the ground.

PLUMBAGO

Perennial Flower
Ceratostigma plumbaginoides

The gentian blue flowers of plumbago appear during the second half of summer, when color in the garden is often in short supply.

Once a fixture in every garden, plumbago is due for a revival in interest. Its name-change half a decade ago, to *Ceratostigma*, certainly caused its popularity to suffer, but today there are many reasons to include this tough plant in your garden. At home in any partially shaded, well-drained spot in Zones 5 to 9, 1-foot-tall plumbago is compact enough to use as an edging, and has a quirky growth schedule that fits in beautifully with several other low-maintenance flowers.

Because it does not emerge until late in spring, plumbago can be planted over daffodils, where it does a great job of hiding their failing foliage. As summer heats up and plumbago's gentian blue flowers begin to appear, it makes a fine partner for orange bloomers such as 'Cosmic Orange' cosmos or 'Profusion Orange' zinnia, or even yellow French marigolds. Blooming continues well into fall. As an added bonus, plumbago's foliage reddens with the onset of cool autumn weather and becomes a show in itself.

Although plumbago is a hardy perennial, you can expect it to flourish and spread into a groundcover in hospitable places. Spreading underground stems, called stolons, help plumbago to form long-lived colonies in open woodlands or other places that get a mixture of sun and shade.

Choosing Plumbago

When shopping through mail-order sources, you may find plumbago classified as *C. plumbaginoides* or *Plumbago larpentae*, an old name that many people prefer. In tropical zones, drought-tolerant Cape plumbago (*P. auriculata*), sometimes classified as *P. capensis*, produces clusters of light blue flowers on 2-foot-tall plants.

Growing Plumbago

Like most plants that are extremely easy to grow, plumbago has one strict cultural requirement: loose, gritty soil. It will languish and refuse to spread in tight clay, but this situation is easily remedied by creating a slightly raised bed amended with sandy topsoil and organic matter. Because plumbago is often used as an edging for partially shaded spots beneath trees, providing the plants with appropriate soil and a hard edging of brick or stone to restrain their movement is best done at planting time. Set out plants in early spring so that they can be well established by the time blooming season begins in midsummer.

After a few years, go through the planting and gently dig out the most elderly crowns which have become woody and show probable signs of crown rot. Younger-rooted stems and crowns will quickly fill in the holes left behind. A light application of an organic or timed-release fertilizer applied in spring will ensure strong season-long vigor.

Plumbago's spreading growth habit makes it suitable for use as a groundcover plant. Here it skirts the ground around a dwarf blue spruce.

Portulaca

Annual Flower
Portulaca grandiflora

If you long for a bright spot of color in a place that seems hopelessly hot and dry, portulaca is the plant you need. Also known as moss rose, this tough little annual, related to the weed known as purslane, has been around for decades. But in recent years plant breeders have made huge improvements in the flower size, color range, and overall vigor of these carefree flowers.

Modern portulacas grow into rounded 12-inch-wide mounds of succulent foliage. The flowers, composed of brightly colored "crepe paper" petals in a rainbow of warm colors, open each morning and close by late afternoon and during rainy weather. This is one flower that demands full sun. It's also wise to get to know the seedlings, which often appear in early summer where portulaca grew the season before. Allow them to prosper wherever they pop up, or use a spoon to lift and transplant them to a fresh location.

Portulaca blossoms are a rich source of pollen, so they are often visited by bees in midmorning, just after the blossoms open for the day.

Choosing Portulacas

Portulaca is not difficult to grow from seed, but bedding plants are widely available in spring and will save you much time and trouble. Besides, portulaca seedlings prefer intense light, which is often difficult to provide in a home setting. Variety names including the 'Sundial' and 'Sundance' series are widely available as mixed flats, and sometimes in individual colors as well. All lend a festive look to any spot in which they are grown.

Planting Portulacas

There is no hurry to get portulacas planted in spring, because the plants prefer warm growing conditions. Do buy plants while the selection is good, and keep them in partial shade until you are ready to plant them. Although portulacas are resilient little water misers, the plants will grow best if they are protected from undue stresses at a tender age.

When planting portulacas in poor soil, work an organic or timed-release fertilizer into the soil prior to planting. Set plants 12 inches apart if you want them to grow together into a mass, and mulch between plants to retain soil moisture and control weeds. Water as often as needed to keep the soil lightly moist for two to three weeks after planting. Thereafter, you will need to water portulaca only during serious droughts. If the plants become thin and leggy in late summer, cut them back by half their size and douse them well with a liquid fertilizer. Encouraged in this way, they will often make a strong comeback.

The blooms of portulaca close in the afternoon and don't reopen until morning. So it's wise to plant portulaca where you'll see it in the heat of the day.

Portulacas are natural water misers, so they are a fine annual to grow in small containers that are difficult to keep moist in hot weather.

PULMONARIA

Perennial Flower
Pulmonaria species

An old-fashioned favorite, 'Mrs. Moon' is an enthusiastic reseeder that will form thick colonies when grown at the base of a tree or another shady, sheltered spot.

Perhaps it's because of its funny common name—lungwort—that this perennial is not more widely grown. And that's a shame, because pulmonaria provides sweet little pink and blue flowers in early spring when precious little else is blooming, and then offers up very interesting, usually silver-spotted foliage for the rest of the season.

The old lungwort name is no accident. The leaves were reportedly used to treat lung ailments in days gone by. But these days, pulmonaria is not just for the medicine cabinet. Rather, it's one of the showiest plants for the shade garden, or for studding into small spaces under trees.

Choosing Pulmonarias

There are numerous good varieties to pick from when looking for lungworts to grow. When selecting a variety, you only need to concern yourself with two things. First, what flower color would you like—white, pink, blue or red? Then, what sort of foliage do you want—solid green, spotted with big silver splotches, or flecked with tiny white specks? You will also need to think about how much you can spend, because newer exotic cultivars cost more than old standards.

'Mrs. Moon' is an old favorite with large silver-spotted leaves and flowers that are pink when they open and then age to blue. A few other cultivars of note include 'Sissinghurst White', with large white flowers and silver-white spotted leaves; 'Roy Davidson', which does well in the South and has heat-tolerant spotted leaves that are longer than they are wide, plus pink flowers that turn blue. Vigorous and heat-tolerant 'Janet Fisk', with heavily marbled foliage and pink flowers that fade to lavender, can really lighten dark areas of the garden. Very showy modern cultivars include 'Berries and Cream', with silvery leaves and rosy pink flowers, and 'Redstart', which has salmon-red blossoms and faint spots on the leaves.

'Little Star' pulmonaria features lovely blue flowers atop daintily spotted leaves. It is an excellent plant to feature in a shade garden, or you can place it along a quiet pathway.

Growing Pulmonarias

The easiest way to get some pulmonarias going in your garden is to pick up a few potted plants at the nursery, or bum some seedlings or divisions of mature plants from a gardening friend. Give this perennial a spot in partial to full shade and it will thrive. Make sure the soil stays moist, although it can be of average fertility. Full sun and/or dry conditions will make the leaves of pulmonaria look ratty by midsummer. If leaves begin to look tattered, shear plants back in midsummer so they'll sprout a fresh display. Many of the pulmonarias will happily multiply by spreading their little seedlings all around if the site is right.

The refined leaf variegation of 'Excalibur' pulmonaria makes it look almost like a houseplant. But it's rugged and durable when grown in any moist, shady spot.

Rose

Flowering Shrub
Rosa species and hybrids

Many modern shrub roses have bloodlines that trace back to fragrant antique strains, and they often have relaxed flower form comprised of numerous loose petals.

Beautiful and fragrant, roses are among everyone's favorite flowers. And although roses have a well-deserved reputation for being difficult to grow, there are numerous modern cultivars that are so vigorous and disease-resistant that they merit a place in a low-maintenance landscape. It is no longer necessary to constantly prune and spray to have roses. But you do need to keep an open mind, because the low-care roses are usually big, spreading bushes rather than stiff, angular plants.

Advances in rose breeding have not changed the basic nature of these beautiful brambles. They still need substantial sun and fertile, well-drained soil. You can grow a small bed devoted exclusively to roses, or use them as part of shrub groupings as long as they are not crowded by other plants. Shrub roses also make great specimen shrubs to grow in an open lawn.

Choosing Roses

The world of roses is so huge and varied that it has its own language. You need not learn all the words for various classifications, because most of the trouble-free cultivars are placed in a new catch-all category called shrub roses. A few, such as 1932-vintage 'The Fairy', are quite old, while others have made their debut in the last 10 years. Some good names to look for include 'Simplicity' (available in pink, red, white and yellow), shade-tolerant 'Scarlet Meidiland' (red) and 'Carefree Wonder' (pink and white). These roses are hardy to Zone 4. If you live in a colder climate, look for roses described as Rugosa hybrids, such as clove-scented 'Hansa'.

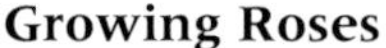

Growing Roses

Dormant roses are often sold bare rooted in late winter and early spring. Later in the season, after they begin active growth, buy them in containers. Early planting is best, because roses grow new roots at the same time they develop leaves and stems.

Dig a planting hole 2 feet wide and deep, and mix about 2 gallons of well-rotted compost into the bottom of the hole. Shape loose soil into a cone-shaped mound, and spread the roots of the rose over it. Then gradually refill the hole, stopping every few minutes to check depth. In cold climates, roses with a graft bulge on the lower stem should have it covered with 2 inches of soil. In Zones 7 to 9, the graft bulge should be just above the soil line. Thoroughly water after planting, and mulch around the plant to keep the soil moist.

Each spring, feed roses with an organic or timed-release fertilizer. Water regularly during dry spells, and periodically trim off dead or diseased branches. With vigorous shrub roses, this should be enough to keep them happy and healthy.

Like other modern shrub roses, pink 'Bonica' grows into a leafy bush studded with dozens of lovely blooms suitable for cutting.

The scourge of rose lovers, rose blackspot is caused by a fungus that spreads whenever leaves are wet. Choose varieties with good tolerance to prevent serious problems.

Salvia

Annual and Perennial Flowers
Salvia species and hybrids

The bold red blossoms of 'Lady In Red' salvia make it attractive to bees and hummingbirds. Blooms open gradually from the lower stem to the tip.

Colorful relatives of the herb called sage, salvias include warm-natured annuals and several short-lived perennials. All produce spikes of tubular flowers that are much loved by bees and butterflies. Salvias need a half day of sun, but once established they typically stay in bloom all summer long. Use them as upright backdrops behind dwarf annuals, or grow them in flowing masses for a vivid display. Because of their spiking form and long bloom time, salvias are among the best companion plants for annuals that produce rounded or daisy-type blossoms, such as marigolds, petunias and zinnias.

Choosing Salvias

Most of the annual salvias sold as bedding plants are hybrids of *S. elegans*. These salvias come in a range of colors, though the red varieties are usually the most vigorous. Preferring morning sun and afternoon shade, red salvias need plenty of water and regular fertilizer to grow into big, robust plants.

For great flowers with less work, look for bedding plants of coral sage (*S. coccinea*), tagged with variety names such as 'Coral Nymph' or 'Lady in Red'. This species thrives with very little attention beyond occasional deadheading to help force out new blooming spikes. On any warm summer day, expect to see lots of bee and hummingbird activity in your coral sage.

Blooming in blue and white, mealycup sage (*S. farinacea*) is a short-lived perennial in Zones 8 and 9. The plants stay covered with blue spikes all summer, making them ideal companions for red, orange or yellow flowers.

Salvias are known for their reds, but other striking colors are available too, such as this deep, rich purple.

In Zones 7 to 10, several other species make fine additions to the perennial bed, including drought-tolerant Texas sage (*S. greggii*) and Mexican bush sage (*S. leucantha*). Look for plants in local nurseries in spring.

Growing Salvias

All salvias are sensitive to salt buildup in the soil, so starting them from seed is slow and difficult. Opt for bedding plants instead, and choose a sunny, well-drained site. Amend the soil with an organic or timed-release fertilizer before planting, and top off the bed with a mulch to retain soil moisture and suppress weeds.

Spikes of salvia make good cut flowers. In the garden, plants will produce new spikes continuously if you trim off the old ones every few weeks. Water during dry spells, particularly if the plants become so dry that the leaves appear wilted early in the morning. Coral sage often reseeds, though the seedlings often do not appear until late spring, after the soil becomes warm. When dug and moved to new locations, the seedlings have a very high rate of survival.

Mealycup sage produces a steady supply of blue spikes all summer. To keep new flowers coming, trim off the oldest spikes every few weeks.

Sedum

Perennial Flower
Sedum species

The flower clusters of 'Autumn Joy' sedum start out pink and gradually age to bronze. Because it blooms late in the season, this is a favorite flower for perennial borders.

The drought tolerance of foolproof sedums will go a long way toward ensuring a successful low-maintenance landscape plan. Persistent and pest free, sedums look good throughout the growing season.

In early spring, fleshy mounds of bright green, blue-green, creamy yellow, or red-tinged foliage emerge. True succulents, sedums' thick, waxy leaves and juicy stems provide unique textural contrast to many other perennials. By midsummer, small, starry flower clusters top those stems in hues of pink, red or white. And when the growing season starts to wane, some sedum flowers even retain their color and form after they have dried.

An eager spreader, S. acre *bursts into bloom in late spring, producing numerous flower spikes topped with sunny yellow blossoms.*

The variety of sedums is stunning—some can reach 2 feet tall and will hold their own in perennial patches, while others are trailing and look fantastic as groundcovers, growing among rocks or creeping in the crevices of a stone wall.

Choosing Sedums

There are so many sedums to pick from that your main task is to decide where you'd like to have sedums growing, and then select ones that fit the bill and strike your fancy.

Among the sedum hybrids, 'Autumn Joy' is probably the most popular, with 2-foot-tall stems topped with rusty pink flower clusters that persist into fall. 'Ruby Glow' is 1 foot tall with rounded purple-tinged leaves and ruby red flowers. 'Vera Jameson' is similar, but with bronze leaves. The parent species of these cultivars, showy stonecrop (*S. spectabile*), reaches 1 to 2 feet tall with flower heads up to 6 inches across. In perennial catalogs or nurseries, look for rosy-red 'Atropurpureum' or rose-pink 'Brilliant'.

Two-row sedum (*S. spurium*) forms mats of wiry stems about 6 inches tall with rounded leaves; 'Dragon's Blood', 'Red Carpet' and 'Ruby Mantle' all have red-tinged foliage, while 'Tricolor' is variegated pink, white and green. Indestructible *S. acre* grows into a green groundcover topped with yellow flowers in the spring.

Growing Sedums

All sedums are tough, easy-to-grow perennials. They prefer average well-drained soils and full sun. Some of the low-growing types will tolerate partial shade in the North. South of Zone 6, part shade is beneficial for all of the sedums. The taller types may get a bit leggy in shade though, and may need to be pinched back or staked to support the flower heads.

To get more sedums, either dig up and divide established clumps in early spring, or take 1- to 3-inch-long cuttings of the fleshy stems in spring or summer and stick them in a moist (but not too wet) pot of soil until they root. Amazingly fast, cuttings are often nicely rooted within a month.

If you want a spreading sedum for a rock garden or other dry spot, two-row sedums such as 'Red Carpet' are colorful and easy to grow.

SERVICEBERRY

Shrub or Tree
Amelanchier species

It's hard to beat this group of native shrubs or small trees for year-round interest in the landscape. The show begins with billowy clouds of small white flowers in spring. Then come purplish black fruits that are juicy and edible. If you can harvest some of the berries before the birds get to them, you're in for a treat—serviceberries make great jam and jelly, and pies that rival the best blueberry pies. In fall, the display continues with foliage that is yellow, gold, orange or red. When serviceberries lose their leaves for the winter, gracefully arched branching structure and attractive gray bark are revealed.

Often called by their botanical name of amelanchier, serviceberries are well suited to naturalized plantings along the edge of a woodland, near ponds, or in similar half-wild locations. In the North, they are sometimes called shadblows, because they were usually in bloom at the time the shad used to run up New England rivers in spring to spawn. Some old-timers still call them saskatoons too.

Choosing Serviceberries

Many species are native to North America, and there have been many outstanding cultivars bred from sturdy native stock. Several well-known varieties with striking fall color include 'Cumulus' and 'Prince Charles' (both *A. laevis*) and 'Autumn Brilliance', 'Princess Diana' and 'Cole's Select' (all *A.* x *grandiflora*). Additionally, internationally known tree expert Michael Dirr of the University of Georgia rated the fruit of 'Prince Charles' tops in a taste test, and 'Princess Diana' seems to resist the leaf spot that plagues many other serviceberries, weakening but not killing the plants.

Growing Serviceberries

In the wild, serviceberries flourish in thickets along the borders of woods, in clearings, and often along the edges of wetlands or stream-banks all the way into Zone 3. So that gives you some insight as to just what sort of site serviceberry prefers—moist yet well drained, with acid soil. But serviceberries are very adaptable, and can be grown in a wide range of soil types and even in drier spots. They'll grow best in full sun, but can even be grown in moderate shade. Most serviceberries slowly grow to 20 to 25 feet tall, so they can be planted where limited height is critical, such as near power lines.

Choose container-grown or balled-and-burlapped trees from a reliable nursery, plant your serviceberries, and keep them watered until they are established. After that there isn't much to growing serviceberries. They rarely require pruning except to remove any dead or broken branches. All you have to do is beat the birds to the berries.

Serviceberries bloom in early spring and then produce large crops of edible berries. These small trees are easy to fit into any landscape, where they need very little care.

Spiraea

Flowering Shrub
Spiraea japonica

The yellowish spring leaves of 'Gold Flame' spiraea will mature to green just before the pink flowers appear. Then the foliage will turn yellow again in the fall.

Truly a shrub for all seasons, Japanese spiraea produces beautiful spring foliage, lovely summer flowers, and then turns golden in the fall. Growing to a height of 6 feet, spiraea maintains a strong winter silhouette that works well with evergreens planted at its sides. The flowers appear in summer long after most shrubs have bloomed, and the rounded clusters of tiny pink blossoms often attract butterflies. An old favorite found in many established landscapes, Japanese spiraea remains a mainstay well worth planting today.

Hardy to Zone 3, Japanese spiraea can tolerate winter temperatures as low as -30°F. In its southernmost range of Zone 8 this shrub benefits from afternoon shade, but elsewhere it blooms most prolifically in full sun. A soil rich in organic matter that can retain moisture well is a plus, but established plants usually manage well with only a good layer of mulch to keep the roots cool and moist.

Choosing Spiraeas

Cultivars vary in size and leaf color, with some variations in flower color too. The leaves of 'Gold Flame' emerge yellow in spring, etched with burgundy, and mature to green before turning yellow again in fall. Its flowers are pink, as are those of 'Neon Flash', which has substantial red tinting in its foliage. These spiraeas grow to 6 feet tall, but if you need something smaller consider 3- to 4-foot-tall 'Shibori', which bears pink, rose and white flowers simultaneously. These and other cultivars often are labeled *S. bumalda*; many are hybrids created by crossing Japanese spiraea with other species. Numerous other cultivars may be available at local nurseries, especially in the North, where this shrub is quite popular.

Two other spiraea species, *S. prunifolia* and *S. vanhouttei*, are commonly called bridal wreath. These shrubs produce arching stems laden with clusters of small white flowers. 'Plena' and other *S. prunifolia* cultivars bloom in spring, while *S. vanhouttei* blooms in summer. Although the bridal wreath show is short-lived, it is extremely dramatic and the plants are very easy to grow. Leave them unpruned for the best show of blooms.

Growing Spiraeas

Set out container-grown plants in spring, and you can expect to see at least 5 inches of new growth each year. Amend the planting hole with compost, and provide enough water and mulch to keep the roots lightly moist through the plant's first summer.

Prune established plants lightly in early spring to shape them and remove weak stems. Japanese spiraeas bloom on the current year's growth, so this type of renewal pruning enhances rather than reduces the show of flowers.

Bridal wreath's dainty flowers are beautiful in the garden and in cut arrangements. The spring-blooming 'Plena' variety is found in many gardens and foundation plantings.

Stachys

Perennial Flower
Stachys byzantina

Some gardeners trim off the flower spikes from stachys, but here they have been left intact to rise up through a sea of lady's mantle and purple loosestrife.

When grown in light shade with good drainage, stachys forms a luminous groundcover. It is at its best when seen early in the morning or in fading evening light.

Affectionately known as lamb's-ears, stachys is perhaps the softest textured plant you can grow in your garden. The gray, heavily felted leaves really do feel as furry as lamb's ears, and they give off a glow that makes everything around them look prettier and more refined. Stachys makes a fine edging plant for partial shade, or you can grow small colonies near the front of sunny flower beds. Either way, it is always a good idea to have a clump within easy arm's reach, because visitors of all ages love to receive a leaf to hold in their hands.

Make the most of stachys's texture by growing it near iris, daylily or other plants with spiking foliage. Color-wise, stachys is lovely paired with pink flowers (such as petunias) and creates an icy cool effect when combined with blue salvia or pansies. Because of its light gray color, stachys is wonderful for areas that are often seen at night.

Good drainage and sufficient sun to promptly dry the leaves after soaking rains will usually keep stachys happy. Stachys is hardy to Zone 4, and often holds its foliage through winter in Zones 7 to 9.

Choosing Stachys

If you are offered a few plants by a neighbor who is thinning a bed, by all means accept this generous offer. There are but a few named varieties, including 'Helen von Stein', often revered for its hardiness and vigor, and 'Big Ears', with oversized leaves up to 4 inches across.

Super-vigorous 'Helen von Stein' is a choice variety for cool climates. This touchable plant is enchanting when added to container bouquets.

Growing Stachys

Set out new plants in spring, barely covering the shallow roots with soil. Provide a mulch to limit the splashing of muddy rainwater onto the leaves. It is natural to see some rotting of older leaves that are close to the ground, but too many of these suggests that plants are stressed by limited drainage or too much shade. Rather than abandoning such a planting, make a habit of rejuvenating it each spring by lifting the healthiest crowns, pulling out the most deteriorated ones, and replanting anew in well-dug soil. At any time, crowns of stachys can be borrowed from beds and put to fine use in containers, where the foliage combines beautifully with most summer annuals.

The fact that this is a member of the mint family can be clearly seen in early summer, when the plants produce knee-high flower spikes studded with small purple flowers. You can cut these off if you want to preserve the groundcover character of a planting, or let the blossoms stand and attract bees and other beneficial insects.

Verbena

Annual and Perennial Flowers *Verbena* species and hybrids

A large pot holds a mealycup sage, strawberry gomphrena and a lacy collar of moss verbena. If sheared back in midsummer, the verbena will flower well into fall.

No matter where you live, there is some type of low-care verbena you can grow to grace your summer garden. Annual verbenas are widely available as bedding plants, and these grow into low, 10-inch mounds of dark green leaves studded with refined clusters of red, pink or white flowers. They are wonderful in containers, and bloom nonstop all summer, especially where summers are cool.

In Zones 7 to 10, most gardeners opt for perennial species that come back year after year, producing similar flower clusters to those seen in the annual form. In addition to these, there are several perennial strains propagated from cuttings sold especially for growing in hanging baskets. Although limited in their winter hardiness, few flowers you can grow in containers can match the heat and drought tolerance of these modern verbenas.

Choosing Verbenas

Among annuals, the 'Peaches and Cream' variety is unsurpassed for soft peach color on dwarf plants, ideal for edging. 'Tickled Pink' has a similarly dainty look, or you can find full, saturated red in 'Quartz Burgundy'.

Perennials that thrive in Zones 7 to 9 include 'Homestead Purple', which is as vigorous as many weeds, and festive red and white 'Peppermint Joy'. Both of these are classified as *V. canadensis*, as are several other named strains that produce pink or lavender flowers. Beware of *V. rigida*, a rampant spreader that is fine for wildflower meadows but is too aggressive for flower beds.

The leading verbenas for baskets work equally well as groundcovers, and come in a range of colors. The 'Tapien' series, in several shades of pink, has finely cut foliage similar to one of its ancestors, moss verbena. Rich red or violet flowers can be had from the 'Temari' series. Although hardy only to Zone 8, you can try cutting back the plants and keeping them in a cool garage through winter. With luck and light watering, they will survive and come back to life first thing in the spring.

Growing Verbenas

All verbenas grow best in full sun, in well-drained soil of average fertility. To keep them in bloom continuously, trim off old flowers every few weeks, and feed the plants monthly with a soluble plant food. Many of the newer hybrids are resistant to powdery mildew, which causes white patches to appear on plant leaves. If this problem does develop in beds, pulling out mildewed plants and fertilizing the survivors will often stop the spread of the disease.

An enthusiastic spreader, perennial 'Homestead Purple' verbena makes a fine blooming groundcover plant in low-maintenance beds.

Viburnum

Flowering Shrub
Viburnum species

The lush flowers produced by linden viburnums in the spring are usually followed by a heavy crop of berries, which birds relish.

Viburnums ask very little of the gardener and give a lot in return. "A garden without a viburnum is akin to life without music or art," according to one plant expert. This great group of garden plants numbers over 120 species, all of which are extremely adaptable and enduring. Viburnums range in size from 2 to 30 feet and bear flowers in white or pink, followed by fruits that may be yellow, orange, pink, red, blue or black. Depending on climate and species, viburnums can be deciduous, semi-evergreen or evergreen, and delightfully fragrant.

Use large viburnums in a shrub border, or let smaller ones add interest to foundation plantings. Viburnums look fantastic when combined with broad-leaved evergreens in the landscape.

Choosing Viburnums

Your choice of viburnums is nearly limitless. Some superior cultivars you may want to consider include: *V.* x *burkwoodii* 'Mohawk', a 6- to 8-foot-tall shrub with abundant dark red buds that open to red-blotched white flowers with a strong spicy clove fragrance. Its glossy, dark green leaves turn red in fall and hang on as winter approaches; 'Mohawk' is hardy from Zones 5 to 8. Deciduous Judd Viburnum (*V.* x *juddii*) reaches a full, round 15-foot height and is a good choice for larger landscapes in Zones 4 to 7. Flowers are pinkish white, and fruits are black. For smaller gardens in Zones 5 to 8, there's *V.* x *carlcephalum* 'Cayuga'. Dark green foliage turns brilliant red and covers the 5-foot-tall shrub well into winter in the South. Pink flower buds give way to clove-scented white flowers in spring, then black fruits later in the season.

Known for its spicy fragrance and bright fall color, 'Mohawk' viburnum can be mixed into foundation groupings or grown as a specimen shrub in a mixed flower bed.

Growing Viburnums

Pick a spot that gets full sun or partial shade with slightly acid, well-drained soil. Keep in mind that viburnums prefer even moisture—not too wet, and not too dry. Transplant balled-and-burlapped, container-grown or small bare-root plants. Firm the soil around the roots, and water well. Keep your new viburnums watered until they become established, usually a couple of months.

Let viburnums grow into their natural shape. Occasionally, you may need to prune off branches that are dead, in the way or are sprouting up from the base of the plant. If you need to prune, be sure to prune after viburnum blooms in the spring. If your viburnums produce berries, be sure to let them ripen so that birds can enjoy them as delicious winter treats.

VINCA

Groundcover
Vinca minor, V. major

Although it is not a strong climber, with a little help Vinca minor *will clothe the base of a low wall with glossy green foliage. Flowers appear in the spring.*

Often called periwinkle or myrtle, vinca is a prime groundcover for shady spots, including sloping sites where little else will grow. The vines take root wherever they touch moist ground, forming a tangle of stems that hug the surface. In spring, starry pink flowers dot the evergreen foliage, though some cultivars bloom white or deep rose.

When used as a groundcover in open woodlands, you can underplant vinca with little daffodils and other small bulbs, transforming the site into a spring wonderland. Vinca also makes a fine plant to clothe the ground around large azaleas or other shrubs. If you like making container bouquets or planting window boxes with annual flowers, try taking up a few rooted pieces of vinca and adding them to your composition. As summer rolls on, the vinca stems will drape themselves elegantly over the sides of the containers.

Choosing Vincas

For a groundcover that never grows more than 5 inches high, choose petite *V. minor*. With glossy green leaves only 1 inch long, the plants always look good mingling with a natural mulch of leaves. 'Ralph Shugert' and a few other cultivars have leaves margined with white. Extremely petite 'Alba' bears white flowers rather than pink ones.

V. major is a taller, rangier plant, growing to 14 inches and appearing almost shrubby at times. It is fine for wild areas that get partial shade, but the most common use of these plants is to plug stems of the white variegated strain into containers in the spring. The variegated form also makes a nice groundcover in beds created to mask the bases of trees.

Variegated Vinca major *is often used in containers and window boxes, or you can grow it as a groundcover beneath large trees.*

Growing Vincas

Set out container-grown plants or well-rooted cuttings in spring, and keep the planted area constantly moist until new growth appears. Pull weeds by hand, and water as needed to keep the area from drying out. Once established, a stand of vinca can tolerate drought, and there is no need to remove pine needles or small leaves that fall on the foliage in autumn. However, should very large leaves form a mat over your vinca, gather them up and use them as mulch elsewhere.

V. major can look tattered at times, and should be trimmed back to within 4 inches of the ground to make way for new growth. To keep variegated *V. major* from year to year to use in containers, bring some pots into a cold garage in the fall, water sparingly through winter, and prune and repot the plants first thing in spring.

Vinca minor *eagerly threads itself among rocks, whether the site is a stone wall or a small stream. In any woodland setting, this groundcover can be grown with ease.*

Zinnia

Annual Flower
Zinnia species and hybrids

A mass planting of 'Bouquet' zinnias in mixed colors becomes a festive hedge, blooming continuously despite high heat and humidity.

The cheery blooms of zinnias are warm-weather staples in the landscape. Because they grow so quickly, compact selections are great for filling in gaps in the flower bed where perennials have yet to take over. Other varieties sport huge blooms atop long, sturdy stems and make beautiful cut flowers. Zinnias are tremendously heat- and drought-tolerant, but regular watering and well-drained, fertile soil are needed to help them reach their blooming potential.

Choosing Zinnias

For large flowers suitable for cutting, grow *Z. elegans* varieties. The 'Benary' (formerly 'Blue Point') series is an especially gorgeous line of jewel-toned, densely petaled, 6-inch-wide blooms. Some *Z. elegans* varieties can reach up to 4 feet tall, so plant them in the back of the flower bed. By continually cutting flowers to bring indoors, you will encourage these types to produce more.

For edging the flower bed and filling in gaps, select narrow-leaf zinnias (*Z. angustifolia* or *Z. linearis*). Their flowers are generally smaller, ringed with a row of single petals, and come in orange, white, yellow or pinkish red. Narrow-leaf zinnias bloom almost nonstop and there's no need to pick off dead flowers. Look for zinnias with 'Star', 'Pinwheel' or 'Profusion' in their name at the nursery to identify reliable narrow-leaf varieties.

For an interesting twist on the zinnia theme, there's Mexican zinnias (*Z. Haageana*), which grow about 2 feet tall with multicolored blooms in red, mahogany, gold, purple, chocolate and cream. Peruvian zinnias (*Z. peruviana*) reach a little over 2 feet tall and are topped with a profusion of single gold, orange or rusty red flowers with button-like centers.

Growing Zinnias

Most of the cutting-type zinnias have large seeds and are fairly easy to start by planting ¼ inch deep in warm soil after all danger of frost has passed. In colder climates, you may want to try starting some inside about 3 weeks before planting out to get a jump on the bloom season. Many of the other zinnias mentioned above have smaller seeds, and it's usually easier to start with transplants purchased at a nursery.

Taller types of zinnias may need staking depending on where you have planted them. Allow some of the seeds from a few dried flowers to fall where they may, and enjoy a return crop of zinnias next year. These volunteers can also be dug and planted to another spot.

Older plants of large-flowered zinnia are often plagued by powdery mildew, which weakens the plants. Where this disease is prevalent, make a second sowing in midsummer to replace the first crop. Young zinnias are always more mildew resistant than old ones.

Long-stemmed 'Red Sun' zinnias are perfect for cutting. Here they meet their ideal match in blue mealycup sage.

Rustic Mexican zinnias feature rich mahogany tones on petals that are typically edged with yellow. They are fine bed partners for yellow marigolds or yellow plume celosia.

CHAPTER 7

Better Gardens You Can Eat

Growing good things to eat can be delicious, nutritious, easy and fun.

Imagine biting into a sun-warmed ripe tomato, or rubbing sprigs of rosemary between your hands to release their wonderful scent. One bite or sniff and you know exactly why home-grown vegetables, fruits and herbs are worth the trouble of growing them. They taste great, and because you can pick them at their peak of ripeness, they are always at their nutritional best. There's nothing fresher, and nutritional content of many foods wanes significantly when they cross the country on a truck or sit on the supermarket shelf.

And perhaps you can grow what you can't buy. Herbs and gourmet salad greens are a cinch to grow, but they can be hard (and high priced) to find in stores. Plus, when you know how your vegetables and fruits are grown, you can avoid harmful chemicals. Need any more reasons to grow your own edibles? The clincher is that nothing beats the fresh air, sunshine and exercise that getting out in the garden provides.

What to Grow

Lettuce is always a winning crop in a home garden. Leaf lettuces such as 'Oak Leaf' become crisp and sweet when they mature in cool weather.

When deciding what edibles to grow, be choosy and keep it simple. The more uncomplicated your plan, the less maintenance will be involved and the happier you will be with the results. The most important thing is to grow vegetables, fruits or herbs that you enjoy eating. That way, you'll stay interested in the project through the entire growing season as you anticipate the delicious reward.

Here are some other questions to ask yourself as you choose what to grow. What is expensive to purchase at the market? What is hard to find? What is easy to find, but not of very good quality? The answers to those questions will guide your decisions. For instance, if all of your neighbors grow zucchini and are leaving bags full of zukes on your doorstep, then maybe zucchini shouldn't be tops on your list of things to plant.

Grocery List Gardening

If you plan your edible garden according to the growable items that turn up time and time again on your grocery list, your collection of vegetables and herbs will save you both time and money. Having things growing in your yard that you eat often makes sense in many ways. When you can go outside and pluck a few parsley stems when you need them, you throw out far fewer half-used bunches, and your parsley is fresher and prettier too. Also, our eating habits are just that, in that we tend to eat the same things over and over. So if your family regularly eats cucumbers or tomatoes or green onions, you know the ones you grow will be appreciated, with little if any heartbreaking waste.

If your partner is the grocery shopper at your house, ask them to pass on their old lists for a few weeks. Old grocery lists are a gold mine of information on excellent edibles for your garden.

Like many other members of the squash family, cucumber vines tend to produce bumper crops all at once, so you will probably want to keep plantings small.

Wondering Why?

Growing Organic

Growing your own edibles organically is the perfect way to get pure, clean food not contaminated with chemicals. In a home garden, it just makes sense. You don't have to handle the toxic stuff and you don't have to eat produce laced with it. Besides, home gardens are naturally low-pest zones because of the diversity of plants grown there. In a mixed-up garden, pests are much less of a problem than they are in huge fields where only a single crop is grown. And if pests do become a nuisance, there are safe, earth-friendly alternatives to chemicals: insecticidal soap, baking soda, oil sprays and others.

All members of the cabbage family are outstanding vegetables to grow in climates where summers are cool. These include broccoli, cabbage, cauliflower and kohlrabi.

Plantings of sweet corn need to be large because there must be plenty of plants to share pollen.

Climate and Quality

Your climate will influence the quality of the vegetables you grow, because most vegetables prefer either cool, warm or hot weather. You can work with these preferences by making use of seasonal weather changes, but you can push things only so far. Gardeners in cool climates will always have great luck with cool-natured vegetables such as lettuce and cabbage, while gardeners in hot climates often have pepper crops that zoom off the charts. Moderate climes often are home to the finest sweet corn and snap beans.

The beauty of well-grown vegetables is more than skin deep. When vegetables are so well matched to the climate and soil that they grow with ease, they often have slightly higher nutritional value too. In other words, happy vegetables in your garden are extra-healthy vegetables on your plate.

Getting into Varieties

Want more reasons to grow some of your own vegetables? If you spend a little time in the pages of seed catalogs (many of which are now on the Web), you'll quickly learn that there are dozens of variations in lettuce, and the same goes for squash, peppers, tomatoes and popular herbs like basil and mint. Some of the most remarkable varieties are never sold in grocery stores! So if you want to taste a yellow zucchini, roast some multicolored sweet corn or float a sprig of crinkled lemon mint in your tea, you may have to grow them yourself.

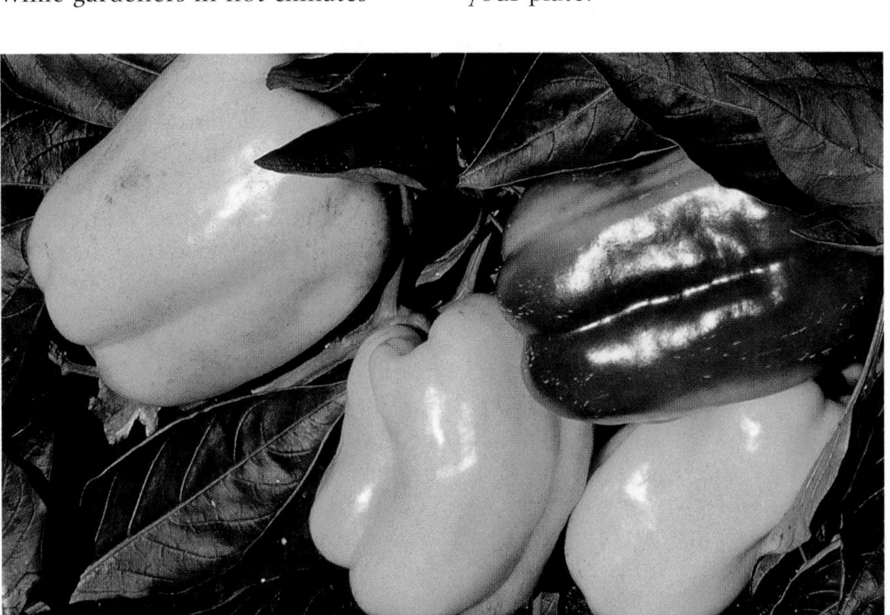

Sweet bell peppers need a long, warm season to ripen from green to their mature colors, which may be red, yellow or orange.

Irish potatoes are really from South America, where they are found in numerous colors and forms. Special seed potato companies make rare varieties available to gardeners.

Intensive Planting

In raised beds where every square inch is planted, you can grow huge amounts of produce in only a little space. Raised beds often warm up quickly in the spring too.

Time-Saving Tip: Pre-Sprout Seed

Get a jump of several days on the growing season by sprouting seeds before you plant them. This works with peas, beans, corn or other veggies with seeds large enough to handle easily. Wrap seeds in a paper towel, insert the towel in a plastic bag and then add some water to dampen the towel. Keep the bag in a warm place for 24 to 48 hours or until you see the seeds swell and send out their first pale rootlet. Then plant the pre-sprouted seed at its normal planting depth.

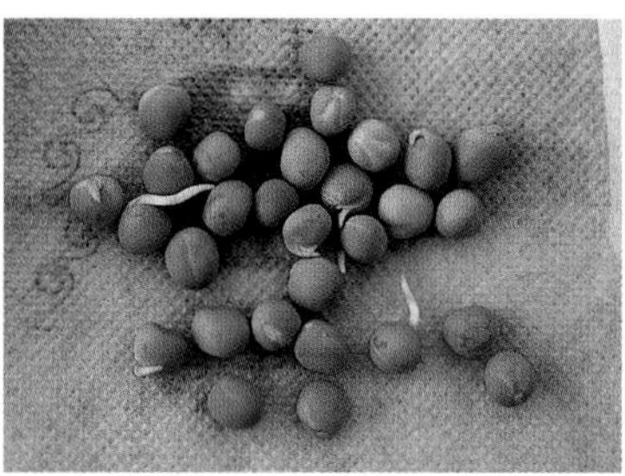

After soaking up water from damp paper towels for 2 days, these snow pea seeds are in perfect condition for planting.

To get the most out of your garden, it pays to learn how to space plants close together. Do away with the conventional method of planting everything in rows, and you can squeeze a lot more in much less space without compromising yield. Most important, planting intensively also saves work. As plants get larger, their leaves will just about touch, which in turn shades or crowds out any weeds that try to invade. That means less work for you in weeding the vegetable patch. Intensive planting always helps conserve soil moisture, which means less time spent watering your vegetables.

WATCH OUT!

Overproductive Vegetables

The following are so eager to produce that it's important to plant only what you can reasonably eat:

Zucchini
Green beans
Cucumbers
Cherry tomatoes
Cabbage
Hot peppers

Zucchini is notorious for producing too well, but you can also find yourself buried in hot peppers or cherry tomatoes if you set out too many plants.

Getting Started

Intensive planting works best if you use beds instead of a row system in your garden. See pages 152-155 for ideas on building beds. Build beds just wide enough so that you can reach across them without stepping on them. By confining foot traffic to paths around the beds, you eliminate the wasted space between conventional rows that often becomes a haven for weeds. The result is bigger yields per square foot of garden space.

If you intend to mulch your crop with something like straw, it is best to spread mulch over the bed *before* you plant, because plants that are intensively planted will be spaced so tightly that it will be hard to cover the ground with mulch later on. After you mulch, use your hands to open a small window in the mulch where you want to plant, drop a seed or plant in the ground, and snug the mulch back over the area.

Be Happy with Your Hoe

Weeding doesn't have to be a chore if you have a good, sharp hoe. There are many designs on the market, many of which do a better job than the standard old hoe. For example, there is the stirrup or "oscillating" hoe, which is actually shaped like the stirrup on a saddle. This type of hoe cuts through tough weeds both on the push and pull motion, so hoeing is fast and efficient. A collinear hoe has a long thin blade, making it easy to weed between plants spaced very close together.

To be happy with your hoe, first try it out in the store. If it feels heavy or awkward, you are not likely to use it in the garden. When using your hoe, hold it as you would a broom (not a push broom) with your thumbs up, and move it in a sweeping motion, as if you were sweeping the floor. The edge of the hoe should skim just below the soil surface. This slices weeds off with a minimum of effort and does not churn up more weed seed. For easy hoeing, work when the soil is dry and keep the edge of your hoe sharp. In less than a minute, you can use a small metal file to restore a sharp edge to your hoe.

When shopping for hoes, try them out first. By handling a hoe before you buy, you will know it is right for your height and build, and the way you move.

Prime Planting Pattern

Arrange seeds or plants in a diagonally offset spacing pattern with all seeds or plants the same distance from each other in all directions. You may see on the back of a packet of seed the recommended spacing for plants within the row and between the rows. Disregard that information. Instead, see the box "Best Vegetables for Intensive Planting" (at right) for the spacings for some common vegetables when using this technique.

If you are new to intensive planting, you may wish to make a small template out of a triangular piece of cardboard to help get the spacing just right. The length of each side should be the same—the distance you wish to have between plants. Lay the template on the soil, and plant a seed or plant at each corner of the triangle. Reposition the triangle, with one corner touching what you have just planted, and plant two more seeds or plants at the other two corners. Continue to move the triangle and plant your bed. As you go, you will get the hang of it and be better able to judge the distance by eye.

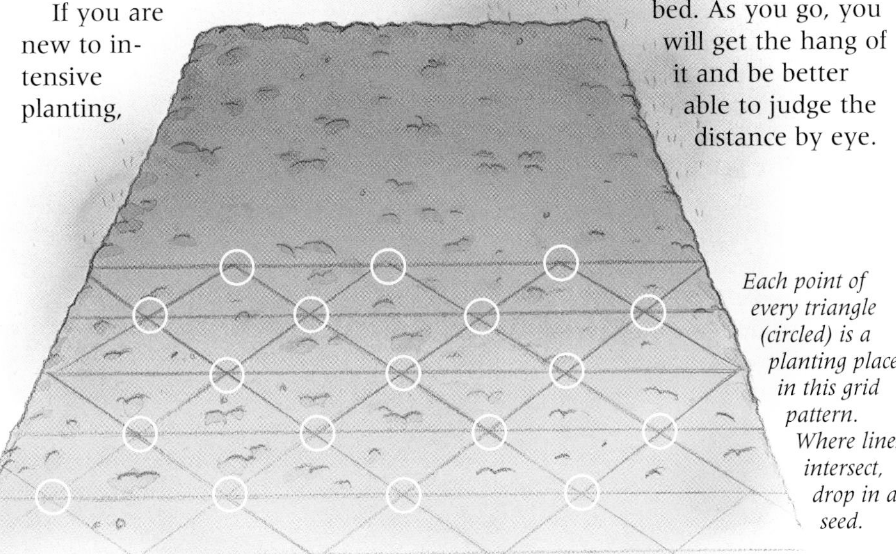

Each point of every triangle (circled) is a planting place in this grid pattern. Where lines intersect, drop in a seed.

Best Vegetables for Intensive Planting

Vegetable	Inches Between Plants
Beets	4
Broccoli	15
Cabbage	15
Carrots	3
Cauliflower	15
Eggplant	18
Kale	15
Leeks	6
Lettuce, head	12
Onions	4
Peppers	12
Spinach	6
Tomatoes	24

Cabbage leaves need space to spread.

Eggplant grows both tall and wide.

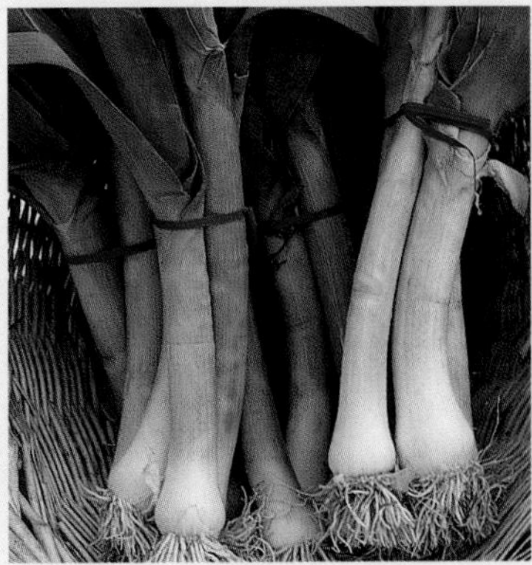

Onions that are harvested young, such as scallions, can be grown only 2 inches apart. But those that you want to mature into fat bulbs need at least 4 inches between plants.

Raised Beds

Neat and compact, raised beds save space and strain on your back. You can fill them with vegetables, flowers, herbs or (best of all) a little bit of everything!

Frame-Less Beds

Don't have time to frame up a raised bed? Or maybe you want to change the shape, size or position of a raised bed from year to year. Then try this fast, easy technique to build a raised bed. Rake soil from what will be the pathway around the raised bed right into the spot for the raised bed. Keep raking until you have a mound of soil several inches high. Level the mound out with a rake, and get planting. For at least one season, the bed will stay intact without a structural border. You can use the exposed sides of the bed for planting too. Be creative and allow a few trailing flowers such as nasturtiums to cascade down the sides and cover the soil.

Raised beds provide a landscape-enhancing package as well as ideal conditions for growing good things to eat. This type of bed is basically a pile of soil that is several inches higher than the surrounding ground, hence its name.

Raised beds allow water to drain quickly, which is critical if you have long rainy seasons or heavy clay soil. They also warm up faster in spring, which allows you to plant sooner. Foot traffic is confined to paths around the beds, so the soil remains loose and easy to work. Loose soil also enables roots to grow deep so that plants can better withstand drought. And, with raised beds filled with nearly perfect soil, you can include more plants in the bed for higher yields from a garden that's almost too pretty to eat.

Frame Basics

Typically, raised beds are built by filling a frame with a mix of garden soil and good quality compost. Frames help to contain the soil and provide a finished look in the garden. On these pages you will discover how to build an economical frame out of wood or plastic lumber. Then see pages 154-155 to find out how to build a raised bed using concrete blocks. For a method to build raised beds without a frame, see "Frame-Less Beds," above right.

When planning raised beds, keep the size of beds relevant to the vegetables you plan to grow. For instance, a 4- x 6-foot bed will make a nice salad patch, but is too small for tomatoes and sunflowers or squash.

Build the bed with ease of use in mind. Make its width about arm's length so you can easily tend the garden by reaching across it, and don't make it so long that you have a hike just to push a wheelbarrow or carry tools around it. Sketch your ideas on paper first, and then go out and measure the area where you plan to put your bed.

Pole beans rise from a raised bed that's been planted with French marigolds, which help control nematodes, a serious soil-borne pest in warm climates.

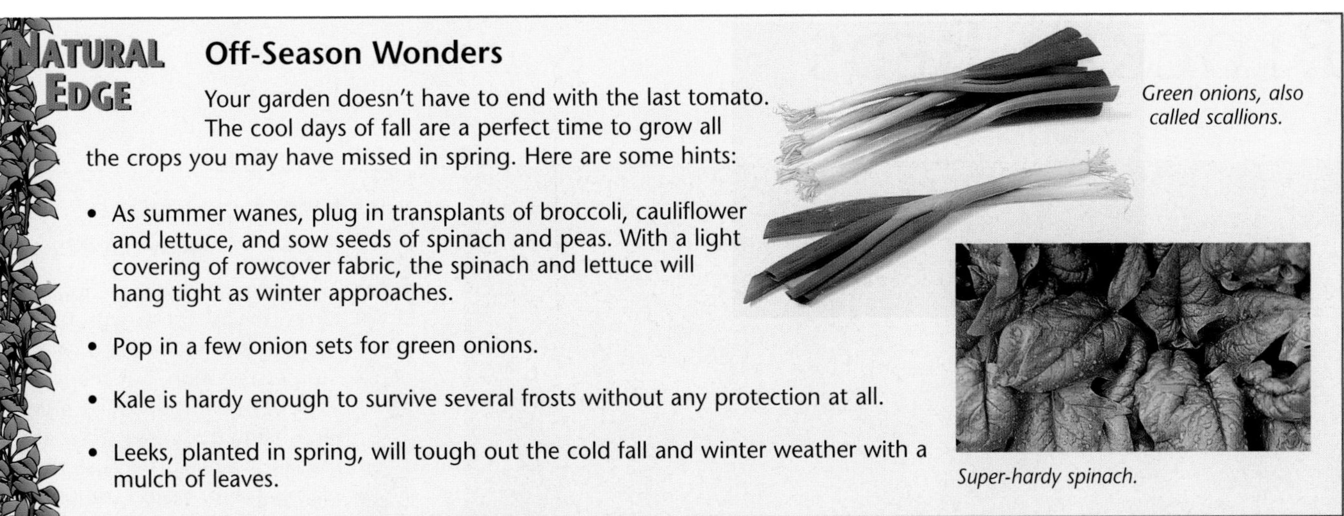

NATURAL EDGE

Off-Season Wonders

Your garden doesn't have to end with the last tomato. The cool days of fall are a perfect time to grow all the crops you may have missed in spring. Here are some hints:

- As summer wanes, plug in transplants of broccoli, cauliflower and lettuce, and sow seeds of spinach and peas. With a light covering of rowcover fabric, the spinach and lettuce will hang tight as winter approaches.
- Pop in a few onion sets for green onions.
- Kale is hardy enough to survive several frosts without any protection at all.
- Leeks, planted in spring, will tough out the cold fall and winter weather with a mulch of leaves.

Green onions, also called scallions.

Super-hardy spinach.

Building the Frame

Use this simple technique to build a frame made of wood or of recycled plastic lumber. Use 2x4 or 2x8 lumber, depending on how deep you would like your raised bed. You may also want to drive stakes into the ground along the bed's exterior perimeter to support the sides against the pressure of the soil. Additionally, if burrowing critters are a problem in your area, it's wise to line the frame of your bed with wire mesh that extends 6 inches into the soil. This usually prevents mice, moles and other critters from tunneling into the bed from the bottom.

Step 1

Cut lumber to the desired lengths. Lay the pieces of lumber on their edges on a flat, level surface in the outline of the bed.

Step 2

Drill pilot holes in each end and screw ends together with wood screws. Reinforce corners by screwing L-brackets to the inside of each corner.

Step 3

Position your bed where you want it. Fill with a mix of soil and compost. Water thoroughly to settle the soil. When the soil has dried, begin planting in the new bed.

WONDERING WHY?

CCA Wood

Wood that is treated with CCA (chromated copper arsenate) may leach chemicals into soil. This is a concern where vegetables and herbs are grown, because you may eventually eat those chemicals. There are many alternatives to pressure-treated lumber to frame raised beds for edibles. Naturally rot-resistant cedar, redwood or locust—or manufactured materials such as recycled plastic lumber or concrete blocks—are all good choices. Also avoid using railroad ties or old telephone poles to build beds planted with edibles, because these materials are preserved with toxic creosote.

Wood frames for raised beds can be any size or shape, though they work best when they are at least 4 inches deep and no more than 4 feet across.

Blocked Beds

In this raised-bed garden built to be beautiful, brick is combined with 6x6 lumber to form raised beds filled with flowers, vegetables and herbs.

Framing a raised bed in concrete blocks offers a lasting option for creating an ideal growing spot. You will never have to replace the frame due to rotting. Concrete blocks are strong enough to withstand the pressure of the soil within the bed, so you can build beds a little deeper than is practical with boards. Because of their weight and permanence, beds built of blocks also play an important role in your landscape's design, dividing areas of use in a precise fashion. Particularly useful on slopes, a series of concrete-framed raised beds can also be used to make a terraced garden in otherwise unusable space.

Block Basics

The following technique will work for concrete blocks or for the more decorative concrete wallstones that are widely available at home improvement stores.

Concrete blocks are made from a stiff concrete mix. They are heavy, but the hollow cores in each block make them easier to grip and place, and help to insulate the soil in the raised bed. Enlist some help when handling concrete blocks—a typical concrete block is roughly 8 x 8 x 16 inches and weighs about 45 pounds. You can plant in the topmost holes in the blocks of your raised bed, or use stone or concrete capstones to close them off. In cold climates, be sure to select "N-grade" blocks for places where a wall will be exposed to freezing and thawing.

Concrete blocks stabilize a tiered garden built on a slight slope. The rows of sturdy concrete blocks double as a walking surface.

Wallstones are solid blocks made from durable concrete. The soft natural colors mimic stone. These blocks have flat edges except for a curved, textured front, making it very easy to position the blocks to form curved walls. Generally, 3 nursery wallstones equal 1 square foot. Because nursery wallstones do not have holes, the top row of blocks has a smooth, finished appearance and makes a nice spot to perch as you tend your raised bed.

Natural Edge

Floating Rowcovers

Floating rowcovers are made from special lightweight fabric that allows light and water to pass through, but keeps out pests and provides a little insulation from cold. They are called "floating" because the fabric simply lies on top of a crop without hurting it (although you can stretch the fabric over small hoops for a tidy appearance). Floating rowcovers are fantastic to extend the growing season—they can be used to protect spring transplants or late-fall crops from frost. Anchor the edges of rowcover fabric with soil, rocks, bricks or pieces of wood. Rowcover is sold in rolls or flat pieces, and can be purchased at well-stocked garden centers or from mail-order or online companies.

As sure-fire protection from pests, a lightweight fabric rowcover is held aloft over kohlrabi seedlings by short pieces of plastic pipe shoved into the ground.

Veggie-Flower Combos

Raised beds provide the perfect opportunity for an ornamental display of vegetables and flowers. Here are a few perfect vegetable and flower combos. Some pairs protect each other from pests, while others just look great together.

- Marigolds and eggplant
- Nasturtiums and tomatoes
- Celosia and chard
- Tansy and potatoes
- Alyssum and broccoli

Nasturtiums can be grown around the base of tomato plants, or you can drop seeds into the ground between plants arranged in rows.

Building the Frame

This particular frame for a raised bed will be made without mortar. The technique is known as "dry wall." A bed is easy and quick to construct without mortar, and the bed frame can be disassembled and moved at a later date if desired. Do not build a dry wall any taller than 2 feet, because increasing the height also increases its propensity to bulge or topple.

Step 1

Dig a shallow trench slightly wider than the width of the blocks (or wallstones) around the perimeter of the raised bed.

Step 2

Line the trench with a layer of gravel to make a stable base for the frame.

Step 3

Begin laying the first course of blocks along the trench.

Step 4

Lay the second course of blocks on top of the first. Stagger the blocks so that a block in the second course spans a joint between two blocks in the first course. That way, joints between blocks will never line up across the courses, and the frame will be much stronger.

Step 5

Continue to lay successive courses of blocks until you reach your desired bed depth.

Step 6

If using concrete blocks, drive several lengths of half-inch iron stakes (called rebar stakes) down through the wall and into the soil where the holes through the blocks line up. This will give the frame added resistance against the pressure of the soil, and against freezing and thawing.

The stability of a concrete block wall depends on its foundation. Use a board-mounted level to make sure the gravel-lined trench is as level as possible.

WATCH OUT!

Perennial Weeds

Be especially vigilant about perennial weeds in permanent raised beds. They can get a foothold because raised beds are generally not tilled or otherwise disturbed every season. Before you know it, you've got an invasion on your hands. Perennial weeds spread not only by seeds, but also by creeping underground roots and rhizomes. Be on the lookout for Canada thistle, kudzu, poison ivy, Bermuda grass, quackgrass, field bindweed and yellow nutsedge. When you find one of these, hack off all the above ground parts of the weed and dig up as much of the roots as you can. Wear gloves and be extra careful in handling poison ivy.

Pry deep-rooted dandelions out of beds or they will quickly shed seeds throughout your lawn and garden.

Sow a Salad Garden

Explore the endless variations in the color and texture of lettuce leaves in your garden. Front to back, here are butterhead, crisphead, red oak leaf and green oak leaf types.

Imagine the crunch of crispy lettuce and cucumbers, the tang of a fresh tomato, the bite of a green onion. Hungry yet? If you are, then you know that a salad of garden-fresh vegetables that you have grown yourself is beyond comparison.

You do not have to have a huge space or a lot of time to reap satisfying salad rewards. A single 3 x 6-foot bed can keep you in salad fixins for months. By using high-yielding vegetables and intensive planting techniques, you can harvest almost 50 pounds of produce from such small space! Here's how.

Build a Bed

Use one of the techniques suggested on the previous pages to construct a 3 x 6-foot raised bed. A raised bed is perfect for a salad garden because it will provide the optimum growing conditions necessary for an intensively planted little patch.

Time-Saving Tip

Cut and Come Again

A quick and easy way to grow salad greens is the "cut and come again" style in which lettuce and other salad greens are sown thickly, and then harvested by the handful when they are baby greens, by shearing them with scissors. This technique works great with lettuce and mesclun, which is simply a mix of different types of lettuces and greens all sown together in one patch. Start snipping leaves as soon as they reach 4 to 5 inches tall, or about 30 days after seeding. Grab a clump of leaves in one hand, and cut them off about an inch above the soil level with the other hand. That inch of stubble will regrow for another 3 to 4 harvests, or as long as cool weather lasts.

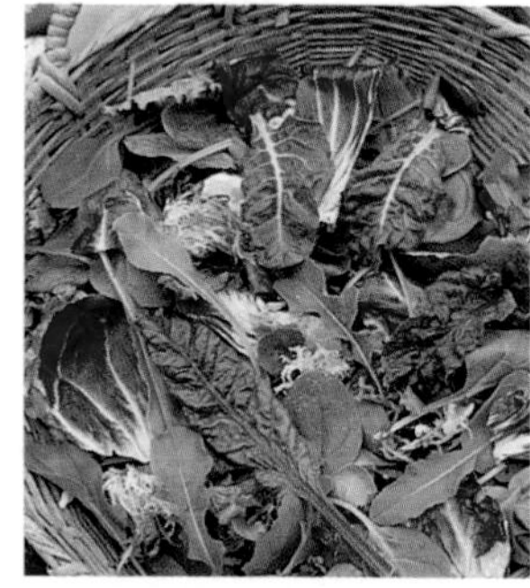

Salad green mixtures called mesclun are expensive to buy yet easy to grow. Just snip, rinse and chill, then mesclun is ready for the table.

Flowers You Can Eat

Toss them in salads or use them as garnishes. These flowers taste as good as they look.

Nasturtiums	Chives
Squash blossoms	Borage
Pansies	Lavender

Lavender.

Spring lettuce is usually ready before tomatoes ripen, but you can have these two vegetables together by planting lettuce again when nights cool in late summer.

NATURAL EDGE

Cherry Tomatoes

The essence of summer in a bite-size package, cherry tomatoes are much closer to their "wild" relatives than their larger, meatier cousins. So they don't need pampering, and they are top choices for a less-work garden. First, forget staking, trellising or tying this baby to a pole. It's like roping the wind, and nothing will frustrate you more than a cherry tomato that's been fenced in and is trying desperately to break out. Instead, position cherry tomato plants at the edge of the garden where they can be allowed free rein. Cherry tomatoes make an attractive cascading border for the garden, or even a fun barrel planting. Don't worry when overripe fruits fall to the ground. Let them rot there, and you will never have to buy a cherry tomato plant again because hundreds of volunteer plants will sprout up next year and every year thereafter. Weed out the seedlings you don't want, and allow a few keepers to grow.

Sprightly cherry tomatoes come in a range of sizes and colors, from tiny red or yellow 'currant' varieties to meatier small globes such as red 'Sweet Chelsea'.

You can replace fast-growing radishes and greens with cucumbers, chard or heat-loving peppers. Divide your bed into sections to make replanting easy.

Pick Your Plants

Let your palate be your guide in choosing what you would like to grow in your salad garden. Divide your bed into 6 squares of the same size (approximately 18 x 24 inches each). In each square, plug in a different salad veggie. The following are some suggestions for crops to start in spring, as well as ideas for what to plant in its space when it is finished. You may also want to plant edible flowers (page 156) around the perimeter of the salad patch for pretty, and tasty, garnishes.

- Onions, followed by kale
- Sweet bell pepper
- Tomato, followed by spinach
- Radishes, followed by cucumbers, then lettuce or onions
- Spinach, followed by peppers
- Carrots
- Lettuce, followed by beets
- Lettuce, followed by chard

Ease Through the Seasons

To push cool-loving salad crops like lettuce and spinach into summer, shield them with some shade cloth. Available at most garden centers, the fabric covering allows just enough light to pass through to promote healthy growth, while filtering out the sun's strongest rays. You may also consider planting a summer salad garden in a lightly shaded area, or let some lettuces grow in the shade of taller plants such as tomatoes.

Keep It Working

By planting a salad garden in a compact area, it will be easy to tend. Keep your crops well watered to promote robust growth. Weeding should be a snap. Because plants are spaced so closely, weeds will have a hard time getting a foothold. Any that do sprout will be easy to see and remove. Harvest crops as soon as they are ready, and as often as possible. This will encourage the vegetables to produce more. As soon as one vegetable is finished, remove it and get the next crop in the ground. By never letting the bed go idle, you can reap big yields from such a small space.

When to Plant

Vegetable	Planting Time
Beets	Spring, midsummer
Carrots	Spring
Chard	Spring, midsummer
Cucumbers	Late spring
Kale	Midsummer
Lettuce	Spring, midsummer, late summer
Onions	Spring, late summer
Peppers	Late spring
Radishes	Spring
Spinach	Spring, midsummer
Tomatoes	Late spring

Carrots.

Radishes.

A Salsa Garden

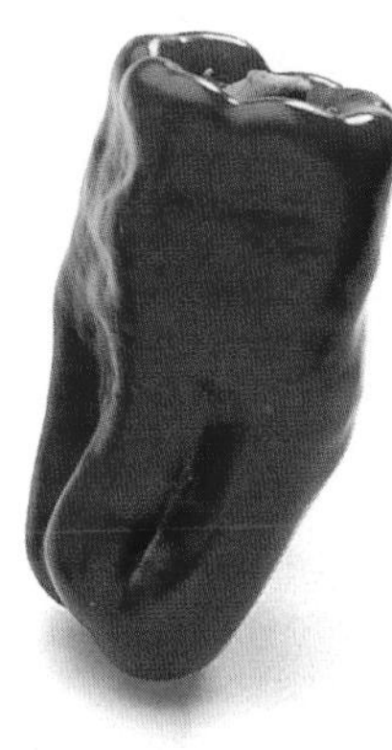

Peppers give salsa both color and flavor. Most hot peppers are green, but sweet peppers in pretty colors are great to use in salsas that include fresh fruit.

Fill a small garden bed with flavor and send your tastebuds on a culinary tour south of the border by growing the essential ingredients for salsa! In a space no bigger than 2 x 5 feet, you can grow all the peppers, tomatoes, onions, tomatillos and cilantro that you'll need to make loads of salsa for you and your friends. And you will probably have enough produce left over for other culinary adventures as well.

The fundamentals for salsa making are fairly basic. At a minimum, you'll only need one plant each of peppers, tomatoes and tomatillos. You'll also need several onions and a few cilantro plants.

Peppers

Anything goes when it comes to peppers suitable for salsa. For most aficionados, the hotter, the better! Jalapeño peppers are a standard for salsa, with their excellent not-too-hot spicy flavor. If you prefer, there are even jalapeño varieties available that are barely hot, so you can enjoy their flavor without as much of the bite. Moving up into more fiery peppers, there are 2-inch-long, fleshy serrano peppers, and heart-shaped, 3- to 5-inch-long ancho peppers. Then there's the habanero—one of the hottest peppers you can grow. If hot isn't your thing, you can grow a bell pepper or two for adding succulent sweetness to a tame salsa. Plant one pepper plant per square foot of garden bed.

Habanero peppers are easy to grow yet too hot for most people to eat. Be sure to wear gloves when handling hot peppers like these.

Onions

The easiest way to grow the onions necessary for great salsa is to plunk a few onion sets (little baby onion bulbs) in the ground in spring. Take your pick from white, yellow or red—any of them will work well. Plant about 16 sets per square foot to get good-sized bulbs.

When onion tops fall over, they are ready to pull. To cure, lay them out to dry for a week or more. But you can eat uncured onions, which are often extra sweet and juicy.

Wondering Why?

Peppers Heat Up in Hot Weather

A compound called capsaicin gives hot peppers their fire. And when it gets hotter outside, your hot peppers get hotter inside. Why? Because stress on the plant makes them turn up the heat. Stress can come in many forms—too little water, not enough nutrients—but the stress most likely to make peppers more fiery is nighttime temperatures. Hot nights stress plants the most and make for hotter peppers. That explains why a pepper grown in one region can be so much hotter than the same variety grown during the same season in a cooler climate.

Anaheim peppers are packed with flavor but usually have very little heat. They make a rich, full-flavored salsa.

Tomatoes

If you only plan on growing one tomato plant, then choose one that will not only make delicious salsa but will also provide great fruits for slicing and otherwise enjoying. That means picking a beefsteak-type tomato with large, juicy, flavorful fruits. If you have the room to grow two tomato plants in your salsa garden, then add an egg-shaped paste tomato. The smaller, meatier fruits will lend a thicker consistency to your condiment endeavors. If you are staking or caging your tomato plant, then place one plant per square foot.

You can use the same tomatoes for salsa that you use for salads and sandwiches. Peel, chop, and you're ready to make salsa.

Tomatillos

These sweet-tart fruits are the secret of the green version of salsa. The tomatillo is actually a relative of the tomato, and requires the same kind of care. In fact, tomatillo means "little tomato." The glossy, firm fruits are clothed in a papery husk. Pick when the husks have just turned from green to buff, but while the fruits are still green. Give this plant at least 2 square feet (or more) to ramble; expect a few volunteers to spring up next year.

Tomatillo plants are tall and rangy, and they produce huge crops in warm summer weather. They can also reseed wildly, so gather up fallen fruits when you spot them.

Cilantro

Salsa gets its pungently full flavor from the leaves of this herb. Cilantro is very easy to grow from seed, and likes cool weather. It will bloom and make seed in no time flat (its seeds are actually the well-known spice, coriander), so sow successive plantings to get enough leaves for all your salsa ventures.

Cilantro is sometimes called Mexican parsley, and it has a distinctive flavor and aroma. It grows best in the cool weather of spring and fall.

Care and Harvest

Keep your plants well watered through summer so they keep pumping out the ingredients for the hot stuff. Harvest any ripe produce regularly so the plants continue to produce. If you have staked the tomato plant, continue to tie it to the stake as it grows. Pull onions as needed before their tops brown. When their tops brown, pull all of them and allow them to dry in a cool, dry place for several days before storing them.

TIME-SAVING TIP

Cardboard Mulch

Instead of carting your old cardboard boxes to the recycling center, recycle them at home by using them as mulch. Cardboard makes a great weed barrier yet still allows moisture to get through to the soil. Don't worry—it eventually breaks down. The cardboard mulching technique is very useful if you have a spot that you'd like to turn into a garden. Layer some cardboard (it will even kill grass!), and pile organic materials such as grass clippings or leaves on top. If you are not planting right away, consider piling manure over the cardboard for a fertility boost. Hose the whole works down to keep the cardboard from blowing away. The following year, poke holes through the crumbly layers and plant away.

The Essential Herb Patch

Herbs are often petite plants, so you can dress up your bed with small flowers such as lobelia or dianthus. The little daisies here are chamomile, used to make tea.

Many herbs thrive with little care and take up small spaces in the garden. In return, they provide fresh flavors and scents that are beyond compare. If you were to buy some of these herbs at the supermarket, you would spend a lot and would probably get limp, flavorless leaves compared to what you can grow yourself. In addition, having fresh herbs within easy reach will encourage you to cook more creatively and healthfully as you substitute their interesting flavors for salt or butter. Here are 12 easy-to-grow herbs no gardening cook should be without. On the following pages, you'll see how to plant and care for a small bed designed specifically for these herbs.

A Dozen Indispensable Herbs

Basil (*Ocimum basilicum*)

Basil is essential to Italian, French and Thai cooking. It is a frost-sensitive annual, so start seed indoors 6 weeks before your last frost date, or purchase seedlings. Pinch the flower buds from the plants to encourage them to keep producing leaves instead of flowers.

Basil.

Chervil (*Anthriscus cerefolium*)

The flavor of chervil is a cross between parsley and licorice, and it's essential to French cooking. Chervil is an annual or biennial depending on where you live, so sow seed of it in early spring. Plants will grow about 2 feet tall.

Chervil.

Chives (*Allium schoenoprasum*)

The mild onion flavor of chives can be used in many dishes, and the lavender flowers can be added to salads for both color and flavor. Chives are perennial, hardy from Zones 3 to 9. Divide the clump every two to three years to rejuvenate it. Plants reach about 12 inches tall, and will self-sow if you do not snip off the flowers.

Cilantro (*Coriandrum sativum*)

The pungent leaves of cilantro are essential in Mexican, Indian and Asian cooking. The seeds of this plant are known as coriander, a citrus-flavored spice for baking or flavoring sauces and marinades. Sow this annual outdoors in spring and fall. Plants will reach 3 feet tall in bloom.

Sample Before You Buy

As you shop for plants for your herb patch, it pays to be picky. Especially where culinary herbs are concerned, you want to know if the flavor of the herb is too strong, nonexistent or just right. Some herbs have been bred for looks, and sometimes their flavor is lacking. So before you buy, pinch a leaf or two from the plant in question and crush between your fingers. Smell the crushed leaves, and taste them if it is something you plan on eating or using in cooking.

Dill.

Dill (*Anethum graveolens*)

The fresh leaves are fantastic with salmon and pasta, and are important to Eastern European dishes. Seeds and leaves flavor pickles. Sow seed of this annual in spring; plants will reach 3 feet tall in bloom.

Cilantro.

NATURAL EDGE

Herbs All Winter

Certain perennial herbs, such as rosemary, cannot withstand very cold winter weather, and other herbs become dormant when left outdoors. To keep them around for winter use, bring a few plants indoors to grow on a sunny windowsill. In early fall, dig them up and plant them in pots at least 6 inches across. Use well-drained potting soil, and water thoroughly. Set them in a shady spot for a few days, then move them indoors before freezing weather comes. Put the pots in a space that gets at least 5 hours of direct sun each day to ensure good growth. Allow the soil surface to dry out between waterings.

Thyme is an easy herb to grow indoors on a sunny windowsill. Frequent clipping promotes the growth of leafy new stems.

Lovage.

Lovage (*Levisticum officinale*)

This herb looks like a giant celery plant, and its leaves also taste like it. It's much easier to grow than celery, and can be substituted for it in soups, stews and salads. Lovage is hardy from Zones 3 to 8, and will prolifically self-sow if you do not cut off the flowers.

Oregano (*Origannum* species)

Oregano goes hand in hand with Italian and Greek cooking. Be sure to sample leaves of this perennial before you purchase it to make sure you are getting a flavorful variety. Plants are hardy from Zones 5 to 9 and grow about 1 foot tall.

Oregano.

Parsley.

Parsley (*Petroselinum crispum*)

Leaves of this biennial are either frilly or flat. For a steady supply of top-quality leaves, treat parsley as an annual and plant anew each year.

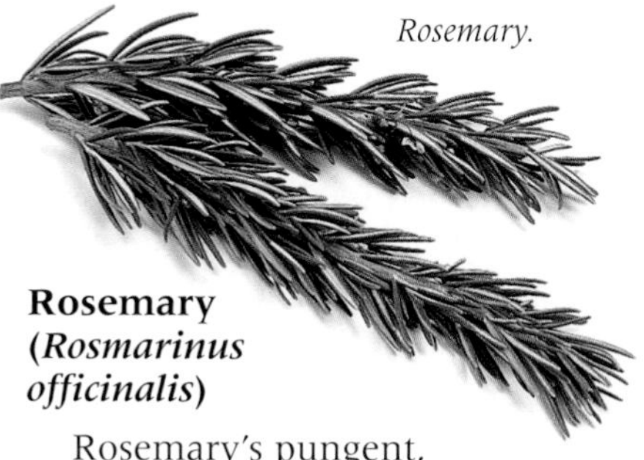

Rosemary.

Rosemary (*Rosmarinus officinalis*)

Rosemary's pungent, needle-like leaves are a classic accent to roasted meats, marinades, eggs, cheese, tomatoes and potatoes. It's a tender perennial that will need to be moved indoors for the winter north of Zone 7.

Sage.

Sage (*Salvia officinalis*)

The bold flavor of sage is the perfect accompaniment to stuffings, meat dishes and cream sauces. It's a perennial that's hardy from Zones 4 to 9 and will reach over 2 feet tall.

Tarragon (*Artemisia dracunculus*)

Tarragon's licorice-flavored leaves are essential to Hollandaise sauce, and complement chicken, salads and cream soups. This perennial herb grows 2 to 3 feet tall and is hardy from Zones 4 to 8.

Thyme (*Thymus vulgaris*)

The tiny leaves of thyme add aromatic punch to soups, stews, stuffings, vegetables, cheese, and egg dishes. It is a perennial that grows about 6 to 12 inches tall and is hardy from Zones 4 to 9.

Thyme.

A Kitchen Herb Garden

Culinary herbs including rosemary, sage, thyme and chervil share bed space with coral sage and nasturtiums. The potted rosemary can be brought indoors in winter.

Keep Mint in Bounds

Mint is a great herb, but it may actually grow too well and crowd out every other herb in the garden if you don't take precautionary measures. The easiest way to keep mint in bounds is to cut out the bottom of a large plastic pot, then dig a hole so the pot can be sunk all the way up to its rim. Fill the area inside the pot with soil, and set your mint plant within the boundary the pot provides. The pot will provide a barrier to creeping underground roots—the key to managing mint.

A half whiskey barrel holds a refreshing crop of mint. Mint strains vary in their appearance and flavor.

You can combine the herbs discussed on pages 160-161 to create a small bed that is as attractive as it is useful. Site the bed in full sun close to your house, so herbs can be harvested quickly and easily as needed. The bed design here is triangular, perfect for tucking into a corner where a walkway, patio or fence meets the house. This planting pattern can be adapted to beds of different shapes and sizes too.

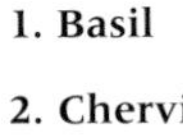

1. **Basil**
2. **Chervil**
3. **Chives**
4. **Cilantro**
5. **Dill**
6. **Lovage**
7. **Oregano**
8. **Parsley**
9. **Rosemary**
10. **Sage**
11. **Tarragon**
12. **Thyme**

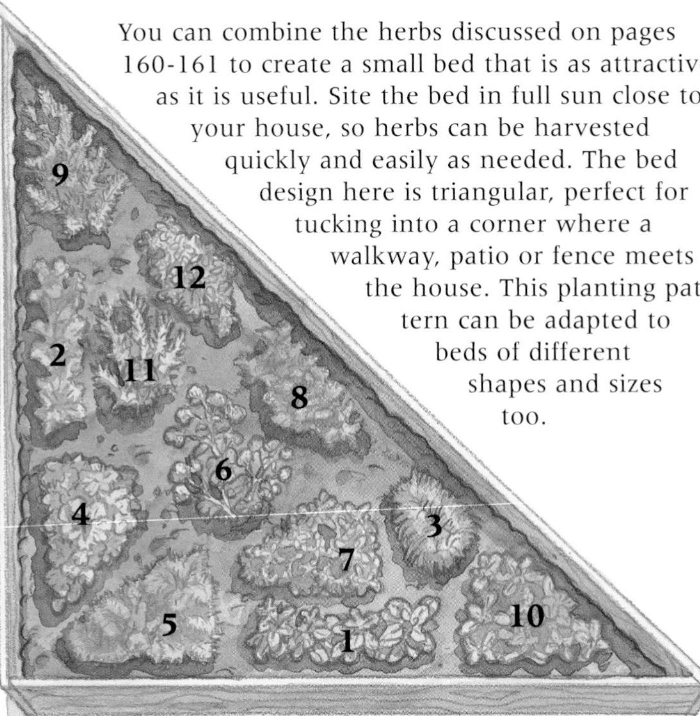

Shopping List

Buy Seeds of: Chervil, Cilantro, Dill

Buy Plants of: Basil, Chives, Lovage, Oregano, Parsley, Rosemary, Sage, Tarragon, Thyme

Planting the Patch

Begin your herb garden in winter by ordering seeds and plants from mail-order or online purveyors. They will send plants to you at the perfect time for planting in your area. If you choose to wait until spring to get started, the herbs in this design can be easily found at garden centers or nurseries.

Prepare the site for the herb garden by outlining the bed on the ground with string or a line of lime or flour. Remove any grass. Be sure the soil is dry enough to work and, using a spading fork, loosen the soil to a depth of about 8 inches. Spread a 1- to 2-inch layer of compost over the bed and dig it into the soil. Rake the soil surface smooth.

Following the planting diagram, start planting in spring. Sow seeds of dill, cilantro and chervil first. Water lightly each day until seedlings appear. Set out herb plants in spring. Wait until after your last frost to plant rosemary or basil.

All-Weather Access

Nothing beats the convenience of an herb garden in the backyard. But did you ever dash out to grab a few sprigs of thyme for that perfect chicken dish in November, only to waste time mopping up all the mud you tracked into the house from your quick jaunt to the herb patch? Consider providing all-weather access to your herb garden by making walkways that won't turn to mud!

You may want to lay permanent steppingstones or spread a thick layer of gravel in the path. Either approach will complement the informal nature of an herb garden. If you do not want to install a permanent path, or if it is too late in the year to do so, simply plop down a few wide planks to provide safe, clean footing as you harvest in less-than-perfect weather.

Caring for the Herbs

Mulch around your herbs to reduce weeding chores and keep the soil moist. Mulch will also reduce the need to water. Start harvesting herbs a month or so after planting by pinching or snipping off leaves. Seed heads of cilantro and dill are ready to harvest when they darken in color. Snip the seed heads off and put them in a paper bag to catch the seeds as they finish drying.

Annual, Perennial or Biennial?

Depending on which herbs you choose to grow, they may stick around for just one season or for several years. The life span of an herb can be discerned by whether it is called an annual, perennial or biennial. Annuals, such as basil and dill, grow and die in one season. You may need to get more seed or plants of these each year. Perennials (such as oregano) keep coming back year after year. Biennials (such as parsley) will grow leaves the first year, and then go to seed and die during the second year. Oftentimes, biennials are treated like annuals and replaced each year.

An annual, basil craves warm weather and quickly produces flowers and seeds. Pinch plants back to keep them leafy, or sow a second crop in mid-summer.

A biennial, parsley flowers and sets seed in its second year. Plant new seedlings each spring and fall to make sure you always have a fresh supply.

A perennial, oregano usually dies back to the ground in winter, though a few leaves near the crown may remain green. It rebounds first thing in spring.

Herbs That Keep on Giving

You can plant several herbs and forget about them—you'll never have to plant them again. Even though both cilantro and dill are annuals—meaning they will sprout, grow, go to seed and die all in one year—any seed that is left on the ground will sprout the following year to start the cycle all over again. Lovage and chives are considered perennials, but both of these will self-seed prolifically as well. Hoe out any seedlings you do not want, or dig them up and trade them with friends.

Kid-Grown Gardens

Little gardeners may just grow up into big ones, and in the meantime they can have plenty of fun nurturing colorful, pickable flowers.

Kids just want to have fun, so let fun happen in a special garden geared just for them. On the next three pages you'll find hints and tips to make an inviting, exciting and enduring flower or vegetable garden for children. A little garden will give children lasting lessons and tangible rewards, far beyond what they can get from a TV show or a video game. Plus they'll get fresh air and sunshine in the process—something we can all use a healthy dose of regularly. Who knows? You may inspire a lifelong passion for all things green and growing.

A Flower Garden for Kids

The beauty of flowers takes on new meaning when you see the delight that flowers inspire on children's faces. And what kid wouldn't want a special patch they can call their own, where they can lovingly pick a handful of posies for Mom or pluck blossoms for their own handmade crafts? Flowers are a perfect place to start for novice gardeners because kids like them, and many require very little care or maintenance throughout the season.

What to Grow

Offer your child a seed catalog with bright, beautiful pictures to get them in on the planning process early in the season. Using the catalog as a guide, ask them what they would like to grow. Steer their choices to flowers that have large seeds, which will be easier for small hands to handle. If you are unfamiliar with a particular flower, look to the "seed count per ounce" for a clue as to how big a flower seed will be. Also stay away from flowers that are known to be poisonous, because a kid gardener may be tempted to taste what's growing. Flowers with unusual colors or fragrance are always kid-pleasers.

Stick to annual flowers, which grow and flower in one season, rather than perennials. Perennials may not bloom in their first year, whereas annuals will guarantee rewards for impatient little gardeners in short order.

Older children can assume much more initiative and responsibility for their gardens, along with enjoying the rewards the garden brings.

Ten Great Flowers for Kids

- Calendula
- Cosmos
- Impatiens*
- Marigolds
- Melampodium
- Nasturtiums
- Pansies*
- Petunias*
- Sunflowers
- Zinnias

* Buy plants. Start others from seed.

Zinnias.

Sunflower.

Signet marigolds.

The more things kids actually do in the garden themselves, the more involved they will be as the season progresses.

flower garden. Many of these flowers are readily available at local nurseries or garden centers. It's great fun to let kids shop for bedding plants to pop into their garden or perhaps into sturdy plastic pots. Kids will get a little instant gratification from the plants, and be able to put their creative skills to work in choosing colors. Don't worry about colors and design, and let them plant purple-and-white-striped petunias with glowing fuchsia geraniums! After all, these are *their* flowers.

Watering Cans for Little Hands

Children love to water just about anything. So make it easy for them to care for their flowers: Provide a personal watering can! Plastic is best, because it is lightweight and can withstand abuse. Look for small cans so that children can handle them when they are filled with water. Ones that have a sprinkling "rose" attached to the spout are especially desirable—the shower effect is always a kid-pleaser. If you cannot find a small watering can where garden supplies are offered, look in the beach or pool toy area of the store: small watering cans that are more than adequate for the job are often sold there.

Young children love to water, so let them have fun with a kid-sized watering can. To kids, filling and emptying a watering can is serious work.

Getting Started

Starting the garden from seed is always exciting for kids because it's nothing short of miraculous to witness a dead-looking little seed sprout into a living, growing plant. For younger gardeners, choose seeds than can be planted directly into the ground. Older children who are looking for more of a gardening challenge may want to start some flowers indoors 6 to 8 weeks before the last frost date.

Some flowers, such as petunias and impatiens, are more difficult to start from seed. But once they're started, they're quite easy to grow and suitable for a kid's

The Nitty Gritty

Depending on the age of your child, you may want to help them create a garden of their own, or have them incorporate their flower patch into one of your larger beds. Help by tilling the soil or spading it, but let them remove any rocks and rake or hoe the soil smooth.

When the garden is planted, encourage your child to visit it every day to see what has sprouted. They can water and weed the garden too. Depending on their age, you may have to help them complete those tasks. As the plants grow and bloom, use the opportunity to show your children basic principles of botany. Point out butterflies or other insects that are drawn to the flowers for mini entomology lessons.

When flowers start appearing, encourage creativity with various flower-centered, age-appropriate activities such as bouquet making and flower pressing.

Kids hate to wait, so fast-growing plants such as radishes are rewarding choices for a children's garden. Radishes can be grown in containers too.

An Edible Garden for Kids

An edible garden for children offers endless possibilities for food, fun and education. It all begins with planting seeds. Then there's watching the weather, creating a scarecrow, observing a caterpillar turn into a butterfly, eating cherry tomatoes by the handful, or hiding under a bean-covered teepee. A garden is always fertile ground for little imaginations!

This can also be a very healthful adventure as children enjoy the outdoors and get some of their "5-a-day" in the process. You'll be amazed that even the most finicky eaters will eat the raw vegetables they have grown themselves, even if they usually refuse the same item otherwise.

What to Grow

Provide a few seed catalogs, especially some with color pictures, for your children to begin planning their garden. Help them choose vegetables that are easy to grow so they do not get discouraged (see "Great Crops for Kids" for ideas). To keep the interest level high throughout the growing season, plant several different vegetables that mature at different times so there is always something to look forward to in the garden.

Don't limit your choices strictly to vegetables. Remember there are lots of other edible delights a kid can grow, such as dainty strawberries, sunflowers for tasty seeds, or delicious herbs like mint.

Children naturally enjoy big and colorful things that come from a garden. Provide a place where they can wash their veggies before sampling them.

Great Crops for Kids

- Baby carrots
- Cherry tomatoes
- Gourds
- Pole beans
- Popcorn
- Pumpkins
- Radishes
- Runner beans
- Strawberries
- Sunflowers

Pole beans are fun to pick.

Help kids decorate miniature pumpkins.

Sunflowers can support morning glories.

Getting Started

Planting a garden from seed is usually the most gratifying for children. Choose seeds that can be planted directly into the ground for younger gardeners. Older children who need more of a gardening challenge may start some seeds indoors, such as tomatoes, 6 to 8 weeks before the last frost date.

You may also want to head to a local nursery or garden center to pick up transplants for the veggie patch. Show kids how to plug the transplants into the garden, and have them use a yardstick or tape measure (think math lesson!) to space the plants. They'll get some satisfaction in seeing several plants already growing in their designated space.

If kids help you in your garden, teach them how to do simple things so they can feel more useful and needed.

The Nitty Gritty

Decide where you would like to have your child's garden. This will probably be dictated by age and skill level. Younger children may be content picking from their own special plants in their parents' garden. Older children may crave the independence that a special garden patch of their own will provide.

If a kid helps grow cucumbers, he or she will eat them. Youngsters may even want to share produce with their friends.

Take a playful approach to designing the garden. Don't just plant plain rows. Use trellises, teepees and arches to add interesting nooks and crannies for a child's play. To satisfy the kids who just love to get their hands dirty, add a worm box or small compost pile. Consider themed gardens, such as a garden of giant varieties, or one that is based on unusually colored vegetables. And even if your yard is tiny, you can still have a kid's garden by growing small delights such as radishes and lettuce in a trough, wooden crate or half-barrel on the porch or balcony.

The level of work children can do to care for the veggie patch will also be decided by their age. You will probably have to prepare the soil by tilling or spading it, but let them remove any rocks and rake or hoe the soil smooth. When the garden is planted, encourage them to visit it frequently to see what has sprouted, how things are growing, and if anything needs to be harvested.

Kids can water and weed the garden too, but you may have to assist them in sorting vegetable seedlings from weed seedlings. Encourage them to spread grass clippings in between plants so weed problems do not become daunting. And refrain from using any chemicals in your child's garden. The hazards of exposing a child to such substances in an area where they are playing and randomly sampling the produce far outweigh the possibility of a bug hole or two.

The veggie garden is a great place to explain basic principles of science, math and even art. As produce matures, you can also bring the classroom indoors to the kitchen and help young chefs prepare their homegrown bounty.

Melons in the Compost

Did you ever notice how well volunteer vines grow in the compost pile? Throw a piece of watermelon or cantaloupe on top, turn your back, and seemingly overnight the pile is covered with a green tangle of vines that sprouted from your cast-offs. Use this method of easy growth to your advantage and get kids to either tend those volunteer vines, or deliberately plant some of their own in the compost pile. The pile provides the ideal growing environment for rambunctious plants such as melons, pumpkins and gourds, because they can grow unfettered without trampling the rest of the garden. If there's a wire bin surrounding the pile, you already have a built-in trellis.

Plug-In Veggies

Best Bets for Spring

- Cantaloupe
- Cucumbers
- Eggplant
- Hot peppers
- Squash
- Sweet peppers
- Tomatoes
- Watermelon

Plant edibles from this list early enough in spring so that they can take full advantage of late spring's and early summer's lengthening days; that's when these plants will grow like mad. Shown: cantaloupe.

Vegetable seedlings grown in containers will quickly take off in your garden—provided they have received regular water and plenty of light.

In these days of hectic lifestyles, it's not uncommon that weeks slip by and you haven't had a chance to think about a garden, let alone plant one. But even if you think the prime planting time has passed away, don't write off having a garden until next year. It's never too late to start a garden if you choose the right vegetables to grow for the season you're in.

And it won't take very long to whip a garden together, either. With all the transplants available at garden centers, you can have a respectable garden planted in a weekend, with very little effort. As an added bonus for procrastinating, you will probably find that many transplants go on sale at bargain-basement prices after spring garden-fever subsides. So what are you waiting for? Time's a-wasting if you want a red, ripe and juicy tomato or sweet, crunchy carrots!

Dig In

Before you head out to purchase transplants, assess your garden site. That way, you'll know exactly what you need and what will fit, so you won't over-buy.

Do any preparation necessary to get the garden ready for planting ahead of time, so when you get home with your new transplants, all you have to do is "plug and play." Remove any dead plants from last year, and hoe or till any weeds that have begun to grow this year. If you do not plan to till, loosen up the soil with a spading fork. Rake the soil level and form beds, if you desire. Get the sprinkler in place.

If you will not be planting for a day or two and the weather has been dry, go ahead and turn the sprinkler on for a little while to soak the ground. If you are going to be planting the same day you get the garden ready, then wait until after you plant to turn on the sprinkler.

Shop Smart

Take a trip to at least two local garden centers or nurseries. There, you'll probably be able to find plants that haven't been neglected too much even though the buying rush is over. Look for plants that are vibrant-green and as compact as possible. Avoid anything that's wilted, brown or otherwise sickly looking.

If you purchase any plants that have fruits on them, such as tomatoes or peppers, pinch off the fruits before you plant. That way the plants will devote more energy into sending out roots rather than developing fruits.

While you're shopping, consider picking up some bedding plants of annual flowers. They will help to dress up your veggie patch and provide a little excitement for the eyes while you wait for the vegetable plants to fill in.

Planting Pleasure

Planting a plug-in garden is a breeze. All you need is a good trowel, and away you go. Simply dig holes, and pop plants in where you want them. That's it!

One advantage to planting a garden in a weekend is that you can develop an overall design scheme with the actual plants rather than guessing what will go where as the season progresses. Snip the six-packs apart so you have individual plants in individual little pots. Arrange your plants until you get the best layout; the little pots will prevent their tender roots from getting dried out. Be creative in your design—vegetable gardens do not require soldier-straight rows with all the same things in rows all by themselves. Mix and mingle the plants for a visually interesting garden that naturally resists pest attacks. Intermingled plantings confuse pest insects, so it's harder for them to find a meal.

Keep plant spacing in mind. Remember that the darling little 6-inch-tall tomato transplant is going to grow into a 4-foot-tall behemoth in short order. Imagine what each vegetable will look like full grown, and space accordingly. Remember to position plants so it is easy to tend them too. Give rambling plants like cucumbers a place near the garden's edge, where they can wander without being stepped on when you're trying to weed.

Best Bets for Fall

Broccoli	Kale
Brussels sprouts	Kohlrabi
Cabbage	Lettuce
Cauliflower	Spinach

Mid-summer is a good time to plant edibles from the list above, timing it so the plants will mature during fall's cool weather. End result? Crisp and sweet produce! Shown: kohlrabi.

Brussels sprouts are best grown as a winter crop from seedlings set out in late summer. Even when frozen, the sprouts are pickable.

Time-Saving Tip

Planting Leggy Tomatoes

When picking up tomato transplants at the garden center, you're bound to run into plants that have grown tall and spindly because they've been kept in a container for too long. These oldsters are fine to plant in the garden if you follow this advice. Pinch off all the lower branches, leaving only the top two or three. Then dig a deep hole or a horizontal trench, and bury that tomato plant all the way up to the top leaves. The plant will quickly form roots all along the buried stem, making a much stronger plant that you will not have to coddle!

The lowest section of a tomato's main stem will quickly sprout roots if it is buried in damp soil. This will lead to a more vigorous and productive plant.

Zone Maps

Throughout this book, the regional adaptability of many plants is summarized by naming the "Zones" in which they grow during the various seasons. The zones on this hardiness zone map, based on average winter temperatures, are the standard numbered zones used in almost all gardening books, magazines and seed catalogs. Sometimes the zone number is followed by a letter, as in Zone 6a or 6b. An "a" means that the area falls within the colder sections within the zone, and the "b" suggests warmer growing conditions than those that prevail elsewhere in the zone.

We have also included maps outlining average dates of the last spring frost, as well as average dates for the first fall frost. Many planting decisions are also made relative to those target dates.

Hardiness Zones

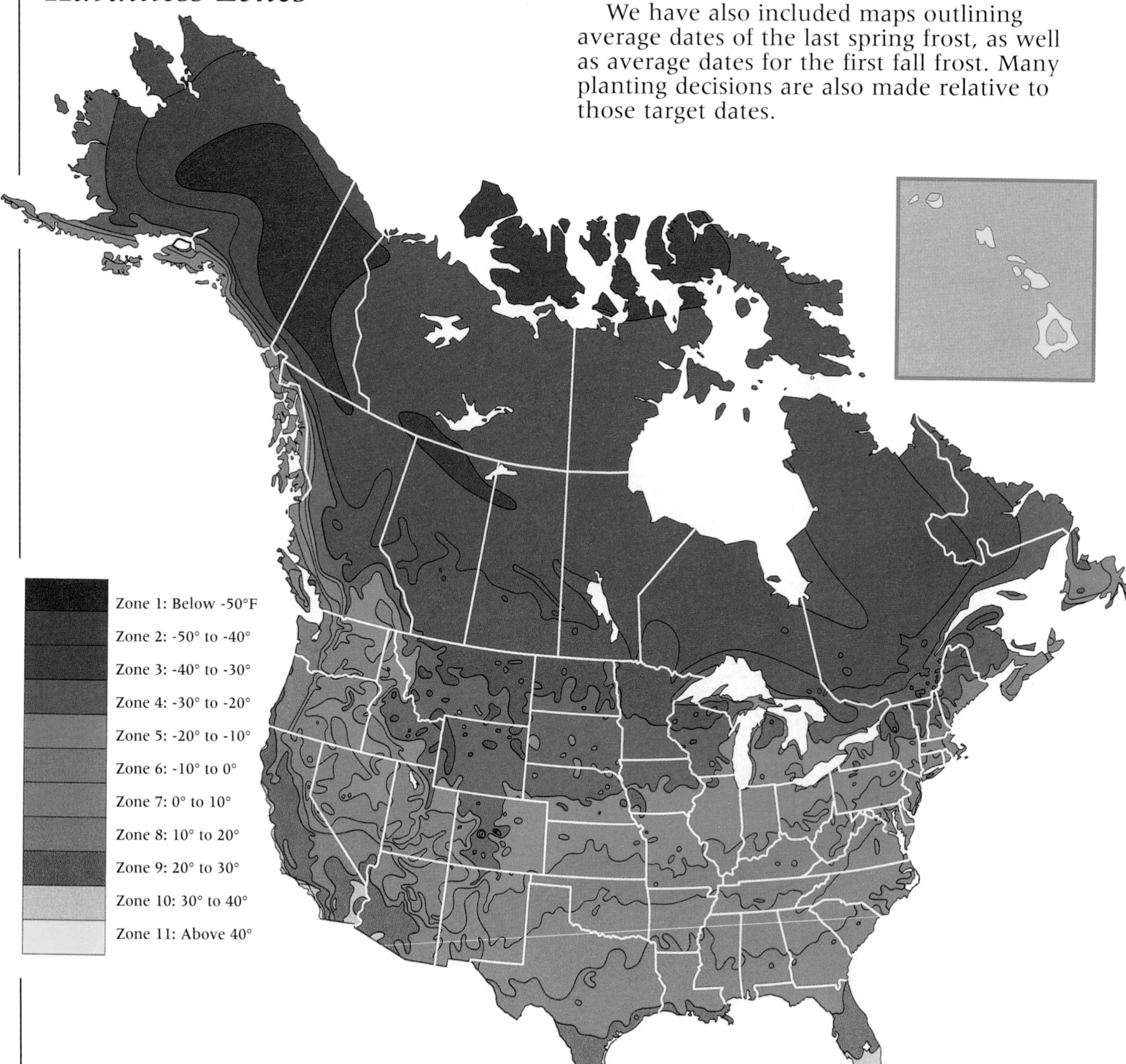

USDA Plant Hardiness Zone Map, indicating areas with similar average low temperatures. This map is a necessary reference tool for every gardener.

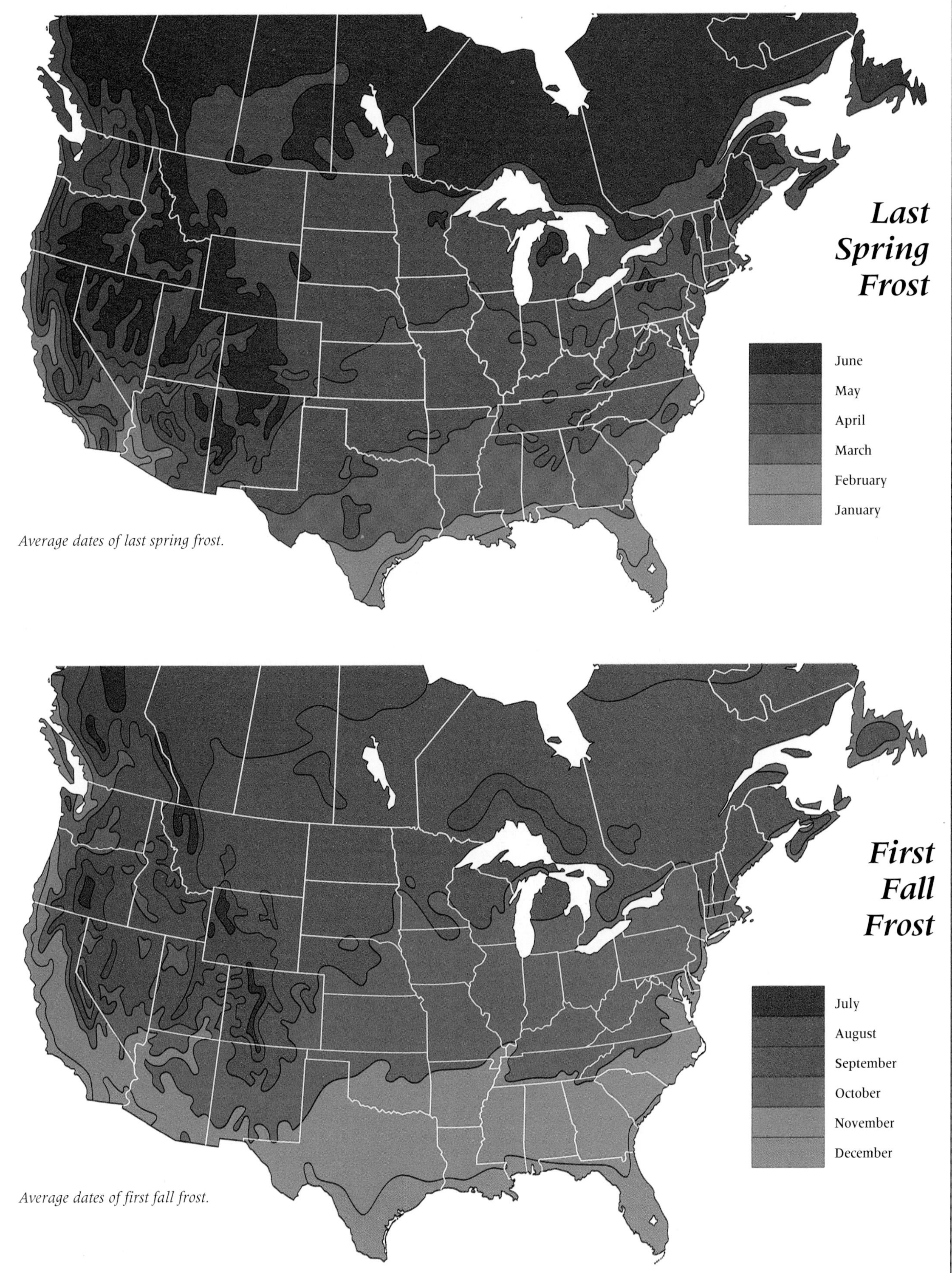

Average dates of last spring frost.

Average dates of first fall frost.

Glossary

Annual—A plant that germinates from seed, then blossoms and produces mature seed before dying, all in one season. Most bedding plants and vegetables are annuals.

Balled-and-burlapped—The way many trees and shrubs are sold after being mechanically dug from nursery fields. Soil from the field remains tightly packed around the roots, and is held in place with burlap that is pinned, nailed or tied to hold the wrapping in place.

Bare-root—The way some trees and shrubs are sold, with their roots bare and loosely wrapped in plastic with a few damp wood chips inside to maintain moisture. This method saves money on shipping weight and reduces chances of spreading disease. Bare-root plants need to be planted or set in temporary pots as soon as possible after they are received.

Cultivar—A plant strain with special characteristics, such as leaf or flower color, that is retained by propagating the plant from stem cuttings, division or other methods of vegetative propagation rather than by seed.

Deadheading—The practice of removing spent flower blossoms, which often encourages a plant to produce new stems and buds.

Deciduous plants—Those that shed their leaves, usually in fall, and grow new ones in the spring.

Evergreen plants—Those that retain their leaves or needles year-round, such as boxwoods and pines.

Foundation—The part of a house that is in contact with the ground, which is often made of concrete blocks and is less attractive than the material that covers the rest of the house's exterior.

Hybrids—Unique varieties created by crossing unlike parents to create a generation with desirable characteristics of both parents. Hybrid plants grown from seed show their superiority for only one generation, and then usually revert to being similar to only one of their parents. Hybrid shrubs, which often involve species crosses, are usually propagated from stem cuttings or other vegetative means of propagation.

Perennial—A plant that regrows each year from winter-hardy roots. Most perennials die back to the ground in winter.

pH—The relative measure of acidity or alkalinity in soil. A measure of 7.0 is neutral. Lower numbers indicate acidic conditions; the slightly acidic range of 6.0 to 7.0 is ideal for many plants, but azaleas and a few others need soil with an even lower pH around 5.5. Alkaline soil has a pH above 7.0.

Variety—A plant strain with special characteristics, such as flower color or flavor, that is retained through normal propagation of seeds.

Sources for Plants, Seeds and Supplies

Brent and Becky's Bulbs
7463 Heath Trail
Gloucester, VA 23061
877-661-2852
www.brentandbeckysbulbs.com
Uncommon and common bulbs for naturalizing and formal display.

Burpee Seeds
300 Park Avenue
Warminster, PA 18974
800-888-1447
www.burpee.com
Broad selection of flower and vegetable seed with emphasis on dependable hybrids.

Dutch Gardens
P.O. Box 200
Adelphia, NJ 07710
800-818-3861
www.dutchgardens.com
Every bulb you might want, in any color or any season.

Cook's Garden
P.O. Box 535
Londonderry, VT 05148
800-457-9703
www.cooksgarden.com
Seeds of edible flowers, herbs and favorite varieties for salad gardens.

Gardener's Supply Company
128 Intervale Road
Burlington, VT 05401
800-863-1700
www.gardeners.com
Nifty tools and supplies to make gardening more fun.

Park Seed
1 Parkton Avenue
Greenwood, SC 29647
800-845-3369
www.parkseed.com
A must-have catalog for every flower lover.

Plant Delights Nursery, Inc.
9241 Sauls Road
Raleigh, NC 27603
919-772-4794
www.plantdelights.com
Cutting-edge perennials including many hostas and superior native plants.

Prairie Nursery
P.O. Box 306
Westfield, WI 53964
800-476-9453
www.prairienursery.com
Nursery-grown native plants for Midwestern prairie plantings.

Shady Oaks Nursery
1101 S. State Street
Waseca, MN 56093
1-800-504-8006
www.shadyoaks.com
Every imaginable plant that thrives in limited light.

Shepherd's Garden Seeds
30 Irene Street
Torrington, CT 06790
860-482-3638
www.shepherdseeds.com
Cut flowers, edibles, fragrant varieties and much more.

Stokes Seeds
P.O. Box 548
Buffalo, NY 14240-0548
716-695-6980
www.stokeseeds.com
Color headquarters for outstanding annuals in every hue.

Wayside Gardens
1 Garden Lane
Hodges, SC 29695
800-845-1124
www.waysidegardens.com
Superior cultivars of perennials, shrubs, vines and trees.

White Flower Farm
P.O. Box 50
Litchfield, CT 06759
800-503-9624
www.whiteflowerfarm.com
Extensive selection of hardy perennials, bulbs and shrubs.

Wildseed Farms
P.O. Box 3000
Fredericksburg, TX 78624-3000
800-848-0078
www.wildseedfarms.com
High-quality wildflower seeds by the packet or the pound.

Index of Plants

General Index

National Home
Gardening Club

National Home
Gardening Club

National Home
Gardening Club

National Home
Gardening Club

National Home
Gardening Club

National Home
Gardening Club

National Home
Gardening Club

National Home
Gardening Club

National Home
Gardening Club

National Home
Gardening Club

National Home
Gardening Club

National Home
Gardening Club

National Home
Gardening Club

National Home
Gardening Club

National Home
Gardening Club

National Home
Gardening Club

National Home
Gardening Club

National Home
Gardening Club

National Home
Gardening Club

National Home
Gardening Club

National Home
Gardening Club

National Home
Gardening Club

National Home
Gardening Club

National Home
Gardening Club

National Home
Gardening Club

National Home
Gardening Club

National Home
Gardening Club

National Home
Gardening Club

National Home
Gardening Club

National Home
Gardening Club

National Home
Gardening Club

National Home
Gardening Club

National Home
Gardening Club

National Home
Gardening Club

National Home
Gardening Club

National Home
Gardening Club

National Home
Gardening Club

National Home
Gardening Club

National Home
Gardening Club

National Home
Gardening Club

National Home
Gardening Club

National Home
Gardening Club

National Home
Gardening Club

National Home
Gardening Club

National Home
Gardening Club

National Home
Gardening Club

National Home
Gardening Club

National Home
Gardening Club

National Home
Gardening Club

National Home
Gardening Club

National Home

National Home

National Home

National Home

National Home